Southern Africa in World Politics

Dilemmas in World Politics

Dilemmas in World Politics offers teachers and students in international relations a series of quality books on critical issues, trends, and regions in international politics. Each text examines a "real world" dilemma and is structured to cover the historical, theoretical, practical, and projected dimensions of its subject.

BOOKS IN THIS SERIES

Southern Africa in World Politics

Local Aspirations and Global Entanglements

JANICE LOVE
University of South Carolina

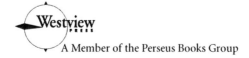

Westview
PRESS

A Member of the Perseus Books Group

Copyright © 2005 by Westview Press, A Member of the Perseus Books Group.

Published in 2005 in the United States of America by Westview Press.

Find us on the world wide web at www.westviewpress.com.

Westview Press books are available at special discounts for bulk purchases in the United States by corporations, institutions, and other organizations. For more information, please contact the Special
Markets Department at the Perseus Books Group, 11 Cambridge Center, Cambridge, MA 02142, or
call (800) 255-1514 or (617) 252-5298, or e-mail special.markets@perseusbooks.com.

Library of Congress Cataloging-in-Publication Data
Love, Janice.
    Southern Africa in world politics / Janice Love.
       p.   cm. — (Dilemmas in world politics)
    Includes bibliographical references and index.
    ISBN 0-8133-4311-9 (pbk. : alk. paper)
       1. Africa, Southern—Politics and government—1975-1994.   2. Africa, Southern—Politics and
government—1994-   3. Globalization—Political aspects—Africa, Southern.   4. Globalization—
Economic aspects—Africa, Southern.   I. Title.   II. Series.
    DT1165.L75 2005
    968'.0009'04—dc22
                                                                                    2004027267

The paper used in this publication meets the requirements of the American National Standard for Per-
manence of Paper for Printed Library Materials Z39.48–1984.

05   06   07   08   /   10   9   8   7   6   5   4   3   2   1

To those who deepened my understanding of racial justice:
The World Council of Churches
United Methodist Women and The Women's Division
Wesley United Methodist Church
Columbia, South Carolina

Contents

Tables and Illustrations

Acronyms

ANC	African National Congress
AP	anti-personnel
APEC	Asia-Pacific Economic Cooperation
ARV	antiretroviral
AU	African Union
BCG	Beira Corridor Group
CBC	Congressional Black Caucus
CIA	Central Intelligence Agency
COMESA	Common Market for Eastern and Southern Africa
CSO	Central Selling Organization
DRC	Democratic Republic of the Congo
EU	European Union
FDI	foreign direct investment
FLS	Frontline States
FNLA	National Front for the Liberation of Angola
FRELIMO	Mozambique Liberation Front
G8	Group of Eight
GATT	General Agreement on Tariffs and Trade
GDI	Gender-Related Development Index
GDP	gross domestic product
GEAR	Growth, Employment, and Redistribution
GM	genetically modified
HDI	Human Development Index
HIPC	Heavily Indebted Poor Countries
IBRD	International Bank for Reconstruction and Development
ICBL	International Campaign to Ban Land Mines
ICC	International Criminal Court
ICRC	International Committee of the Red Cross
IFIs	international financial institutions
IGOs	intergovernmental organizations
IMF	International Monetary Fund
INGOs	international nongovernmental organizations
JSE	Johannesburg Stock Exchange
LMT	Land Mines Treaty
MDC	Movement for Democratic Change
MMA	Southern Africa Multilateral Monetary Area

MMD	Movement for Multiparty Democracy
MNCs	multinational corporations
MNR	Mozambican National Resistance
MONUA	UN Observer Mission in Angola
MPLA	Popular Movement for the Liberation of Angola
MTCT	mother-to-child transmission
NAACP	National Association for the Advancement of Colored People
NAFTA	North American Free Trade Agreement
NEPAD	New Partnership for Africa's Development
NGOs	nongovernmental organizations
NICs	newly industrializing countries
NP	National Party
OAU	Organization for African Unity
ODA	official development assistance
ONUMOZ	UN Operation in Mozambique
OPEC	Organization of Petroleum Exporting Countries
PAC	Pan Africanist Congress
PMA	Pharmaceutical Manufacturers Association
PTA	Preferential Trade Area
R&Rs	restructurings and debt reschedulings
RDP	Reconstruction and Development Program
RENAMO	Mozambique National Resistance
SACU	Southern African Customs Union
SADC	Southern Africa Development Community
SADF	South African Defense Forces
SAPs	structural adjustment policies
SWAPO	South-West Africa Peoples' Organization
TANs	transnational advocacy networks
TRC	South African Truth and Reconciliation Commission
TRIPS	Trade-Related Aspects of Intellectual Property Rights
UDI	Unilateral Declaration of Independence
UN	United Nations
UNDP	UN Development Programme
UNHCR	UN High Commissioner for Refugees
UNTAG	UN Transition Assistance Group
UNVEM	UN Angola Verification Mission
WBG	World Bank Group
WCC	World Council of Churches
WFP	UN World Food Programme
WHO	World Health Organization
WTO	World Trade Organization
YMCA	Young Men's Christian Association
YWCA	Young Women's Christian Association
ZANU	Zimbabwe African National Union
ZAPU	Zimbabwe African Peoples Union

Introduction

"All politics is local," declared "Tip" O'Neill many years ago. A renowned Speaker of the U.S. House of Representatives, O'Neill argued that the problems and concerns of towns and cities around the United States affect the actions of their representatives in Washington, D.C., and to some degree determine their future as officeholders.

With the acceleration of globalization in the twenty-first century, might one also declare that "all politics is global?" Do the worries and issues of one local group or community shape those of others far away? Do the policies and actions of one set of government officials in one country have an impact on people in distant places, even if those who have a stake in the decisions have no "remote control"?

Increasingly, the answer to such questions is yes. These days, politics often seem to be local and global simultaneously. This makes for considerable conceptual difficulty and thus challenges citizens, politicians, and scholars to sort out what is domestic from what is international and how the two are related.

Scholars usually designate the study of different forms of domestic or national politics as comparative politics. Generally, the investigation of what happens across and between various national arenas is labeled world politics or international relations. A classical definition of politics is "who gets what, when, where, how, and why." A more contemporary one is "prices, police, and preachments."[1] Both imply that the study of politics necessarily involves a number of other subjects, too, such as government, the economy, the military, culture, and the environment.

This book deliberately attempts to cross these intellectual boundaries by refusing to separate the domestic arena from the foreign, or the national from the international, or politics from broad processes that affect societies and the world. Using the region of southern Africa, this study explores the complex realities that cause local and global politics to become intimately interwoven, sometimes inextricably so. Furthermore, the book reveals that for this region, like many others, such linkages are not new. They have existed for decades, if not centuries. Yet the current era is different from previous times when human communities found themselves closely intertwined, and this study examines what has changed in recent decades.

To begin contemplating the blurred lines between domestic and foreign arenas or between the local and the global, consider the following illustrations. From a political point of view, who is doing what to whom, when, where, how, and why in these snapshots of events?

- Grammy-winning musician Carlos Santana raised more than $2 million to fight the global pandemic of HIV/AIDS by devoting the proceeds of his U.S. twenty-three-city tour in the summer of 2003 to groups working in Africa.[2] Southern Africa will receive a share of the funds because South Africa holds the distinction of having the highest number of HIV-positive people in the world. Due to the impact of this disease regionally, the average life expectancy is now forty-eight years in South Africa, forty in Botswana, thirty-five in Lesotho, and thirty-two in Zambia. Such demographic trends could destabilize the region, the continent, and perhaps the world.
- The worst flood in 150 years hit Mozambique in 2000. An area as large as the combined acreage of Rhode Island, Connecticut, and Massachusetts was under water. TV crews on the scene filmed some dramatic rescues, triggering massive international response. Air forces from nine governments, including the United States, formed the largest air rescue operation ever mounted in such a short time. Under the command of the United Nations, these governments deployed the largest number of military aircraft ever used in a coordinated way in a natural disaster. Deeply moved by the media coverage, individuals in a number of countries donated more than $100 million. South African individuals and companies donated 850 tons of food and other goods. Forty-five thousand people were rescued, although 700 people died. About 500,000 people fled their homes into nearby accommodation centers so well administered that no serious malnutrition or major outbreaks of disease occurred. This degree of success among local, regional, and global governmental and nongovern-

mental organizations in the delivery of vital services offers a model for coordinated responses to other natural disasters.[3]

- Does anyone on earth not know the name Nelson Mandela? Perhaps, but if measured by the adulation, accolades, and honors he receives inside and outside his country (including the Nobel Peace Prize), Mandela is one of the world's greatest living heroes. Universally admired for leading South Africa to newfound democratic freedom in 1994 without the racially charged bloodbath that most people expected the country to suffer, he models for many the concept of more just and peaceful race relationships. For example, he met and sought reconciliation with some of those responsible for keeping him in jail for more than twenty-seven years, an act that continues to inspire many to find more compassion for their adversaries.

- The United States and the European Union imposed sanctions on Zimbabwe in 2002 and the Commonwealth suspended its membership after Robert Mugabe, president since 1980, claimed victory in deeply flawed elections that were neither free nor fair. Meanwhile, numerous international aid agencies sent food shipments to the country to address a widespread famine caused by drought and economic mismanagement. Angered by opposition party supporters who waged a vigorous campaign against him during the election, Mugabe systematically denied their followers access to the aid supplied by foreign donors.

- The World Bank and the International Monetary Fund are international financial institutions that loan money to poor countries on the condition that they follow certain policies. In recent decades, these institutions have rescheduled loan repayments and specified particular economic strategies in chronically debt-ridden countries like Mozambique and Zambia more frequently than citizens have had opportunity to vote for elected officials who are charged with guiding the national economy. Under conditions where global institutions determine a country's basic policies, what does democracy mean?

- Since the 1950s, newly engaged women the world over, both wealthy and middle class, have come to expect a diamond ring from their future husbands as a symbol of the couple's impending union.

This global cultural trend grew out of a post–World War II marketing strategy adopted by the De Beers Group, a South Africa–based
diamond mining corporation that controls much of the world's
supply. In 1947, a New York public relations firm hired by De Beers
coined one of the most noteworthy advertising slogans ever
penned: "A diamond is forever." Since then in many cultures far beyond where the jewels or slogan originated, a diamond engagement
ring has come to signify a couple's commitment to marry.

But diamonds are not only "a girl's best friend." In an effort to
stop the use of "blood diamonds" to finance wars in places like Angola, activists in a number of countries waged a campaign using the
Internet and other communication networks. They pressed governments to adopt legally binding regulations on the international
diamond industry. As one of several responses, the United Nations
imposed sanctions on the transfer of gems from countries with il-
licit trade. Certifying the origins of diamonds, however, has proven
to be very difficult. Yet researchers in Belgium working with the Diamond High Council recently invented a process for identifying
the chemical fingerprint of diamonds and have begun to analyze
samples from every operational mine in the world.[4]

- In July 2003, a coalition of animal rights advocates filed lawsuits
in Washington, D.C., to try to block the importation of eleven
African elephants from Swaziland even though the U.S. Fish and
Wildlife Service approved the transfer. After an extensive investigation, the agency gave permission to zoos in San Diego, California, and Tampa, Florida, to purchase the animals. The Swaziland
government argued that the animals needed to be culled from
herds too large for their environment and had planned to devote
profits from the sale to poaching-prevention programs. Activists
asserted that the region contained sufficient space for the elephants, which need not be subjected to the transfer. The U.S.
courts have still to decide the Swazi elephants' fate.[5]

- By some estimates in mid-2004, about 1,500 South African soldiers
and police officers were serving in Iraq as private security contrac-
tors, or mercenaries, as some call them. They performed many du-
ties, some guarding L. Paul Bremer, the chief U.S. envoy to Iraq, and
others patrolling the Green Zone, headquarters of the U.S. com-

mand. What circumstances brought these men to Iraq? When apartheid fell in South Africa in 1994, hundreds of white and black soldiers became unemployed. Others quit rather than work for the new, black government. Thus, men with superior training and excellent management skills became available for deployment in a wide range of military causes throughout the world, including Ivory Coast, Papua New Guinea, Angola, Sierra Leone, and Iraq. Furthermore, at a cost of $10,000 to $15,000 per month, most work for about half the wage demanded by ex-U.S. or British special forces soldiers. Before leaving home, some sought and received pardons from the South African Truth and Reconciliation Commission (TRC) for atrocities they committed under apartheid. Alarmed by these trends, the South African government passed legislation that forbids mercenary activities. This means that those who survive the war in Iraq will not be able to return home without the probability of facing prosecution, and those who die will forever be known as Africans fighting a U.S. war in the Middle East.[6]

These small vignettes illustrate how blurred the lines now are between local and global, domestic and foreign, and national and international, the categories often used to study these issues and events. Individuals, groups, corporations, governments, international organizations, and other such actors operate in and impact local-to-global politics, economics, environmental issues, military matters, and more. How they do so is complex and often perplexing. Many analysts increasingly use the term "globalization" to describe such interactions.

This book examines how the interplay of local, regional, and global actors and arenas shapes the lives of the people and nations of southern Africa. Students of international relations, comparative politics, and African studies will find the region's experience instructive in understanding larger trends in the world. Students particularly interested in Africa will gain insight not only about this region but also about its significance for the whole continent.

Southern Africa offers an interesting case study of the dilemmas facing virtually all nation-states: How can governments cope with globalization—that is, the fast-paced, complex, and intense penetration of global forces—and harness these forces in order to respond to the needs and desires of the nation? Can individual states create or shape global trends to benefit their country as a whole?

In economic arenas, for example, large multinational corporations (MNCs) have an enormous impact on southern Africa. The global sales of some corporations are larger than the gross domestic product of some countries. Other key global economic actors such as international financial institutions wield more resources than the national budgets of many governments. Under these circumstances, what possibilities exist for the region's people and states to shape their own economic future? What obstacles and opportunities do these nations face, and what policies might they adopt to lessen the obstacles and increase the opportunities?

In political arenas, all the countries of southern Africa claim to be democracies. How can these governments contend with the power of intergovernmental organizations that have a significant influence on their countries, such as the European Union or the United Nations, while at the same time ensuring the local democratic processes of participation, consultation, transparency, and public accountability? How do global and regional institutions enhance national governance, and how do they undermine it? Furthermore, how can governments gain the loyalty and productive participation of their citizens and respond to local needs and aspirations, which themselves sometimes pull people in separate directions? What obstacles and opportunities do these nations face, and what partnerships might they forge, since governing a country involves coping with multiple layers of powerful political actors across the world and the region as well as inside the country? Can a government be locally, regionally, and globally accountable to sometimes crosscutting pressures all at the same time?

In military arenas, such global trends as the Cold War of the twentieth century and colonial conquest in earlier times played key roles in creating and perpetuating wars or other forms of violent conflict in a number of countries in southern Africa. Now that armed conflict no longer actively wreaks havoc, do global and regional actors have any obligation to help reconstruct the war-torn societies? Moreover, how can the national governments that have been party to devastating conflicts regain the loyalty and productive participation of their citizens who fought on the other side? Can populations that endured chronic war or civil strife for generations rediscover and re-create social patterns that deemphasize and delegitimate the use of violence as a normal way of life?

Global and regional actors, structures, and processes have a profound impact on southern Africa now, but in many respects this same claim is true for the past, too. Analyzing historical and current events and institutions can shed light on some of the dilemmas and complexities of the multilayered interactions characteristic of globalization, regionalization, and localization in the twenty-first century. By engaging in this exercise, readers will not only understand more about southern Africa but will also begin to gain insight into the kinds of questions that might be asked about other regions.

Chapter 1 organizes the book by providing a conceptual framework that defines and discusses the terms "globalization," "regionalization," and "localization." The chapter explores the complexities of these dynamics through a discussion of such domains as politics, economics, culture, and the military and provides a brief history of globalization in these arenas.

Chapter 2 briefly outlines the history of Southern Africa up to the mid-twentieth century in relation to the framework presented in chapter 1. The chapter portrays the keen interest in southern Africa displayed for centuries by many actors across the world, especially those from Europe, as well as the reactions they met from the Africans already living in the region. This discussion places particular emphasis on a process somewhat peculiar to southern Africa: the establishment of white minority rule by large numbers of settlers and its persistence across several centuries.

Starting with the mid-1900s, chapter 3 focuses primarily on military globalization and the wars and other violent confrontations fought in southern Africa. The chapter examines the region's various guerrilla groups that fought for black majority rule, some of which became governments, and then analyzes the wars in Mozambique and Angola in some depth. These case studies demonstrate the interplay of local, regional, and global military dynamics in recent decades. Conflicting regionwide efforts either to preserve or to abolish white minority rule in Zimbabwe, Namibia, and South Africa were imposed on the struggle for independence in these Portuguese colonies, exacerbated by the imposition of the Cold War confrontation between East and West.

Chapter 4 focuses primarily on political globalization. The discussion analyzes how local, regional, and global politics have interacted since World War II to shape events and institutions in the region. The chapter also examines models of political leadership that the region offers to the rest of the world. The analysis includes a look at empires, nation-states, the United Nations, activists, social movements, individual leaders, and other actors in world politics, all of which fit into the framework outlined in chapter 1. This part of the book also contains a brief discussion of dictatorship and democracy in the region.

Chapter 5 examines economic globalization and addresses a wide range of topics, all of which help to reveal the complexities associated with the prospects for sustained economic development in the region. Debates about the overall relationship of governments to economies provide the context for examination of each country's connections to the regional and world economies through trade, finance, and debt. The chapter investigates the governmental policies that guide the economies and assesses their performance in addressing basic issues such as poverty, HIV/AIDs, and women in development.

Chapter 6 concludes the book by summarizing what the region elucidates about the interaction of global, regional, and local dynamics in world affairs, about what is new and what is old concerning globalization. In this way the book uses southern Africa to display the development and impact of globalization across time. Local and regional actors and arenas sometimes challenge global dynamics and at other times reinforce them. This analysis attempts to show how such processes have worked and continue to work in this significant region of Africa.

Notes

1. James F. Barnes, Marshall Carter, and Max J. Skidmore, *The World of Politics: A Concise Introduction* (New York: St. Martin's Press, 1980).

2. Andrew Bridges, "Grammy Winner Carlos Santana Raises Millions to Fight AIDS in Africa," Associated Press State and Local Wire, July 15, 2003.

3. Frances Christie and Joseph Hanlon, *Mozambique and the Great Flood of 2000* (Bloomington: Indiana University Press, 2001).

4. "Researchers Decipher Origin of a Diamond; Chemical 'Fingerprint' Helps Locate the Mine, a Breakthrough in the Fight on Illegal Sales," *Los Angeles Times*, July 26, 2003.

5. Michelle Morgante, "U.S. OKs Import of African Elephants for San Diego, Florida Zoos," Associated Press State and Local Wire, July 10, 2003.

6. Sudarsan Raghavan, "Iraq, a Land of Opportunity for South Africa's Apartheid-Era Troops," Knight Ridder Washington Bureau International News, May 17, 2004; and "The South African Mercenary Question in Iraq," Africa Analysis, Financial Times Information, February 6, 2004.

1

Globalization and Localization

WHEN VIEWED FROM THE PERSPECTIVE OF SOUTHERN AFRICA, CURRENT debates in world politics warrant skepticism. Analysts, particularly from the North—the rich countries of the world—describe the increasing political convulsions and turbulence in international affairs in the last decades of the twentieth century. Some argue that the rapid pace and consequences of social, political, and economic change imply a fundamental transformation in international relations, the opening of a new era. However, when viewed from the South—the poor countries of the world, such as those of southern Africa—world events often look different from the way they do in the North. As in many other parts of the globe, southern Africa has also experienced dramatic changes in recent decades. But historically the region has frequently been caught up in the whirlwind of major events and transitions that originate in other parts of the globe. What, if anything, is new about current trends?

Chapter 1 begins to address this question by providing theoretical concepts to organize the analysis. These are then applied to the region of southern Africa in succeeding chapters. This chapter provides a conceptual basis for examining two major, seemingly opposing forces in world politics. Within the first force are the processes drawing people and places across the world more closely together, blurring boundaries and leaping over barriers. The second force includes the processes pulling people and places apart from one another, often referred to as fragmentation, disintegration, or devolution. Here, groups and organizations seek to heighten boundaries and barriers between themselves and others, trying to isolate their piece of the world from others. The term "globalization" has come to be the most widely used concept to describe the first set of trends. The term "localization" describes the second set of trends. "Regionalization" lies somewhere between the two.

The discussion that follows demonstrates that these patterns and tendencies that seem so contradictory frequently interact significantly to reinforce and even shape each other. Often they coexist in particular places and may or may not be opposed to one another. Furthermore, both can be seen as having positive or negative consequences, depending on the values of the viewer.

CONCEPTUAL FRAMEWORK

Globalization

The term "globalization" has become a key buzzword for anyone studying or even casually reading about international relations. Its widespread use began in the 1980s, with its popularity soaring in the 1990s. Across these two decades, as with any new and unfolding concept, its meaning has varied considerably in use. Yet many have now come to agree that globalization points to a process occurring across the world and accelerating significantly in the late twentieth century. This increasing conceptual consensus about globalization being a process contrasts with earlier assertions that defined globalization as a particular outcome or end-state that the whole world would reach at a given point in time.

Despite such agreement, several important debates about globalization continue. The first is raised in the opening paragraph of this chapter: What is new and what is old about this process? Haven't previous periods of history also shown intense interaction of people, groups, and governments across national boundaries? If so, how is this era different? A second debate centers on whether globalization defines a single process or many. Does globalization occur in a number of domains of social activity simultaneously, or does it spring from a dominant process that then spills over into others?

To begin to answer these questions, the definition used here is that of Anthony Giddens: Globalization may be defined as "the intensification of worldwide social relations which link distant localities in such a way that local happenings are shaped by events occurring many miles away and vice versa."[1] In other words, culture, politics, economics, and other social activities are stretched across national boundaries such that "events and decisions taking place on one side of the world have a significant impact on the other."[2] What seems to be local may be very global, and what we presume to be global may be at the same time very local.

This definition has several advantages. It leaves open for investigation the possibility that the concept of globalization may be applicable to more than one time period in history. The definition also allows for globalization to be viewed as multifaceted and either positive or negative in its consequences. Building in part on Giddens's work, David Held and colleagues have offered a rich and complex framework that allows exploration of various dimensions of the concept.[3] Their analysis invites useful questions about the nature of globalization in any given period of time. For example, in looking at different historical eras, analysts need to consider how far geographically international activities and interconnections extend across the globe. How intense are these interactions? How fast do they flow? What is their impact? What kinds of institutions and infrastructure facilitate, promote, and sustain global transactions and processes? Are they evenly or unevenly spread, and who controls them? Are they imposed, as through military might, or entered into willingly, as in cooperative arrangements?

Such inquiries quickly turn attention to facets of this concept, described by Held et al. as the domains of globalization. When asking how far geographically global interconnections extend, one might reasonably conclude that the question should be narrowed to consider various domains or arenas, for instance, politics and culture. During the colonial period of the nineteenth century, for example, when one nation physically occupied a number of others, the geographic stretch of *political* globalization extended much further than the reach of *cultural* globalization, since television, radio, and other forms of mass communication had yet to be invented. Or, to give another illustration, the intensity of *environmental* globalization has strengthened considerably since much of the world became industrialized, in contrast to the time when agriculture provided the economic base of most societies. As these examples demonstrate, drawing a distinction among various domains of globalization, such as the environment and the economy, offers greater possibilities for multidimensional analysis, refines the concept, and makes its applicability more meaningful.

Six prominent domains of globalization can be defined as follows:

Political domain: the reach of political power, authority, and forms of rule.

Military domain: the network of worldwide military ties and relations, as well as the impact of key military technological innovations, from steamships to reconnaissance satellites.

Economic domain (trade, finance, and production): trade—a system of regularized exchange of goods and services across regions and continents leading to the emergence of worldwide markets; finance—the emergence of worldwide flows of credit (such as loans and bonds), investment (such as foreign direct investment, equities), and money (foreign exchange); production—the emergence of worldwide organization for producing goods and services, primarily through multinational corporations (MNCs), companies that produce goods or market their services in more than one country.

Migration domain: the movement of people across regions and between continents, for example, labor migrations, diasporas, and migrations of colonial settlers.

Cultural domain: cultural flows and institutions across regions, civilizations, and continents, with culture defined as the social construction, articulation, and reception of meaning, a lived and creative experience for individuals, as well as a body of artifacts, texts, and objects.

Environmental domain: the transformation of entire ecosystems or components of those ecosystems resulting in an adverse impact on the economic or demographic conditions of life and health of human beings; in addition, processes explicitly acknowledged by human beings that in some sense offend, contradict, or come into conflict with their aesthetic or moral values, irrespective of their practical or personal biological consequences.[4]

Examining these domains offers the opportunity to probe history for different eras of globalization and their distinguishing characteristics. This, in turn, helps to address the question of what is new and what is old about global interactions and interconnections in today's world. Using this framework, Held and his coauthors concluded that throughout history, human societies have been interacting significantly across considerable distances with varying degrees of globalization occurring in a variety of domains. They divided the history of globalization roughly into four broad time periods: premodern (prior to 1500), early modern

(1500–1850), modern (1850–1945), and contemporary (1945–present). To situate this book on southern Africa within a broader context of world politics, it is useful to briefly summarize the historical periods demarcated by Held et al. First, however, the discussion will turn to defining two other key concepts: localization and regionalization. As stated earlier, globalization is not the only important trend in international relations, nor is it the only force with which nation-states like those in southern Africa must cope. These two other seemingly contradictory forces also shape world affairs in the region and elsewhere.

Localization

At the same time that globalizing forces seem to bind people and societies together across vast geographic distances, other powerful forces seem to be separating people from one another, fragmenting the world into smaller decentralized social units. James Rosenau, a scholar known for his work on the interaction between centralizing and decentralizing processes, described this countervailing trend as follows: "[L]ocalization derives from all those pressures that lead people, groups, societies, governments, institutions and transnational organizations to narrow their horizons and withdraw to less encompassing processes, organizations, or systems."[5]

If globalization generates transcontinental or interregional relations, localization concentrates activity and the exercise of power much closer to home—within subnational or national arenas. Globalization encourages similarity and uniformity among people, groups, and social systems, whereas localism[6] fosters differences. Localism separates "us" from "them," whereas globalization seeks to combine "us" and "them" to create a merged "we." Globalization expresses the human desire and need to expand our horizons to take in goods, services, and ideas unavailable to us at home, whereas localization embodies the human need for close community offered by family, neighborhood, and culture. Just as globalization can have such negative consequences as imperialism, so localization can be manifest in unfortunate tendencies such as xenophobia. But both also have positive potential.

In general, localism can be analyzed according to the domains of globalization described above, meaning that this tendency to narrow borders and interactions can be found in political, military, economic, environmental, and cultural arenas as well as in issues of migration. For example, attempts to prevent the movement of goods and services into a particular area, as with protectionist trade policies, constitute a form of economic localization. Attempts by subnational groups to break away from nation-states represent a form of political localism, an effort that is often called self-determination, especially when supported by democratic processes internal to the subnational group. Both the resurgence of previously suppressed cultural practices and the rise of various kinds of religious fundamentalism demonstrate aspects of cultural localization.

Globalizing trends often produce localizing reactions. For example, news media brought home to people all over the world the pictures and stories of voters in South Africa in 1994 casting their ballots in the first democratic elections ever held in that country. Activists living under authoritarian regimes in Indonesia, Zaire (now Congo), East Timor, and elsewhere gained inspiration from witnessing dramatic change in South Africa, prompting these activists to redouble their efforts to achieve democracy in their own locations. In another example, workers in rich countries whose jobs are threatened by cheap imports have lobbied governments to impose measures to protect their industries against trade competition.

However, globalization also often subverts localizing trends. For example, governments and other institutions that try to eliminate their citizens' access to cultural influences from abroad find themselves undermined by satellites, computers, and other technology that beams in music, commentary, and images from afar. Furthermore, to make the situation still more complex, those who promote a focus on the local often take advantage of the infrastructure of globalization. For example, guerrilla organizations fighting for independence for a subnational group might communicate with each other via cell phones and e-mail. Or xenophobic leaders attempting to mobilize one ethnic group to fight another might use the technology of mass media to communicate their message.

When viewed across the historical periods to be discussed below, most analysts believe that the interaction between globalization and localization has been and will continue to be complex and unevenly spread across the world. Yet globalizing tendencies historically dominate localizing ones, and this pattern is likely to continue into the future. As the brief discussion on the history of globalization will show, at the turn of the twentieth century, globalizing processes had a very extensive reach and operated very intensively. They also had substantial impact across the world. However, the cataclysmic events of two world wars and the Great Depression reversed this trend for the most part. Nonetheless, globalizing tendencies won out again after World War II and into the twenty-first century. Why? James Rosenau has suggested an answer.

[R]ecorded human experience is a history of expanding horizons—of individuals, families, tribes, and societies driven by their own growth as well as by technology and industrialization to build ever more encompassing forms of social, economic, and political organization. To be sure, no less historically conspicuous than the movement along these lines have been the resistances to globalizing dynamics, counter-reactions driven by the need for identity and the psychic comforts of shared territory and culture to retreat into narrower forms of social, economic, and political organization. . . . Still when the globalizing and localizing dynamics collide and interact, the latter seem unlikely to offset the consequences of technological innovation, the skill revolution, and the global scale on which economic processes are now conducted. . . . [I]t is difficult to anticipate the breadth and speed with which globalizing processes will outpace those fostering localization . . . [and] . . . it seems doubtful that globalization will be so predominant as to overwhelm localizing processes and reduce local communities to mere appendages of global institutions. The local entity, in short, is likely to mark the human landscape as far as one can see into the future even as it will also be continuously assaulted by the requirements of a global economy and the intrusion of communications technologies.[7]

Therefore, in addition to facing the opportunities and obstacles presented by global trends, governments like those in southern Africa must also cope with decentralizing pressures from below, such as ethnic groups that want more access to power or to separate from the country as a whole. One mechanism that governments sometimes use to address both kinds of pressures is that of regionalization.

Regionalization

Held et al. have defined this term as "a clustering of transactions, flows, networks and interactions between functional or geographical grouping of states or societies."[8] In other words, states that share borders or have other deeply held common interests get increasingly interconnected. As with localism and globalization, regionalism can be manifest in political, military, economic, cultural, and environmental domains, virtually all of which can be found in southern Africa. Frequently, however, regions take shape around the concentration of economic transactions or the coordination of foreign economic policies among geographically proximate nation-states.[9]

One of the most famous regional organizations, the European Union (EU), began primarily as an effort in economic integration. The EU evolved from a series of intergovernmental agreements dating back to the 1950s. Although it is the most well known, the EU is but one of many such institutions. According to the World Trade Organization (WTO), seventy-six regional economic organizations have been founded since the end of World War II, with about half of them initiated after the end of the Cold War.

Many regional dynamics mark the history of southern Africa, and these will be examined in later chapters. The region itself, however, will be defined as the ten nations shown in Map 1.1: Angola, Botswana, Lesotho, Malawi, Mozambique, Namibia, South Africa, Swaziland, Zambia, and Zimbabwe. Most analysts include these ten countries in a definition of the region to acknowledge an important common theme among them. For several centuries, large numbers of white European settlers and their descendants dominated the area. Only in the late twentieth century did black Africans regain political control in the region, a process permeated by wars and other forms of contention that drew significant international involvement. Thus, not only do these countries sit contiguously in the lower one-third of the African continent, they also share an important history that intimately bound their local fortunes with other nations and people across their region and the globe, as will be shown in chapter 2.

This definition differs, however, from that used by some of the regional organizations that affect southern Africa. The Southern Africa Development Community (SADC), for example, has fourteen members, including some islands off the coast as well as nations as far north as the Democratic Republic of the Congo (DRC) and Tanzania. Other regional organizations, as discussed in Chapter 4, either include a large number of countries other than those in the SADC or hold in their membership only a few of

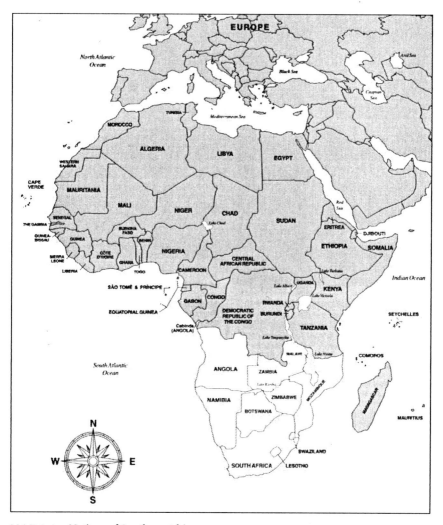

MAP 1.1   Nations of Southern Africa
SOURCE: F. Jeffress Ramsay and Wayne Edge, *Global Studies: Africa*, 10th ed. (Guilford, CT: McGraw-Hill/Dushkin, 2004), p. 118.

the ten countries listed above. This text will stick with the ten-nation group described above.

Southern Africa's history and its local, regional, and global dynamics can best be understood in the context of how events have unfolded across the whole world. Globalization is nothing new for these nations, and its larger manifestation elsewhere provides the backdrop against which to understand the region.

Key Periods in the History of Globalization

Only very brief descriptions of the premodern and early modern eras of globalization will be covered here as a means of illustrating how interconnections across human civilizations have been important to the world throughout history. In analyzing southern Africa in world affairs, the modern and contemporary periods, spanning the years from 1850 to the present, are the most important and will be given more attention.

As one might expect, "thin" globalization characterizes the *premodern period*, dating roughly prior to 1500. Political and military empires as well as migration and world religions (i.e., cultural globalization) constituted the key domains. Most encounters between regions or civilizations occurred across the Eurasian landmass. The famous, ancient empires such as those of the Indic civilization (300–1200), Han China (206 BCE–220 CE), and the Roman Empire (31 BCE–410 CE), although remarkably impressive at the time, had considerably less than a global reach and could sustain little routine intensive oversight even within their territories. Their infrastructure (such as roads, shipping routes, and trading networks) was confined and uneven, and few processes were institutionalized across the whole area. Religion, an important aspect of culture, was initially contained within one or two regions or civilizations until Islam became the first to break this pattern after the sixth century CE. Settled agriculturalists moving into territories held by hunter-gatherers represented the most significant migration of people during this time period, although conquests such as those made by the Mongols from the twelfth to fourteenth centuries also left a lasting impact.

Early modern globalization dates from around 1500 to 1850, and includes periods of great European global exploration as well as significant colonial conquest in the Americas. Large-scale migrations and their environmental impact (including epidemiological flows) led globalization in this period, with political and military empires from Spain, Portugal, the Netherlands, Britain, and France making this possible. By the close of this period, "European peoples, empires, religions, flora, fauna and microbes had transformed the Americas and the Caribbean and were getting to work on Australia and the rest of Oceania."[10] Another European nation, Russia, began stretching its power all the way to its Pacific coast.

Europe could not sustain substantial penetration of Africa and Asia, but Africa endured substantial impact nonetheless. Colonization in the Americas and the Caribbean, where the wholesale destruction of indigenous people and societies left plentiful land but scarce labor, stimulated 400 years of Atlantic slave trade.

Large trading companies like the Dutch East India Company and the Hudson Bay Company initiated new forms of economic globalization, regularizing trade and economic transactions. Military, political, migratory, and economic globalization extended much further than in previous eras; yet due to still limited transportation and communication technology, the speed of interaction, infrastructure, and institutionalization of these domains remained limited. For example, Europeans could conquer the Americas, but they had difficulty holding onto their empires there. Notably during this period, however, Europeans established a crucially important institution within their region and began asserting its form across the world: the sovereign nation-state, together with the emergence of regulated interstate relations.

Even though vast areas, particularly in Asia and the interior of Africa, remained relatively isolated from these trends, globalization increased significantly from the previous period and affected much of the world. Ironically, the largest impact may have been on the region from which the coercive imperial rivalries sprang—Europe. Vast wealth in precious commodities imported from the New World, the export of discontented masses who otherwise might have stirred trouble back home, and the stimulus of military and political rivalries among the colonial powers all contributed to the development of new technologies, economic processes, and institutions that would transform Europe itself and spill over into the rest of the world in the second half of the nineteenth century.

Modern globalization occurred over the century between about 1850 and 1945, a period defined by the political, military, and economic spread of European and American empires, often known in part as the age of imperialism. Each empire contained a genuinely global network. As the largest of the imperial powers, Britain and France expanded already substantial holdings by moving into previously inaccessible territories in Africa and Asia. Italy, Germany, Belgium, Spain, and Portugal joined Britain and France in the "scramble for Africa." Although the Dutch earlier lost their colony in southern Africa to the British (who struggled until 1902 to fully gain control there), the Netherlands maintained its long-standing holdings in the East Indies, just as other imperial powers continued to hold possessions gained in previous decades. The United States undertook expansion across the continent to the West Coast and then further to Alaska, Guam, the Philippines, and the Midway, Hawaiian, and Wake islands. Japan gained colonies nearby in Asia. Altogether, the period demonstrates an unprecedented extension of globalization, as illustrated by the following statistics.

> What amounted to a quarter of the land surface of the globe was distributed between a few states between 1876 and 1915. Great Britain's colonial possessions grew in this period by 4 million square miles, France's by 3.5 million, Germany's by more than a million square miles. Portugal added 300,000 square miles of colonial territory, and the United States and Japan 100,000 square miles each.[11]

Due to advances in technology and the use of fossil fuels, remarkable new possibilities for globalization's infrastructure developed. These included railways and mechanized shipping as well as new communications capabilities through telegraph and telephone. Together with industrialization, such infrastructure facilitated an explosion of economic transactions, created massively more powerful military capabilities, and made political control over greater distances more intense. Imperial rule continued as an important type of global interaction from the early modern era, but a significant new and powerful mode of globalization was introduced: secular Western ideologies such as liberalism, Marxism, nationalism, and science, the diffusion of which would profoundly transform cultures and practices of people everywhere. The spread of Christianity to Africa and parts of Asia increased cultural globalization.

Certainly during this period European and American interests dominated global networks, but with their vast empire the British maintained hegemony. For example, London became the financial capital of the world with institutionalization of the gold standard. An important consequence of the global stretch of imperial rule was more pronounced stratification among nations and peoples. Ruling elites in African, Asian, and other non-European societies, as well as the peoples and systems they governed, were destroyed or declined dramatically as a result of conquest and incorporation into empires. A few countries such as Turkey, Japan, and China succeeded in staving off Western domination through domestic modernization.

Trade, investment, and other economic interactions intensified. Most economic exchange occurred between imperial nations and their colonies. Empires often decisively shaped the economies of many of their colonies, usually to their disadvantage for decades to come. Meanwhile, investment and migration from overseas became key to the industrialization of the United States, northern and eastern Europe, and parts of Latin America. Migration grew to be more global with increased transatlantic flows, augmented by a massive exodus of Asians to many parts of the world. The United States gained much needed labor, and the emigration of Europe's poor, landless, and unemployed allowed that region to escape greater social instability.

This modern era embodies a remarkable paradox, however, of the fairly rapid rise and decline of globalization. The world had never been so tightly interwoven as it was at the turn of the twentieth century, demonstrated in part by the founding of a number of global organizations to undergird the growth in international relations. When comparing the prewar world with today, some analysts argue that in many respects, particularly in economics, globalization reached its greatest heights during the modern era.[12] The sustained momentum of increasing global interactions and interconnections, however, collapsed with World War I. The imperial powers mobilized their forces worldwide to fight each other, and most regions of the world were drawn into the conflict, virtually ending global trade, investment, and production. Furthermore, after the Great Depression of the 1930s, the world economy fractured into imperial blocs, eliminating what little was left of free trade as well as the gold standard. Two new nation-states, the Soviet Union and Germany under the Third Reich, even attempted economic autarky.

Although World War I drew much of the globe into conflict, it proved to be no precedent for the scale of war unleashed in World War II. With the exception of Latin America and southern Africa, every continent and ocean became embroiled in the second global conflagration. The world had never experienced the vast expanse of destruction or the levels of human suffering brought on by World War II. The devastation brought with it the demise of European and Japanese empires, although in most cases, the formal transfer of power from colonial masters to newly independent governments in the former colonies took another decade or so. The efforts made after World War I to build global political institutions such as the

League of Nations evaporated with the onset of World War II, but many leaders emerged from the second global descent into sustained bloodletting more convinced than ever that such organizations are necessary. With much of the world in ruins, the only nation left with any sustained capacity for global leadership was the United States, the new hegemonic power that would initiate fresh international mechanisms through which the revival and reinvigoration of globalization would occur.

Contemporary Globalization: What's New?

The era of *contemporary globalization* begins in 1945 with the end of World War II, a watershed in world affairs and a significant turning point in the history of globalization. In a brief span of about three decades early in the twentieth century, two world wars and the Great Depression devastated the nations of Europe economically, politically, and militarily. In contrast, the United States emerged from the war recovered from the depression and stronger than it had been in many years. Furthermore, with such a foundation, U.S. leaders were ready to assume the mantle of world leadership. The country's superpower status was challenged only by the Soviet Union. These two nations embarked on a Cold War confrontation between East and West, complete with competing military alliances and other antagonistic encounters that reverberated throughout the world. These and other significant changes that mark the beginning of the contemporary era can be further described somewhat systematically using the domains of globalization: economic, military, political, environmental, migration, and cultural.

In assuming a hegemonic role, the United States undertook an ambitious plan of establishing global institutions and practices that would help to reshape world affairs. In the short span between 1945 and 1950, nations of the world came together to create a number of intergovernmental organizations (IGOs), including the United Nations (UN), the World Bank (or International Bank for Reconstruction and Development—IBRD), the International Monetary Fund (IMF), and the General Agreement on Tariffs and Trade (GATT). Building on the League of Nations as precedent, the United Nations sought to encompass all the independent nation-states of the world, although through its Security Council, the UN lodged substantial power in the hands of the victors of World War II. In contrast, the IGOs established for economic matters, such as the IMF, IBRD, and GATT, embodied the concerns, perspectives, and practices of only one part of the world, the West, and they lodged substantial control particularly with the United States. These institutions are known collectively as the Bretton Woods system, named after the New Hampshire locale where British and American leaders reached agreements about establishing such organizations. Together with multinational corporations (significant actors in international business—see chapter 5), these IGOs became key instruments in the process of economic globalization.

Some analysts assert that economic globalization lies at the heart of all other domains of globalization.[13] They point to evidence that U.S. governmental and business leadership in international trade and investment led to significant growth in the world economy in the early decades after World War II and helped to shape trends thereafter. Several economic crises occurred in the early 1970s, however, to interrupt these trends briefly, including oil price hikes by the Organization of Petroleum Exporting Countries (OPEC) and a massive influx into international banks of dollars earned by oil-producing nations. In the 1980s, a wave of domestic neoliberal economic deregulation in several large countries followed these crises, and together with new communications technology, these changes unleashed a dramatic acceleration of economic globalization. By the 1990s, trade and investment had spread to Eastern Europe and the former Soviet Union, too. Now almost all economies, and certainly all those with some industrial base, find themselves enmeshed in institutions and patterns of global trade and finance, which themselves have exploded in growth. These institutions and patterns certainly affect the nations of southern Africa profoundly (see chapter 5).

Another major historical trend in the contemporary period, the Cold War, helped to shape other domains of globalization. Simultaneously with the launching of new intergovernmental organizations immediately after World War II, the two military superpowers, the United States and the Soviet Union, formed rival alliances in pursuit of their Cold War objectives. The characterization "cold" came from the fact that these two nations rarely engaged each other directly in armed conflict (to make the war "hot"). The two superpowers opposed each other with the largest military forces in the world, including nuclear arsenals. They perceived each other as aggressively pursuing the worldwide spread of their respective ideologies, communism in the case of the Soviet Union and capitalism in the case of the United States. They each created formal, institutionalized military blocs, locking member states into collective defense arrangements. They escalated the global arms trade and made decisions on the sale and transfer of arms on the basis of their opposition to each other. Although a few nations in the world managed to maintain a stance of nonalignment, refusing to take sides in this struggle, it provided one of the key dynamics in world affairs for most of the second half of the twentieth century. Directly or indirectly, this conflict affected every part of the globe, spreading military globalization worldwide, including to the region of southern Africa.

By the 1990s, the Soviet Union had broken up into a new set of nation-states, and with its demise came the end of the Cold War. The United States stood alone as the sole military superpower with the capability to mobilize for war anywhere in the world. Yet across the globe, reliance on regional military alliances continued and in some cases was strengthened, as most governments continued to believe that they could not achieve military security unilaterally. The United States and Russia reduced their nuclear arsenals somewhat, while the trade, transfer, and acquisition of military weapons continued, although at a lower pace. Whereas the Cold War had prevented the United Nations from developing much capacity for military intervention, the end of this conflict resulted in a remarkable growth in UN peacekeeping activities, including in southern Africa (see chapter 3). This development, in turn, further promoted and legitimized the globalization of military matters.

Another major historical trend in the contemporary period is that of decolonization. As former colonies gained independence, two important aspects of political globalization occurred: the universal spread of the nation-state as a form of political organization, and the emergence of global governance.

From 1947 through the mid-1960s, the imperial powers relinquished control of their colonial possessions in Africa, Asia, and other parts of the world in relatively peaceful transitions. Colonial intransigence in southern Africa represented an exception to this trend, yet overall, widespread decolonization and the proliferation of newly independent nations marked a significant shift in the political structure of the world. For the first time in history, one political form—the modern nation-state—became a desired norm for all people and societies, even if, as in most of southern Africa, they had yet to achieve this status.[14]

There is considerable variation in strength and coherence among the nation-states of the world, but they all conform to some degree to two characteristics. As a European invention dating back to the Peace of Westphalia in 1648, the modern nation-state came to be known as: (1) a legal entity recognized to be a government capable of exercising control over a community of people within a well-defined territory; governments of nation-states are assumed to hold a monopoly over the means of coercion within their own territories such that no rival political authority can exercise force within their country; and (2) sovereignty, meaning that no higher legal authority has jurisdiction over the nation's government. Although these characteristics may not apply perfectly to all countries at all times, this political structure is universally held to be normal for the whole world. Decolonization made this possible, and the nation-state system in international relations became key to the process of political globalization.

Once having gained their independence, former colonies embarked on the often enormous task of nation building, that is, forging some semblance of common identity and purpose for the people living within the newly founded nation-state. Imperial powers had drawn colonial boundaries often with no regard to the preexisting societies, and the newly established postcolonial governments had little desire to renegotiate these borders. Therefore, these independent countries had to face the dilemma that this book addresses with regard to southern Africa: how to form nations of diverse people often pulled to more local identities, while at the same time entering the international arena to face the challenges of globalization.

A second key element in contemporary political globalization is the emergence of global governance. As more nations gained their independence after World War II, they joined the United Nations and other IGOs, whose membership, if not political control, eventually became genuinely global. For example, UN membership now stands at nearly 200 independent nation-states from all over the world, compared to its founding in 1945 when fifty-four countries joined, primarily from Europe, North America, and Latin America. Furthermore, the number of IGOs increased dramatically as governments found more issues they wanted to address cooperatively, for example, health, the environment, military defense, economic matters, and human rights. Many IGOs are global, but some are specific to particular regions or issue areas that are not worldwide in scope. Yet all of them create legal and other norms that seek to shape or circumscribe the actions and policies of governments. In the contemporary era, virtually all nation-states now expect supervision and regulation by political actors outside their boundaries, a remarkable shift in world politics to embrace a norm that had been systematically rejected since the fifteenth century.

A similar explosion in transnational activity occurred in business, with rapid growth in the number of multinational corporations (see chapter 5), and in international nongovernmental organizations (INGOs), institutions whose members are private individuals or groups, that is, not officials of national governments. Since World War II, INGOs have used increased communications and transportation opportunities to work across national boundaries to address various issues. Examples of such organizations include Amnesty International, Greenpeace, and the International Red Cross. INGOs have had such impact that some analysts see a rise in what might be called transnational civil society, that is, networks of activists and other concerned people from religiously based organizations, social service providers, foundations, women's groups, and other kinds of grassroots organizations. In some respects, these networks form a new kind of global public, in contrast to national publics. Such networks had a profound impact on efforts to achieve black majority rule in southern Africa (see chapter 4).[15]

Furthermore, alongside the universalized nation-state and the rise of INGOs and their transnational campaigns, yet another norm has emerged in the late twentieth century to leave its imprint on political globalization: democracy. In sharp distinction to other eras of globalization, the vast majority of nation-states in the contemporary period claim to be democratic, as do those in southern Africa. Whether or not this claim is true in all or even most cases, it creates an expectation inside and outside any particular country about how the political system *ought* to operate and how the government *should* behave. This norm also shapes expectations for decisionmaking in most INGOs, although rarely is it extended to IGOs involved in political, economic, or other decisions that affect the world.

As should be clear, in the contemporary era national governments must share the global arena with a plethora of agencies, organizations, pressure groups, and corporations. Political authority and sources of political action have become diffuse and complex, and all of these actors in world affairs must cope with the unprecedented level of interactions, formal and informal agreements, and networks that now flow across the world. Therefore, global politics can be described in part as a system of multilayered global governance. This means that nation-states and the interstate system are enmeshed, or entangled, within a world of "multiple, overlapping political processes" through which "political authority and mechanisms of governance are being articulated and rearticulated."[16] The territorial nation-state, which became ubiquitous with decolonization, continues to shape global politics, but not by itself. It is caught up in the world arena with more novel forms of political power embodied by IGOs, INGOs, and MNCs, all helping to mold political globalization. Thus, every government, including those in southern Africa, faces the dilemma of how to cope with the challenging penetration of global forces and how to recast them to respond to the needs and desires of the nation-state (see chapter 4).

Environmental globalization represents another domain where the contemporary era has brought significant changes. Since World War II, industrial production and consumption for the first time stretched across the entire globe, although unevenly, and with them came massive pollution. New environmental problems such as acid rain, toxic by-products, and nuclear wastes refused to acknowledge national borders. Furthermore, for the first time in human history, environmental threats to the climate system, the atmosphere, the oceans, and the polar regions began to affect the entire planet. As in other regions of the world, environmental issues have become key to the economies of southern Africa (see chapters 3 and 5).

Another domain—migration—also experienced important shifts in the contemporary period. For about three decades after World War II, the economies of northern and western Europe needed labor. They got additional workers from their ex-colonies and from southern Europe, thereby reversing the migration flows of earlier eras out of Europe. Similarly, Latin American and Asian migrants moved to North America, and those from Middle Eastern countries and from South Asia went to work in the newly rich oil-producing countries around the Persian Gulf. Furthermore, the number of refugees and asylum seekers exploded across the globe during this period, as natural and human-made disasters (e.g., wars) left many without homes. Within southern Africa, migration has always been a key economic factor (see chapters 2, 3, and 5).

Cultural globalization also underwent transformation in the contemporary period. Older technologies such as undersea cable, radio, television, cinema, and print became much more highly developed and were joined with the creation of new technologies offered by satellites and computers. The scope and intensity of telecommunication flows changed dramatically in qualitative and quantitative terms. Indeed, some analysts assert that the growing speed and flow of communications represent a primary source of globalization itself, or at least a major foundation in the infrastructure of globalization. Cellular phones as well as the Internet and cyberspace connect people who have never been linked before. In related developments, popular culture grew worldwide, together with transnational media companies, and the English language came to stand unparalleled at the center of global communications. The power of cultural globalization to affect southern Africa is mentioned throughout this book.

In summary, then, what is new about globalization at the turn of the century and the millennium? The contemporary era transformed every domain of globalization: economic, military, political, environmental, migrational, and cultural. Furthermore, new and increasingly sophisticated forms of communication and transportation technology provide an unprecedented infrastructure capable of facilitating global flows. Legal mechanisms for ensuring and regularizing communications and transportation (e.g., naval and air traffic control; joint ventures in satellite technology) enhance the communication and transportation infrastructure considerably. Just as unprecedented, large numbers of institutions and legal norms exist at national, regional, and global levels to promote and reinforce the movement of goods, services, people, ideas, religion, culture, and so on across the world. Global networks and relations have become embedded in the practices and operations of governments, groups, households, and individuals. As will be shown later in this book, although the modern nation-state still dominates world politics, in the region of southern Africa it functions in and competes with the multilayered governing structures that surround it.

The types of interaction and the primary instruments of power, often called the modes of globalization, are more diverse than in previous times. Rather than being primarily coercive (e.g., the physical occupation by formal empires) as in earlier times, today's modes are cooperative, competitive, or forceful. Political, economic, and military force continue to be significant in the contemporary era. However, coercion alone dominated the premodern and modern periods, whereas globalization is now also spread through cooperation or, alternatively, competition of culture, ideology, ecology, and migration. As was the case in the modern era, those now actively promoting various aspects of globalization may have conflicting visions of world order, as would, for example, those who promote land mine removal in Angola, versus those who promoted the trade of armaments to supply warring parties there.

These various organizational dimensions of globalization combine to produce unprecedented outcomes in both space and time. The world has never before experienced globalization that reaches so extensively across so much territory, functions with such strong intensity, and operates with such speed and impact in virtually every domain. Furthermore, the infrastructure is greater than ever before, as is the degree of institutionalization, with more varied modes than in previous periods. All of this makes the contemporary era new and different from previous periods. Yet despite these overall conditions, there is considerable stratification and imbalance among peoples regarding controlling, accessing, and participating in globalization. For example, rural peasants in Mozambique do not communicate using sophisticated technology, except when a tragedy happens (like massive flooding). When such events occur, news media from across the world will report briefly through their satellites on conditions in the country. Ordinarily, however, rural Mozambicans have no access to telephones, televisions, or computers, a condition increasingly labeled "digital apartheid." However, they do own radios and through this medium may be familiar with music, religion, and other aspects of international culture. Stratification exists in every domain and helps to demonstrate that globalization can be both positive and negative. This significant feature of globalization will be discussed in various chapters of this book.

CONCLUSION

Globalization and localization have interacted, sometimes at odds, sometimes synergistically, throughout human history. Today's world, in contrast to previous periods in history, represents far greater degrees of globalization. Localization in many forms also remains prominent, as people, societies, and governments attempt to hold fast to that which is close to home.

The world's impact on southern Africa and southern Africa's influence on the world provide an excellent case study in the dynamic interaction of globalization and localism. The region exhibits all the components of the dilemma facing every contemporary government: How can nation-states use global trends for the benefit of the country or region as a whole, gaining the loyalty and productive participation of their citizens and responding to local needs and aspirations, which themselves sometimes pull people in separate directions? The next chapter begins to address this key question with a short history of the region.

Notes

1. Anthony Giddens, *The Consequences of Modernity* (Cambridge: Polity, 1990), p. 64.

2. David Held, ed., *A Globalizing World? Culture, Economics, Politics* (New York: Routledge, 2000), p. 15.

3. David Held et al., *Global Transformations: Politics, Economics and Culture* (Stanford: Stanford University Press, 1999), p. 16. The entire discussion of globalization presented here draws heavily on this authoritative book.

4. Adapted from ibid., pp. 32, 88, 149–150, 190, 237, 284, 328–329, 377.

5. James Rosenau, *Along the Domestic Foreign Frontier: Exploring Governance in a Turbulent World* (Cambridge: Cambridge University Press, 1997), p. 81.

6. For ease of reading and discussion, in this text the word *localism* will be used interchangeably with *localization,* as they are in much of the literature. Likewise, the word *regionalism* will be used interchangably with *regionalization.*

7. Rosenau, *Along the Domestic Foreign Frontier,* pp. 95–96.

8. Held et al., *Global Transformations,* p. 16.

9. Edward D. Mansfield and Helen V. Milner, eds., *The Political Economy of Regionalism* (New York: Columbia University Press, 1997), p. 3.

10. Ibid., pp. 418–419.

11. Eric J. Hobsbawm, *The Age of Empire: 1875–1914* (New York: Vintage Books, 1987), p. 59, cited in Rodney Bruce Hall, *National Collective Identity: Social Constructs and International Systems* (New York: Columbia University Press, 1999), p. 215.

12. Paul Hirst and Grahame Thompson, *Globalization in Question* (Malden, MA: Blackwell, 1996).

13. Kenichi Ohmae, *The End of the Nation State* (New York: Free Press, 1995), and William Greider, *One World Ready or Not: The Manic Logic of Global Capitalism* (New York: Simon Schuster).

14. Prior to the imposition of colonialism, political groupings of people of various kinds—some quite powerful and highly organized—existed in Africa, Asia, Latin America, and elsewhere. The Zulu in Southern Africa represent one remarkably sophisticated and powerful nation prior to colonialism, for example. But analysts do not consider the Zulu or other such political entities, even those in Europe prior to the seventeenth century, to be nation-states as the term came to be defined in the modern era.

15. Ronnie Lipschutz, "Reconstructing World Politics: The Emergence of Global Civil Society," *Millennium* 21, no. 3 (1992): 389–420; and Paul Wapner, "Politics Beyond the State: Environmental Activism and World Civic Politics," *World Politics* 47 (April 1995): 311–340.

16. Held et al., *Global Transformations,* p. 85.

2

The History of Southern Africa:
An Overview

In 1995 at Langebaan Lagoon, about sixty miles north of Cape Town, a South African geologist and anthropologist discovered the oldest known skeletal tracks of an anatomically modern human, that is, a person like us. The 117,000-year-old footprints probably belonged to a female. Some paleoanthropologists believe this fossil may come from the oldest ancestral group of humans, thus some journalists have nicknamed her "Eve."[1] If southern Africa is the site where our species originated, the region obviously played a rather significant role very early in premodern globalization.

This chapter will analyze some of the history of southern Africa, placing subsequent discussions of contemporary globalization in a larger context. Long after someone left footprints at Langebaan, ancient civilizations as well as some powerful, highly organized precolonial African societies existed in southern Africa. The region, particularly through Indian Ocean trading routes, played an important role in world affairs hundreds of years before the European colonial period began in the fifteenth century. Imperial competition and conquest developed in earnest in the 1600s, as European empires sought to secure this strategic area, a region they found so appealing that it eventually attracted large numbers of permanent white settlers. Having resisted conquest for three centuries, once colonization was complete African groups organized to seek independence and majority rule across many decades of the twentieth century. They used petitions and campaigns and eventually waged guerrilla war against colonial powers and white settler governments determined to prevent black rule. Africans and their allies also appealed to the conscience of the world to invite their aid with pressure and assistance from abroad. Some of the wars did not end with independence, however. A more complete picture of these wars and civil strife continues in chapter 3.

EARLY AFRICANS AND EARLY EUROPEANS

Africa, and southern African in particular, lays claim to ancient wonders. One such marvel is the city called Great Zimbabwe. Dating back to Europe's medieval period, only the ruins remain, now frequented by tourists and researchers in the country named for this old regional power. The ancestors of today's Shona people built the famous complex structure of granite walls, one of Africa's grandest cities. At its height, from about 1100 to 1450, Great Zimbabwe dominated a large area, perhaps stretching into current-day Botswana, Mozambique, and South Africa. Once home to about 18,000 people, this society based its wealth on cattle and military might. Demonstrating premodern globalization, Great Zimbabwe also grew rich from Indian Ocean trade in gold, ivory, animal skins, and slaves. The settlement eventually declined, most likely because it either exhausted local natural resources or was otherwise disrupted by competitors.[2]

Due to deeply ingrained prejudices, many white explorers, colonists, and government officials in the region could not or would not believe that Africans had the organizational capacity to build such a remarkable city as Great Zimbabwe. Although the Portuguese arrived in the 1500s and found the area already in severe decline, later European colonists only discovered the old ruins in 1868. These newcomers searched for alternative explanations for who might have built such a large and impressive city, and some even spun whimsical tales about it. For example, one of the most popular novels at the turn of the century was the 1885 classic adventure *King Solomon's Mines*, a book that sold more than 650,000 copies before the author's death in 1925 and was subsequently filmed five times. The author, Rider Haggard, served in South Africa as a British colonial official in the 1870s. His story built on settlers' speculation that linked the abandoned Great Zimbabwe to King Solomon's gold mines in the biblical land of Ophir. Although fantastic and gripping, the novel fit neither the legend of King Solomon and his gold or the historical facts of African mining in Zimbabwe, but this mattered little. Whatever conception most people in the West had of Africa at this time came from the fiction of *King Solomon's Mines*.³ Early in the twentieth century, however, through careful research, archaeologists demonstrated that the Shona produced Great Zimbabwe, a conclusion many white settlers refused to acknowledge for decades thereafter.

Two overall types of African societies, with important variation within each group, were established in southern Africa prior to European colonialism. The two groups were the ancestors of the people now known as Khoisan and the Bantu-speaking peoples. The Khoisan resided primarily in the southwestern part of the region where the Dutch began settling in the seventeenth century. The term "Khoisan" includes the Khoikhoi, who made their living through herding, and the San, who made their living as hunter-gatherers. Europeans derisively called the Khoikhoi by the name Hottentot, and they referred to the San as Bushmen. The Bantu-speaking people practiced mixed agriculture and cattle raising to the east and north of the area dominated by the Khoisan. The Europeans referred to members of the Bantu-speaking group with the derogatory term "kaffir." Prior to colonization, the Khoisan and Bantu-speaking peoples encountered each other regularly, in both cooperation and conflict. Map 2.1 shows the ethnic groups in their approximate locations as they existed in the mid-nineteenth century.

European interaction with southern Africa began with trade but developed over time into colonization. These processes brought a variety of Europeans as well as Asians to the region, and Europeans eventually conquered the indigenous African societies. The emergence of this complex mix of populations—a fascinating part of the history of the region—laid the foundation for the conflict and compromise in race relations that still exists today.

During the European "age of discovery" in the era of *early modern globalization*, the Portuguese made the first attempts at building an empire. They became a mercantile power in the sixteenth century and were the first Europeans in southern Africa, with explorers reaching the coast of Angola in 1483. They eventually made an alliance with the Kongo king, who converted to Catholicism in 1491. Having rounded the Cape of Good Hope in his famous voyage of 1497–1498, the explorer Vasco da Gama continued up the east coast of Africa, founding the colony of Mozambique prior to continuing his journey across the Indian Ocean. Traders and missionaries soon followed.

At first the Portuguese focused on lucrative trade in the east. Using their superior navy and firepower, Portugal routed the Indian Ocean Islamic traders, who dominated the various island posts and the Mozambican interior. By the end of the sixteenth century, the Portuguese began exporting

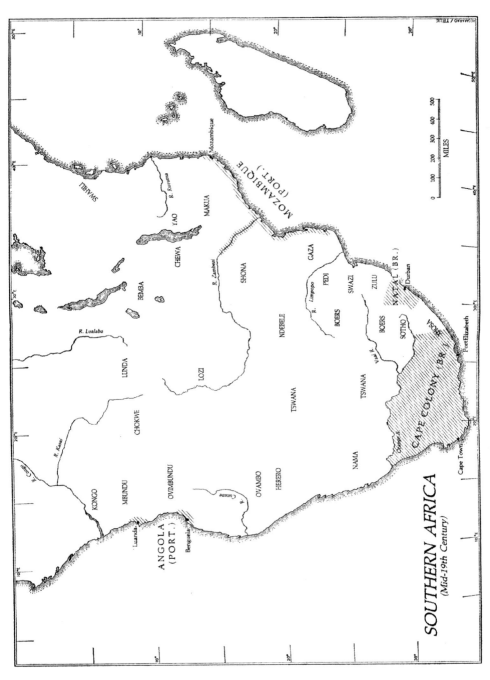

MAP 2.1   Southern Africa, Mid-Nineteenth Century

SOURCE: William Minter, *King Solomon's Mines Revisited: Western Interests and*
the Burden of History on Southern Africa (New York: Basic Books, 1986), pp. 6–7.

slaves from Mozambique and, in far greater quantities, from Angola. The slave traders took their cargo to the Portuguese colony of Brazil as well as to the Caribbean islands. Between the late 1500s and the middle 1800s, the Portuguese exported as many as 4 million slaves from Angola alone.

Like other imperial powers, Portugal often experienced fierce resistance from Africans living in these territories. One queen famed for both her diplomacy and military might against the Portuguese is Nzinga of Angola. "So powerful is her legend that a prehistoric imprint of a footprint on a rock in the natural fortress near the Cuanza river is known as Queen Jinga's [sic] footprint, as if her very feet could mark solid stone."[4] Nzinga lived from about 1581 to 1663 and ruled the Ngongo, a part of the Mbundu people, from 1624 until her death. She claimed the title of ruler *(ngola)*[5] after her brother, the former *ngola*, died. The Portuguese attempted to put a puppet ruler in his place, but she eventually outmaneuvered them all by retreating to the interior to build a base of support to pursue three objectives: ending the war with the Portuguese that was devastating the Luanda plateau; obtaining the same diplomatic recognition the Portuguese had already granted to another African group, the Kongo to the north; and establishing regular trade with Luanda. Allied with Dutch slave traders in the 1630s and 1640s, she earned considerable wealth, consolidated her power, and waged a continuous war against the Portuguese. She eventually concluded a treaty with them that largely achieved her goals and ensured her a prominent place in history.[6]

As a small European power, Portugal repeatedly proved unequal or unwilling to sustain an intensive penetration of the interior through colonial conquest and settlement. Portuguese presence in southern Africa remained primarily in the form of garrisons and trading posts until late in the nineteenth century. White settlers did not migrate in large numbers until the twentieth century, the modern era of globalization, and one analyst has asserted that if the Portuguese had vacated by 1875, "their physical legacy would have been minimal,"[7] except for the devastation wrought by the slave trade in Angola.

As with Spanish colonialism in the Americas, a small mestizo population that arose from the union of Portuguese men and African women became the main agent of mercantile trade in Mozambique and Angola. Many in this population spoke Portuguese, but in most other respects fit well into African societies. Yet their influence reached to commanding local armies, leading trade caravans, operating incipient agricultural estates legally recognized by the Portuguese as Crown land grants, and transmitting bits of imperial culture and religion. In many respects, for centuries Portugal was able to reap the benefits of trade without the costs of occupying its colonies through these middle managers, who themselves wanted to be as free as possible from the imposition of direct rule.

Meanwhile, another country, the Netherlands, facilitated greater globalization in the early modern era, rising as a commercial and sea power in the early 1600s. In 1652, the Dutch East India Company established a stopover station in southern Africa, seized by force from the Portuguese to service trade routes across the Indian Ocean. The station became Cape Town. At first, the Dutch settlers traded with the indigenous people, the Khoikhoi, for supplies, but as more Europeans arrived and sought land for farming, the two groups increasingly came into conflict. Eventually the settlers killed tens of thousands of Khoikhoi, confiscating their sheep and cattle and reducing their numbers to several thousand. The few remaining natives suffered near extinction from a smallpox epidemic in the early 1700s. Without sufficient labor to work the station, the Dutch began importing slaves from southern Asia as well as from Madagascar, Angola, and Mozambique. Racial mixing among the male Europeans and these slaves (as well as the remaining Khoikhoi) created the ethnic group that came to be known as the "Cape Coloured."

By 1780, the European population of the Cape reached more than 10,000, with fresh arrivals from Germany, France, and the Netherlands. Many made their living as farmers and ranchers and came to be known as Boers, derived from the Dutch word for farmer. The Boers pushed far enough east to increasingly encounter substantial numbers of Bantu-speaking Africans, such as the Xhosa, for the first time. As one scholar noted, "On the unsettled interior frontiers, adventurers of all races traded, fought, grazed cattle, and produced children, some assimilated into the white or African communities, others later to be classed 'Coloured.'"[8] Inevitably, with more Europeans moving east, competition for land and water between them and the Bantu-speaking African groups brought further conflict.

By this time, other powerful European nations rose to promote their interests in early modern globalization. During the Napoleonic Wars, Britain seized the Cape Colony from the Dutch in order to keep it out of the hands of the French and gained full control recognized by other European powers in 1806. Like the previous imperial nation, Britain wanted the Cape for strategic reasons related to its key colony, India. But the British also inherited a somewhat rowdy, complex mix of Europeans scattered over the western half of what we now know as South Africa. In order to ease population pressures back home, Britain further complicated the situation by exporting from home thousands of new settlers to the Cape, an illustration of the migration domain of globalization. Physically separated from other Europeans, these British settlers came to be known as the "English-speaking whites." The Dutch and other Europeans who had already been in the area for more than a century called themselves Afrikaners. Afrikaners spoke Afrikaans, a language first adapted by Africans from Dutch.

Tensions among the various populations now at the Cape—Afrikaners, English-speaking whites, Coloureds, and various African groups—began to rise. More immigrants meant more pressure for land and more conflict with the Xhosa to the east. Unable to defeat the Xhosa themselves, Afrikaner and English-speaking settlers needed British imperial troops to complete the task, which they did by the mid-1800s. British control, however, also meant the imposition of British law. Britain abolished its own slave trade in 1807, and under pressure from the London Missionary Society, finally outlawed slavery in the Cape in 1833. On the one hand, this had little positive impact on former slaves' economic opportunities, because African indigenous economies in the area had long since been destroyed. On the other hand, the slave owners, the Afrikaners, resented abolition's negative economic impact on farming.

British law also imposed the exclusive use of English in all aspects of official undertakings, and British merchants came to dominate most commercial interests. Accustomed to their previously established patterns of life and culture, Afrikaners increasingly found the imposition of British rule unbearable, while African societies still resisting conquest increasingly found themselves outgunned by imperial troops. Conflicts among the population groups in the Cape grew.

As this heated mix began to get volatile, two important events occurred. One, the *mfecane,* has to do with Africans living in the north and east, and the other, the Great Trek, concerns Afrikaner expansion into this same territory.

Mfecane is a Zulu word meaning "the time of troubles, weakness, or emaciated from hunger." The Sotho word equivalent, *difaqane,* conveys the sense of forced removals.[9] In the early 1800s, substantial turmoil began among different Bantu-speaking groups to the north and east. There are contending explanations for these developments: the demographic pressure of growing human and cattle populations; the desire by some powerful African leaders, for example, the Zulu chief Shaka (discussed below), to consolidate their rule over nearby groups; pressures on African societies from slave raids and ivory trade by the Portuguese in Mozambique; and the strain of Cape colonists pushing the frontier of the colony eastward. Whatever the explanation for these events, wars between various African groups began around 1817 and lasted for about two decades. The consequences were devastating. As one historian of the region has recounted:

> Thousands died violent deaths. Thousands more were uprooted from their homes. Village communities and chiefdoms were eliminated. . . .
>
> Besides the destruction, the immediate consequences of the wars were twofold. First, thousands of Basotho and Batswana from the highveld, as well as Mfengu and Xhosa from the coastal area, poured into the Cape Colony in search of subsistence which they were able to obtain by working for white colonists. Second the wars provided Whites with unprecedented opportunities to expand into the eastern part of southern Africa. In much of the central highveld, the population was sparse throughout the 1830s. The surviving inhabitants, fearing further disruptions, tended to conceal themselves from intruders, which gave white travelers the impression that the area was uninhabited and unclaimed. In fact, however, the rulers of the newly created Zulu, Ndebele, Swazi, and Sotho kingdoms assumed that, jointly, they had dominion over the entire region, though they contested its distribution among themselves.[10]

One of the region's most famous leaders, Shaka, arose during this period and helped to shape the *Mfecane*. Born around 1787 to a repudiated wife of the Zulu chief, Shaka grew up stigmatized and humiliated in exile. At twenty-three, he became a warrior in the army of Dingiswayo, a Mthethwa chief who quickly recognized Shaka's extraordinary military skills. When Shaka's father died in 1816, Dingiswayo backed Shaka's claim to the Zulu chieftainship and helped to assassinate the designated heir, Shaka's half brother. Shaka immediately reorganized the Zulu warriors, bringing innovations in tactics and weaponry, and shaped them into a fierce military machine that gave no quarter in battle. Within a year, Shaka had conquered and absorbed neighboring groups, quadrupling the number of his subjects in the Zulu nation. After Dingiswayo was killed in battle in 1817 by a rival group, Shaka began to consolidate his hold over other neighboring chiefdoms. He used diplomacy when possible and conquest when required. A number of groups simply took flight from his rule, fleeing as far north as modern Tanzania and as far south as the Cape Colony. Others were subordinated through the payment of tribute and further conquests. Some argue that his ruthlessness resulted in part from being "psychologically disturbed throughout his life and obsessively fearful of being supplanted by an heir."[11]

Shaka gave permission to British traders and hunters to settle in what is now Durban. They provided firearms and a channel through which Shaka tried unsuccessfully to establish diplomatic relations with the British at the Cape. Soon thereafter, his half brothers, with the blessing of other members of his family, assassinated him in 1828 at his royal residence. By that time, the region and the Zulu had suffered a decade of war, but more was to come. One half brother, Dingane, succeeded Shaka as ruler of the Zulu.[12]

Meanwhile, back at the Cape Colony, the second big event of this period, the Great Trek, began to unfold. Deeply resentful of British rule and the changes it brought, Afrikaners responded with a mass migration to the north and east, outside of the Cape Colony territory. Well organized and armed, thousands left the Cape from 1836 to 1854, seeking freedom and independence from British imperialism. They fought Africans along the way. Most notably, an Afrikaner commando group defeated the Zulu army in 1838 at what the Afrikaners call the battle of Blood River, an event that looms large in Afrikaner mythology. The Afrikaners established the republic of Natal on the eastern seaboard of what is now South Africa, a development that alarmed the British. Under pressure from missionaries concerned about the plight of Africans, as well as for strategic trade reasons, the British seized Natal in 1843 and set about importing indentured Indians to work sugar plantations there, bringing yet another population group to the region's complex mix of people.

Believing themselves again in an untenable situation, the Afrikaners left the coastal area of Natal to trek back to the interior, this time to establish two republics, the Transvaal (1852) and the Orange Free State (1854). With these independent territories, Afrikaners accomplished their goal of separating themselves from imperial powers in the region. Nonetheless, the republics remained fragile, dependent on trade with the British and partially circled by independent African chiefdoms with which they occasionally warred. The territories boldly claimed borders they could not enforce.

In summary, by the mid-1800s, due to global and regional dynamics, southern Africa held quite a complicated mix of disparate African groups, European settlers and traders from a variety of locales, Indians imported by the British, and mixed-race people, known as Coloureds. About 250,000 whites lived in the area, with Africans outnumbering them by a factor of ten.[13] Numerous resilient African groups remained intact and fairly independent, but they had been pushed progressively north and east. Africans whose societies were more thoroughly disrupted by conquest lived as laborers and servants in the white colonies, where Europeans depended enormously on them. Except for a few privileges in the Cape Colony where those with property could vote, Africans living under colonialism had no political rights. Whether still living in fairly independent societies or incorporated as subservients into colonial life, Africans increasingly gravitated to Christianity and made use of imported Western commodities.

The entire region existed under the protection of the British Empire, with the imperial government determined to keep control over the Cape's strategic sea routes. The Portuguese, who had very close relations with Britain at the time, held a number of trading posts in Angola and Mozambique frequented by traders from all over the world. Having consolidated their rule over the Cape Colony and Natal, the British government allowed the Afrikaners to separate themselves nearby in the Orange Free State and the Transvaal. This volatile combination of peoples and powers would become more tense in the next phase of history, the modern era of globalization, when the discovery of diamonds and gold in the region together with other factors set off the imperial "scramble for Africa."

MODERN GLOBALIZATION AND SOUTHERN AFRICA

The *modern era* (1850–1945) brought a lasting imprint of globalization, regionalization, and localization. The legacy of changes wrought during this time period are still evident in southern Africa. Globalization fixed the boundaries of the nations of the region, began the process of incorporating southern Africa into the world economy, and rooted powerful new cultural forms and ideas there. Regionalization linked the various parts of the area together in sustained economic and political processes, including interactions among races of people, while localization took hold in a number of arenas, exacerbating ethnic rivalries.

The Impact of Modern Globalization

Political and Economic Domains.   As discussed in chapter 1, intense imperial rivalry marked the first half of the modern era of globalization. The rising industrial powers of Germany, France, and Italy challenged British hegemony in many parts of the world, but particularly in Africa. Prior to this time, except for the British in southern Africa, most colonial interests stayed confined to coastal trading posts and slave raiding. Informal control rather than formal colonial occupation dominated the early modern era. In the modern period, however, the entire continent, with one exception (Ethiopia), came under European control within a short span of about forty years. In addition to imperial rivalry, two crucial discoveries spurred the race for formal colonization in southern Africa: diamonds in 1867 and gold in 1886, both in the territory that came to be known as South Africa.

Analysts assert that a number of features mark the "scramble for Africa": unprecedented speed and scope of expansionism; the transfer of sovereignty (and thus formal, legal political control as the Europeans understood it) from African hands to the colonizer through conquest or unequal treaties; the demarcation of formal boundaries for the colonies, in disregard of the territorial integrity of most African societies; unaccustomed ruthlessness and aggression in acquiring colonies; and intense competition and tension among European powers. At the diplomatic initiative of German chancellor Otto von Bismarck, the colonizers finally agreed on an orderly partition of the continent at the Berlin Conference of 1884–1885.[14]

Map 2.2 shows the outcome for the entire continent. Table 2.1 chronicles more fully the colonial heritage of southern Africa throughout the twentieth century. It also demonstrates the current placement of various ethnic groups that became divided across the colonies when imperially established boundaries ignored and abolished historic territories often recognized by African societies. In addition, Table 2.1 displays each nation's current population and political system, to be discussed later in this chapter.

Britain acquired the lion's share of the region. Consolidation of the territory now known as South Africa came at a high price. Several factors contributed to the British government's determination to take control of the Afrikaner republics of the Orange Free State and the Transvaal, including

34

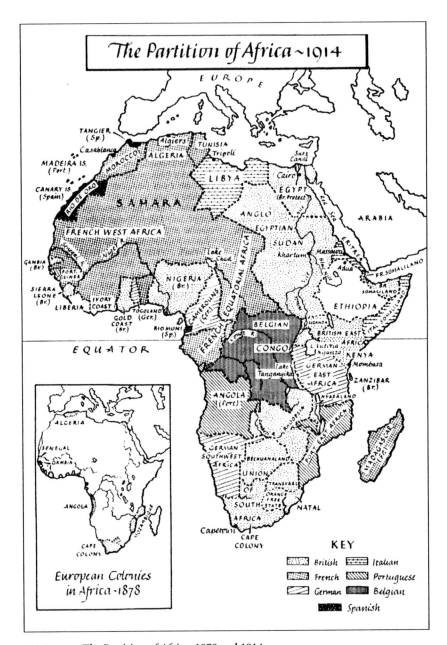

MAP 2.2   The Partition of Africa, 1878 and 1914

SOURCE: William L. Langer, ed., *An Encyclopedia of World History*
(Boston: Houghton Mifflin Co., 1972), p. 864.

TABLE 2.1   The Countries of Southern Africa

Country	Political System	Current Ethnic Groups	Population (million)
Angola	1483-1975 Portuguese colony 1975-1992 dictatorship (and civil war) 1992- multiparty democracy (and civil war) 2002- end civil war	Ovimbundu 37% Mbundu 25% Bakongo 13% Mestizo 2% White 1% Other 22%	13.5
Botswana	1885-1966 British colony of Bechuchanaland 1966 - multiparty democracy	Batswana 95% Basarwa, Kalanga, and Kgalagadi 4% White 1%	1.6
Lesotho	1871-1966 British colony of Basutoland 1966-1970 multiparty democracy 1970-1993 dictatorship/military government 1993- single party democracy	Sotho 99%	2
Malawi	1889-1891 British South Africa Company rule 1891-1964 British colony of Nyasaland 1964-1994 dictatorship 1994- multiparty democracy	Chewa 90% Nyanja, Lomwe and Other 10%	10.7
Mozambique	1497-1975 Portuguese colony 1975-1994 dictatorship (and civil war) 1990 – multiparty democracy	Makua-Lomwe 50% Tsonga, Malawi, Shona, Yao and Other 50%	18.1
Namibia	1484-1885 Portuguese colony 1885-1915 German colony of Southwest Africa 1915-1990 South African trustee/occupation 1990 – multiparty democracy	Ovambo 50% Kavango 9% Herero 7% Damara 7% Khoikhoi, San and Other 27%	1.8

South Africa	1652-1795 Dutch East India Company rule
	1795-1803 British colony (at Cape)
	1803-1806 Dutch colony (at Cape)
	1806-1910 British colony (w/Natal an Afrikaner
	  republic 1838-43, Orange Free State an
	  Afrikaner republic 1854-1902, and South
	  African Republic [Transvaal] an Afrikaner
	  republic 1860-1902)
	1910-1961 Union of South Africa, a dominion
	  in the British Empire
	1961-1994 Republic of South Africa, white minority
	  dictatorship
	1994 - multiparty democracy
		Black 75%, incl
		Zulu, Xhosa,
		Pedi, Sotho,
		Tswana, Tsonga,
		Swazi, Ndebele,
		Venda
		
		White 14%
		Mixed Race
		  (Coloured) 9%
		Asian/Indian 3%
			43.6

Swaziland	1894-1902 Transvaal dependent 1902-1968 British colony 1968 – monarchy/dictatorship	Swazi 97% Zulu, Tsong, Asian, and White 3%	1.1

Zambia	1889-1925 British South Africa Company rule
	1924-1964 British colony of Northern
	  Rhodesia
	1964-1991 single party democracy
	1991 – multiparty democracy
		About 70 different
		Bantu-speaking
		Groups such as
		Bemba, Nyanja,
		  and Tonga, 99%
			10

Zimbabwe	1893-1923 British South Africa Company rule 1923-1964 British colony of Southern Rhodesia 1964-1980 break away colony with white minority dictatorship called Rhodesia 1980-2002 single and later multi-party democracy 2002 dictatorship	Shona 82% Ndebele 14% Other African 3% · White 1%	11.4

SOURCES: Kwame Anthony Appiah and Henry Louis Gates Jr., *Africana: The Encyclopedia of the African and African American Experience* (New York: Basic Civitas Books, 1999); U.S. Government, CIA, *The World Factbook 2002,* www.odci.gov/cia/publications/factbook/print/ao.htm; F. Jeffress Ramsay and Wayne Edge, *Global Studies: Africa,* 10th ed. (Guilford, CT: Dushkin/McGraw-Hill, 2004); and The World Bank Group Country Briefs, www.worldbank.org.

the discovery of precious minerals, increasing conflict among the white population, the ongoing need for a large military force to defeat the remaining African kingdoms, and the threat from imperial rivals (especially Germany). A protracted war between "Brit and Boer" ensued for three years, from 1899 to 1902. The British call it the Boer War, and Afrikaners refer to it as the Second War of Freedom. Most scholars now call the conflict the South African War.

Just as white settler wars against Africans had been brutal and ruthless, the British fought the Afrikaners with the same intent to crush resistance, especially as Afrikaner militias increasingly adopted guerrilla tactics.

> [British commander in chief Lord Kitchener] burned Afrikaner crops and destroyed thirty thousand farmsteads. He exiled captured commandos . . . and removed the civilian population to camps, where they suffered great hardships under inefficient administrators. Nearly 28,000 Afrikaner civilians, most of them children, died of dysentery, measles, and other diseases in the camps. . . .
>
> Britain and the republics had claimed that the war was among Whites only and denied that they were using Blacks for military purposes. In fact, both sides made extensive use of black labor, and Africans as well as Afrikaners suffered from the scorched earth policy. Peter Warwick has shown that "at least 10,000 and possibly as many as 30,000 Blacks" had fought with the British army and that "almost 116,000 Africans had been removed to concentration camps, in which over 14,000 refugees lost their lives."[15]

Together with the Cape Colony and Natal, these republics became provinces of the Union of South Africa, granted independence as a single country in 1910. Because the British government moved so quickly after conquering the Afrikaners to make South Africa fully self-governing, many argue that Britain won the war but lost the peace. As they had for over two centuries, whites held the reins of political power and increasingly controlled the economic wealth of the new union. Therefore, political globalization became somewhat less extensive in southern Africa than other domains, which remained robust.

As had been the case before the war, the union excluded Africans from voting in three of the four provinces (the Cape being the one exception where literate, propertied Africans could vote). White women gained the franchise, but only white men could hold office. Having formed their own political party, Afrikaners regained political control of the Transvaal and the Orange Free State.

When granting the new union independence, Britain retained control of three territories intimately tied to South Africa: Bechuanaland, predominately inhabited by Tswana people and now known as Botswana; Basutoland, home to many Sotho people and known today as Lesotho; and Swaziland, still called by the same name and primarily populated by Swazi people. Britain also continued to hold a huge territory north of South Africa called Rhodesia, which the British had gained through the ambitious adventures of Cecil Rhodes, one of the most famous Britons associated with the colonization of Africa (see below). Rhodesia separated Angola from Mozambique and prevented the Portuguese from extending their hold clear across the continent. With white settlers from the Cape Colony concentrated in the southern part of the territory, the British divided the colony into Northern Rhodesia, known today as Zambia, and Southern Rhodesia, now called Zimbabwe. Through Rhodes, the British also acquired a small colony east of Zambia, and it, too, eventually hosted a large number of white settlers. Known at the time as Nyasaland, the country is now called Malawi. The following brief overview of the pre–South African war period helps in comprehending all these acquisitions.

Having persuaded Britain to annex Bechuanaland in 1885, Cecil Rhodes extended British colonialism northward into what is now Zimbabwe and Zambia by tricking the Ndebele ruler, Lobengula, in 1888 into granting exclusive mining rights in Matabeleland and Mashonaland. The British South Africa Company (organized in 1889) then ruled the new territories, named Rhodesia in 1894, until the British government took formal control in 1925, some years after Rhodes's death in 1902. These acquisitions, however, were only part of his accomplishments.

Born in 1853, Rhodes first made his way from England to South Africa in 1870 to join his brother on a cotton plantation in Natal. Together they became diamond prospectors, and by the age of nineteen, Rhodes had acquired a large fortune. He returned to attend Oxford in 1873 but did not receive his degree until 1881 because of his repeated journeys to South Africa. In 1880, he formed the De Beers Mining Company, then the second-largest diamond-mining company in the region (see chapter 5). Travels through the Transvaal and Bechuanaland in 1875 apparently inspired his ambition that Britain would rule the whole region, later enlarged to a vision of British dominion "from the Cape to Cairo."

Rhodes entered the Parliament of the Cape Colony in 1888, where he served until his death. Accruing political power there gave him a foundation from which to act on his vision of British expansion throughout the region. He became prime minister in 1890. During his term, he reformed education and restricted the franchise to literate people, reducing the African vote. He was forced to resign as prime minister in 1895 because of his role in conspiring to overthrow the government of the Afrikaner republics, against which the British government fought the South African War a few years later. He then devoted most of his time to work in Rhodesia, although he commanded troops at Kimberley during the war. He died at an early age, before the war's conclusion, and left almost all his fortune to promote public service, primarily through the Rhodes Scholarships to Oxford University. They benefit students from the (now former) British colonies, the United States, and Germany. Rhodes is buried in Zimbabwe. He continues to be known as one of the foremost British imperialists, famous for his combining of political and economic exploits.[16]

In the face of British expansion northward, Portugal struggled to keep its claims on Angola and Mozambique, and eventually succeeded. Its imperial rivals, Britain and Germany, signed but never implemented a secret agreement in 1898 to divide the two territories between them, should the Portuguese lose control. Portugal, a poor country with a weak economy, needed the colonies as a source of capital and endeavored to take more direct control by increasing its expropriation of African land and exploitation of African labor. For example, a 1875 vagrancy statute allowed local administrators to force "nonproductive" Africans into nonpaid labor, a practice reminiscent of slavery. By 1900, the colonial administration insisted that taxes be paid in cash, forcing Africans out of subsistence agriculture and into the wage economy of plantations and the mines nearby in British territories. Yet, facing fierce resistance from some Africans as well as political instability and economic crises both at home and abroad, Portugal did not fully conquer and colonize the territories of Angola and Mozambique until the 1920s. Ironically, British and German economic interests provided key support for Portuguese penetration of its own colonial interior, a matter discussed under regionalism below.[17]

A latecomer to the region, Germany acquired South-West Africa, the nation known today as Namibia, at the Berlin Conference in 1885. From the

THE RHODES COLOSSUS
STRIDING FROM CAPE TOWN TO CAIRO.

FIGURE 2.1   Cecil Rhodes
SOURCE: *Punch*, December 10, 1892, p. 266.

early 1800s, German, British, Finnish, and American missionaries had operated trading posts on the coast. The discovery of diamonds there in the
1850s brought renewed interest by Portuguese traders from Angola. The
Ovambo people in the northern part of the territory avoided full colonial
control until 1915, but elsewhere in Namibia the Germans deliberately and

systematically eliminated nearly 80 percent of the Herero and more than half the Nama and Damara peoples.[18] Later, with the defeat of Germany in World War I and the occupation of its colonies by Allied nations, the fledgling League of Nations (predecessor to the United Nations) assigned South Africa to hold Namibia as a mandate territory, responsible eventually for bringing it to independence. In effect, this meant that South Africa occupied the area, settling Afrikaners there to replicate their own nation's political and economic policies and practices.

To summarize political globalization in the modern era, by the end of World War I Britain held colonial control over Botswana, Lesotho, Swaziland, Malawi, Zambia, and Zimbabwe. As a newly independent nation, South Africa occupied Namibia, and as a defeated nation, Germany had no colonies. Portugal held Angola and Mozambique. Firm political control offered opportunity for intensifying economic globalization.

During the modern era, mining and minerals became the primary means through which southern Africa participated in the global economy. Gold, diamonds, and copper became and continue to be prominent exports of the region. They profoundly shaped the regional economy, a development discussed below. South Africa produced gold, as did Zimbabwe in much less quantity. Zimbabwe also ranked among the world's top producers of chromite at the time. South Africa, Namibia, and Angola produced diamonds and continue to do so. Copper comes primarily from Zambia. Coal from South Africa, Zambia, and Zimbabwe fueled both the mines and the railways built primarily to serve the mines. In exchange for these minerals, imports of both goods and finance came mainly from Britain.

Another crucial development incorporating southern Africa into the world economy occurred when South African entrepreneurs used American and European financing to birth what would become one of the world's largest global companies, the Anglo American Corporation. Founded in 1917 and led by Ernest Oppenheimer, Anglo American developed into a key player in regional mining ventures. As early as the 1890s, Cecil Rhodes monopolized diamond mining and marketing in a company called De Beers Consolidated Mines. Using the strength of Anglo American, Oppenheimer took over De Beers and the diamond monopoly in 1929. Then Anglo American dramatically expanded its holdings of gold mines and ventured next into copper. A financial giant, the company soon acquired significant holdings across the region. Anglo American illustrates the interest investors from

the United States and Europe took in southern Africa through locally organized companies as well as through other ventures. (See chapter 5 for more
discussion of these multinational corporations.)

By the end of the modern era, economic globalization extended across
southern Africa with substantial intensity and impact. Chapter 5 discusses
in more detail how the region interacts with the world economy, but at
this point one further domain of globalization needs attention. Cultural
forms of global penetration also proved powerful during this period, significantly facilitating the spread of the economic and political domains
discussed above. An accelerated outpouring of Christian missions and the
introduction of racist ideology came with colonialism, and the region
continues to show evidence of this cultural impact.

The Cultural Domain.   Just as European governments set out to colonize
the world during the modern era, Western Christian missions set out to
convert the world. Missionaries had some positive impact, but they were inextricably part of colonial conquest. In their drive to win converts, these
men and women sometimes catalyzed imperial subjugation of chiefs and
native peoples who resisted the intrusion of foreign religious influence.
When the missionaries got into trouble, imperial troops were sent to rescue
them. Missions also often directly supported conquering colonial forces and
popularized imperial causes back home. These religious workers also helped
to sustain the long-term development of colonies through education and
socialization of clerks to staff imperial administrations, as well as through
theological and biblical justifications for keeping Africans in inferior social,
economic, and political positions.[19] As one common saying in Africa puts it:
"When the missionaries came, whites had the Bible and we had the land.
When the missionaries left, whites had the land and we had the Bible."

One of the most famous missionaries to Africa was David Livingstone,
whose writings during the Victorian era made him a household name
and inspired many others to dedicate their lives to spreading the Christian faith to Africa.[20] Part of his public appeal also stemmed from his explorations. Described as "irascible and single-minded," between 1841
and 1873 Livingstone, who was also a medical doctor, investigated the
Zambezi River region and introduced Europeans for the first time to
Victoria Falls. His writings in part helped to popularize colonialism, but
the information he provided on the slave trade, which he encountered

frequently, generated considerable wrath among readers, contributing to the determination by many to end slavery. By the year 1871, however, no one had heard from him for some time. The *New York Herald* commissioned the journalist Henry Morton Stanley, a British émigré to the United States, to "find Livingstone," which Stanley did in 1871 on the shores of Lake Tanganyika, greeting him with his famous remark, "Doctor Livingstone, I presume." In failing health, Livingstone continued his explorations of the African Great Lakes region. In the meantime, the Royal Geographical Society sent a relief expedition to bring him home. The group arrived in early 1874, but Livingstone had already been dead for almost a year. His embalmed body was returned to Britain and buried in Westminster Abbey.[21]

In contrast to the negative influence of missions, Livingstone's work on the whole demonstrates that they also had some positive influence. As one scholar puts it, "Imperial Christianity, even at the height of imperialism, retained some elements of Christianity."[22] In a number of places, those like Livingstone provided the conscience for colonialism, playing an important role, as mentioned earlier, in the abolition of slavery across the world and particularly in southern Africa. As an alternative to the lucrative marketing of slaves, missionaries promoted investment in other forms of trade and in this way continued to promote colonial penetration. They also on occasion led campaigns against the abuse of workers or excessive taxation in the colonies. Missions provided virtually the only access to Western-style schooling and medical attention available to Africans, although offsetting this latter benefit, Africans suffered disproportionately from the diseases Europeans brought as well.

In addition to religion, a second type of cultural globalization came in the form of racist ideology, often buttressed by distorted forms of Christian theology and biblical teachings. An ideology is simply a set of assumptions, ideas, and principles about the way people and societies ought to behave. Defining racism is more complex.

One authoritative source, Andrew Hacker,[23] has asserted that racism can be expressed in three different but related ways, and only the last of these three can be characterized as an ideology. The first is individual racism, as when people make and act upon limited impressions of another person based on the color of that person's skin or some other inherited or immutable characteristic.[24] For example, in southern Africa, Africans and whites rarely socialize with each other or attend church together, historically or currently.

The second way to express racism is through regularized policies and practices that knowingly or unknowingly favor one group and discriminate against another. This is called institutional racism. In southern Africa, colonial administrations and white settler governments knowingly and deliberately designed labor, land, franchise, and virtually all other policies to ensure white control and African subservience, as will be seen later in this chapter and in this book. Even after Africans had been elected to head all the governments of the region, institutional racism or its legacy persisted in some arenas. That is, a few Africans rose in economic, political, or social ranks, but most remained poor and essentially disenfranchised.

For example, black officials who now head the Zimbabwean government campaigned on promises of meaningful land reform that would help Africans reclaim some of the territory taken during colonial conquest 100 years earlier. Yet at the turn of the twenty-first century, white farmers still controlled more than one-half the fertile land, even though they made up less than 2 percent of the country's total population. Beginning in spring 2000, some Africans illegally took over a number of white farms, claiming that the now twenty-year-old promises for land reform should be fulfilled. Some of the squatters were men who fought during the 1970s in guerrilla armies to achieve black majority rule. Many who support land reform decried the veterans' violent tactics in taking over the farms, but they insist that the government address the exclusion of most African farmers from access to good land, a powerful legacy of white minority rule and thus a form of institutional racism.[25]

The third form of racist expression is "the belief that members of the black race represent an inferior strain of the human species."[26] This kind of racism took the form of an ideology that, although fully developed and articulated in the nineteenth century, can still be found today.[27] Most colonialists of the nineteenth century understood their conquests as part of a "civilizing mission" or a "white man's burden" to bring a superior Western way of life to "backward" or "savage" Africans.[28] In the ideology's seemingly more palatable form, whites characterized Africans as children who could be peaceful, innocent, and caring, but they could never fully grow up to achieve adulthood. Therefore, they must always be under the care of whites.

Often labeled "social Darwinism" or "biological determinism," this seemingly "scientific" perspective arose at the same time that Charles Darwin's theories of evolution in biology were gaining ground. According to biological determinism, blacks were slaves (or poor, or less intelligent, or backward, or any other inferior condition) because the process of natural selection had found the best place for them. They simply were biologically inferior, the argument goes. In contrast, whites were masters (or well-to-do, or more intelligent, or civilized, and so forth), also due to natural selection and their biological superiority. From this perspective, intermarriage would produce "mongrelization" or a "dumbing down" of the whole human species and therefore must be avoided.[29] The superior race, the only ones who really could be characterized as fully human (rather than subhuman) should govern. The inferior race, those not fully human, should have no access to political participation.

As one scholar put it, anyone and any society can be racist. But this Western ideological form grew to outperform all others:

> [T]he Western strain of the virus has eclipsed all others in importance. Through the colonial expansion of Europe racism spread widely over the world. . . . [N]o other brand of racism has developed such a flourishing mythology and ideology. In folklore, as well as in literature and science, racism became a deeply ingrained component of the Western *Weltanschauung*. Western racism had its poets like Kipling, its philosophers like Gobineau and Chamberlain, its statesmen like Hitler, Theodore Roosevelt and Verwoerd [a former prime minister of South Africa]; this is a record not even remotely approached in either scope or complexity by any other cultural tradition.[30]

This racist ideology, an aspect of cultural globalization relevant to many parts of the world, flourished in the modern era when southern Africa became fully colonized by European powers and white settlers. Such ideas profoundly shaped virtually all aspects of life in the region, as will be demonstrated in this chapter and others. Overall, globalization in a number of domains fully penetrated southern Africa, elevating the region in world affairs. These processes shaped regional economic and political patterns that continue to have impact, the next subject of discussion.

Regionalism and Localism in the Modern Era

Prior to the modern period of globalization, southern Africa could hardly be characterized as a region. Instead, it resembled a patchwork of disparate territories informally held by colonial powers ambivalent about their acquisitions. Nineteenth-century imperialism and white settler governance, however, forged regional coherence among formally demarcated colonies, particularly in the political and economic domains. On the whole, regionalization served the interests of globalization, shaping government, the use of land and labor, mining operations, and infrastructure.

There was some variation in local administration among the ten territories in southern Africa, but by the end of the modern era, significant patterns of racial domination emerged across the entire region. In those places with substantial numbers of white settlers such as Zimbabwe, Malawi, and South Africa, British colonial authorities allowed whites limited participation in politics. For example, they elected parliamentary representatives who legislated local matters. British-appointed governors filled executive offices and could veto any legislation. Once independent, the South African government ensured that only whites participated in governance and then applied this system to Namibia as well. In those places with few white settlers such as Zambia, Botswana, Lesotho and Swaziland, Britain used Africans in a system of indirect rule. Colonial authorities took charge of significant policy issues and appointed African chiefs to collect taxes as well as to govern over matters pertaining to each ethnic group.

The Portuguese lagged behind Britain by allowing chartered companies and plantation concessions (some controlled by British and other non-Portuguese financial interests) to govern Angola and Mozambique under the general guidance of colonial authorities well into the twentieth century—long after the practice had ended elsewhere. These companies had the power to tax, control labor, and perform other governmental functions in their areas. They also had the military responsibility for conquering African groups resistant to colonial rule.

Despite the efforts of the Portuguese government, few whites settled in the colonies until the 1940s, and strict differentiation among racial groups did not develop until early in the twentieth century. In the modern era of globalization, Portugal exiled convicts to Angola and Mozambique, and together with traders and government officials these men constituted the white population. Portuguese women did not accompany the men, and a sizable mestizo population resulted. One scholar has noted that in the nineteenth century and earlier,

> Portuguese men intermarried with women of other racial groups, acknowledged the children of these unions, frequently arranged for their education back in Portugal, and saw that they obtained jobs in the colonial administration. The strong position of the father in the Portuguese family, and the pride taken in paternity, helps to explain this readiness to accept half-castes into the white community. Many of the leading figures in colonial society, including governors, military commanders, parliamentary deputies and mayors, were of mixed descent.[31]

This pattern changed soon after the turn of the century, however, when Portuguese administrators explicitly adopted the attitudes and some of the practices of the British colonies nearby. The trend of racial segregation accelerated with greater immigration from Portugal in later decades. Colonial authorities, however, always theoretically allowed for the possibility of African "assimilation" into white Portuguese society as *civilisados*, a policy they proudly contrasted with what they viewed as more racist laws of nearby territories. To be recognized as a *civilisado*, however, Africans had to attain a certain level of education, pay large sums of money, and wade through corrupt bureaucracies. Few Africans had the capacity to fulfill these requirements and fewer still bothered to try. By 1950, only 30,000 Angolans and 5,000 Mozambicans had acquired the status of *civilisado*.[32]

Therefore, by the end of the modern era of globalization, unlike most other colonial territories on the continent and elsewhere, sizable numbers of white people had migrated to and settled in the region. They dominated the political systems of six of the ten territories in southern Africa, even as most of these remained under colonial rule. This pattern of entrenched white political domination would continue to have significant impact on all the countries of the region well into the period of contemporary globalization.

The economic domain demonstrated a similar model of white control, and once again, South Africa led the way. In 1905, under British colonialism, a Native Affairs Commission recommended the permanent territorial segregation of Africans from whites. In 1913, the newly independent South African government enacted the Natives Land Act, which allocated about 7 percent of the country to African reserves and prohibited Africans from purchasing or leasing land outside these areas from people who were not Africans. By 1939, the total land for the reserves had increased to 11.7 percent, in areas later designated by the formal structures of apartheid as "homelands." They became "reservoirs of cheap, unskilled labor for white farmers and industrialists."[33] Without good land, previously prosperous peasants could no longer compete, and Africans could no longer feed themselves. Poor nutrition became the norm, and over 20 percent of the children died in their first year. Missionary societies provided what little education there was for Africans. Municipal, provincial, and central governments all imposed taxes, forcing many who had previously engaged in subsistence farming to migrate away from the reserves into the wage-labor force. All African males who worked outside the reserves were required to carry passbooks that indicated their rightful place and their purposes for temporarily being in a white area.[34] Afrikaners were renowned for their racial prejudice and would later refine this structure of control over Africans, formally naming it "apartheid" (see below). Important to note, however, is that a government led by English-speaking whites first passed and implemented laws to remove Africans from their land, to confine them, and to control their labor and movement.

Other territories with sizable white settler populations instituted similar measures. Zimbabwe's controls resembled those of South Africa. When South Africa brought Namibia under its control, it used the blueprint of its system there. Angola constitutes an atypical case for some of these general conditions, but Mozambique does not. In Angola, because of the uneven and inefficient implementation of Portuguese colonial control, large numbers of Africans continued to prosper through the 1960s as landowning farmers.[35] In both countries, but more commonly in Mozambique, however, the colonial government assigned prime land to chartered companies, plantation concessions, and (eventually) white settlers, forcibly removing Africans when necessary. This land produced export crops like coffee, rubber, cotton, sugar, copra, sisal, and tea. African men carried passbooks, which recorded the district or geographical area to which they were assigned as well as tax and labor obligations. The colonial government instituted hut taxes and vagrancy laws to force men off their farms and into wage labor for local employers. In essence, the law defined an African not employed in the colonial economy as a vagrant. Labor conditions were notoriously bad, at times attracting international indignation and criticism, regularly driving Africans to migrate to other parts of these colonies or to other territories.[36]

Labor migration within and between countries forged another feature of regionalization in southern Africa. Even in the late 1800s, prior to the Portuguese gaining full control of Mozambique, African men from the southern part of the territory migrated to the mines in South Africa. This pattern profoundly shaped the economy of the country as well as the region, and continues to do so. In 1955, one estimate suggested that in southern Mozambique, "half the men of working age were absent in South Africa at any one time, and that most of the men between the ages of seventeen and sixty have spent more than half their adult years in the Union of South Africa."[37] Although work conditions were difficult in the mines, the Mozambican miners preferred them to forced labor back home. The mining companies coordinated the recruitment of labor outside of South Africa through the Witwatersrand Native Labour Association and drew men from across the entire region, except for Angola. Separated from their families, these men worked short-term contracts and lived temporarily in compounds built by the companies.

In addition to patterns of labor migration, the mining companies shaped other aspects of regionalization as well. Infrastructure bears a clear imprint of the mining industry. Largely completed by 1902, the current railways in the region were built with state financing or state-guaranteed loans to service the mining companies. Railroads and ports for commodity transportation came to be dominated by South Africa.

In summary, a number of factors established a clear pattern of regionalization in the economic domain. With the notable exception of Botswana, Lesotho, Swaziland, and parts of Angola, white settlers or other commercial colonial agents owned or controlled the land. Financing for developing the land, the infrastructure, and a budding industrial sector lay in white hands, administered either privately or by colonial authorities. In particular, South African whites had a disproportionate amount of this control and ownership across the entire region. The mining industry profoundly shaped southern Africa's economic dynamics, including the transportation system and a migratory labor system that drew from virtually all of the territories. Throughout the region, Africans, including even those who could remain on their own farms, were forced to work for wages in the predominately white economies in order to pay newly imposed taxes and to avoid prosecution under vagrancy laws.

Localization began to emerge in several ways. As is clear from earlier discussions in this chapter, some historic enmities existed among African groups prior to colonialism. Compounding these, colonial powers were quick to pit one ethnic group against another in military conflict or in social and economic competition. In the British areas, native reserves designated land predominantly according to ethnic group, and the mines often separated men of different ethnicities. African ethnic rivalries did not begin in the modern period, but imperial conquest and white settler rule added new dynamics to these conflicts. In South Africa, English-speaking whites and the British on one side and Afrikaners on the other finished their bitter war, but conflict between them remained. The English-speaking whites dominated mining and other industry and held themselves to be superior over the Afrikaners, who dominated agriculture. These groups and the other whites in the region closed ranks when dealing with Africans, however, to ensure white minority rule.

Thus, the modern era ended with globalization extended throughout southern Africa, which had become a fairly coherent region for the first time in history. These global and regional processes stimulated new forms of localism, some of which exacerbated old ethnic tensions.

CONTEMPORARY GLOBALIZATION IN THE REGION

The remainder of this book portrays in some depth the contemporary era of globalization, particularly in the military, political, and economic domains. In the section below, the discussion of events that unfolded after 1945 will be confined to a portion of the political aspects of global and regional developments and to additional dynamics in the cultural domain. The most significant developments were the achievement of independence and the democratic election of governments. This return to African control came at a heavy price locally, nationally, and regionally. This story only begins here and will be more fully developed in chapter 3 on military globalization.

For five of the territories under British colonialism with fewer white settlers, movement toward independence developed much as it did in other parts of Africa. In the Portuguese colonies and in the three other places with substantial numbers of white settlers, however, independence and the possibility of majority rule came much more slowly and only after decades of warfare and civil conflict. A clear commitment to sustained democratic governance in the region came even later and remains fragile. The Cold War between the world's superpowers exacerbated the difficulty of attaining these goals. Southern Africa became one of the regions of the world that would bear the burden of global conflicts between West and East, capitalism and socialism, along with the more familiar and deeply entrenched division between black and white.

As noted in chapter 1, World War II devastated and exhausted European nations. Eventually, most colonial powers began to rethink the costs and benefits of holding onto their far-flung territories. At the same time, leaders among colonial subjects began to campaign for political freedom. The war gave new impetus to their long-standing efforts to resist and in some cases even to rebel against foreign occupation. Western imperial governments had drafted soldiers from the colonies to fight against German and Italian fascism. At war's end, these returning soldiers and others in the colonies who supported the war effort pointedly criticized the victors' hypocrisy. How could the Allies fight for the cause of freedom from tyranny while continuing to occupy others' territories?

Most imperial powers began to plan for their colonies' transition to independence in the distant future, in another thirty to forty years. Organizations devoted to independence for colonial subjects sprang up fairly quickly in most territories, however, despite heavy and fairly common repression against indigenous political activity. In a few cases, armed rebellions, which had erupted occasionally since the beginning of colonialism, accelerated. With the costs of occupation rising and world opinion beginning to turn in favor of ending formal empires, most imperial governments granted their colonies independence by the mid-1960s, a mere twenty years after the end of World War II. Notable exceptions to this trend were the white settler colonies of southern Africa.

Cultural Globalization: The Power of Ideas

What swayed world opinion, including the public in imperial nations, to urge nations to withdraw from occupying others' territories? Leaders of independence movements in the colonies used powerful and persuasive ideas for organizing their campaigns: nationalism, sovereignty, self-determination, human rights, socialism, passive resistance, and in the case of Africa, Pan-Africanism. Ironically, all but one of these ideologies originated in Europe or the United States. Their application across the world on behalf of peoples subjected to Western imperialism demonstrates yet another aspect of cultural globalization.

Notions of nationalism, sovereignty, and self-determination contributed significantly to political globalization in the contemporary era. Nationalism promotes the idea that nations should have their own state. A nation is a group that understands itself to have a common heritage and identity based on language, history, and culture. A nation-state, as noted in chapter 1, is recognized to be a government capable of exercising control over a community of people within a well-defined territory. Chapter 1 also defined the concept of sovereignty, the idea that no other authority has jurisdiction over a nation's government. This concept dates back to 1648 in European politics. Later, the French Revolution in 1789 was the first source of clearly articulated nationalist sentiments, which then spread throughout Europe in the nineteenth century. Nationalism helped to forge Germany and Italy as nation-states, for example, and demonstrated the power both to unify people into new political entities and to fragment existing ones.

Even though most African colonies contained diverse ethnic groups, African leaders seized on the old idea of nationalism and combined it with a more recently created concept of self-determination to rally their supporters around a unifying theme of independence. The Covenant of the League of Nations (1919) and the UN Charter (1945) formally embody the concept of self-determination, but the notion dates back to the U.S. Declaration of Independence in 1776 and the French Declaration of the Rights of Man in 1789. Self-determination means the right of a group that considers itself a nation to determine what political authority will govern its members as well as what territory they will occupy. This concept played a powerful role in arguments against colonialism in world political arenas.

In the contemporary period, the United Nations also gave important currency to another concept employed in independence movements. Human rights became a globally prominent idea with the UN Universal Declaration on Human Rights in 1948, parts of which echo some of the sentiments of the American and French revolutions. Furthermore, African elites watched and met with African American leaders in the United States, who, beginning in the 1950s, very effectively organized campaigns to achieve their own civil and political rights (a topic discussed in more detail in chapter 4).[38]

Unlike the concepts of nationalism, sovereignty, self-determination, and human rights, some ideologies specifically featured race at the center of their promotion of cultural globalization. A famous American intellectual, W. E. B. Du Bois, originated the concept of Pan-Africanism, which at the time (1897) he called "Pan-Negroism," and he organized the Pan-African Congress of 1919 in Paris. Du Bois became a close friend of the first president of Ghana, Kwame Nkrumah, who actively promoted Pan-Africanism and helped to found the Organization for African Unity (OAU) as one concrete, albeit limited, expression of the concept. Although this ideology encompasses a range of ideas, it focuses on linking the whole black race for political, cultural, and artistic purposes. In particular, many Pan-Africanists advocated the unification of Africans into a single political entity, with some arguing for the return of African Americans to this united African state. Du Bois had identified "the color line" as the twentieth century's primary problem, and Pan-Africanism gave colonial subjects and former slaves in the Americas and the Caribbean a strong foundation for pride in their race and its accomplishments.[39]

A variation on the concept of Pan-Africanism became particularly important to southern Africa, an idea called Africanism. Some groups campaigning for freedom considered themselves Africanists. They placed emphasis on a racial understanding of Africa as the land of black people. They stressed that Africans or blacks must work only among themselves to regain majority rule. No alliances could be made with white people or Indians, no matter how committed some in these groups might be to change. Africanists often tended on the whole to be hostile to socialism, on the grounds that like imperialism, it was a foreign force. (A further variation on this theme, Black Consciousness, developed in the 1970s in South Africa, particularly among students involved in movements for social change.) In contrast, other leaders of independence groups found inspiration in the U.S. civil rights movement and leaders such as Martin Luther King Jr., who sought justice in America at the same time that Africans organized to work for their independence. Strongly influenced by Christian theology, these elites welcomed opportunities for linkages across the races, and unlike the Africanists, they advocated the concept of multiracialism, meaning that all races of people should work together for change.[40]

Some of those who led the campaigns for majority rule also advocated some form of socialism, another concept spread through cultural globalization. Socialism basically asserts that economies should be characterized by public ownership of productive assets (by the state or some other collective entity) and by planning as a mechanism for decisionmaking about the production and distribution of goods and services, undergirded by a driving force to meet human needs[41] (see also chapter 5). Socialist thought originated in Europe in the first half of the eighteenth century but became officially embodied in governmental institutions only after the Russian Revolution of 1917. The Chinese Communist Revolution followed some decades later, in 1949.

Colonial peoples identified capitalism and imperialism with the West, the source of their subjugation.[42] As part of their revulsion with imperialism, these leaders also rejected the notion that their national economies should be modeled on those that had exploited them so badly. The primary alternative model—socialism—held great appeal, and in contrast to Western powers, the Communist governments of the Soviet Union and China assertively supported independence movements.

In Africa, most leaders' articulation of anticapitalist sentiments and ideologies did not equate with uncritical support of communism in the Soviet Union, China, or elsewhere. Many African elites sought to pursue economic systems that would simply ensure a decent standard of living for the people of their country and preserve community life.[43] The various ways in which nation-states organize their economies will be left for a fuller discussion in chapter 5. Important to consider here, however, is the Cold War context in which Africans and other independence movement leaders criticized capitalism and argued in favor of some form of socialism. Some Western governments grew increasingly alarmed at the possibility that socialists would come to power in one or more colonial territories, and on occasion the United States intervened militarily or fought wars to prevent such outcomes, as in Vietnam and various other parts of the world. In their colonies, the British government nurtured and supported moderate African leaders to take the reins of government when the colonies became free, which served as a tactic to undermine the possibility of socialists coming to power.

In summary, virtually all the movements for independence in Africa and other colonial territories embraced ideologies spread through the cultural domain of globalization: nationalism, the pursuit of self-determination and sovereignty, and respect for human rights. Some also enthusiastically promoted Pan-Africanism, and some actively demonstrated their sympathy with socialism. At times, various groups hotly disputed and even fought over contending ideologies. As will be seen in the next chapter, all these ideas had their proponents in southern Africa. New and powerful activist methods for waging campaigns, however, originated in southern Africa and subsequently spread across the globe. One of the world's most admired political leaders, Mohandas K. Gandhi, pioneered the new and creative use of mass mobilization and direct action.

Gandhi came to South Africa in 1893 after legal training in London. In 1906 he became a leader in Indian efforts to resist pass laws that restricted the movement of Indians in South Africa. Later, in 1913, he led a number of campaigns to address unfair taxes, property rights, and various restrictions on Indians, including some on marriages. During these political protests, Gandhi developed the technique of *satyahraha* (soul force), in which large numbers of activists, using nonviolent methods, deliberately broke the laws that offended them and accepted the consequences of imprisonment and suffering for their actions. Other labels for this method are "passive resistance" and "direct action." The point of such mass mobilizations was to arouse the conscience of those loyal to the government and to convince the authorities that reform was in their own interest. After numerous arrests and a prison sentence, Gandhi left South Africa for India in 1914, but a powerful legacy remained.[44] Many resistance leaders in colonial territories adopted his techniques of mass mobilization and direct action (as did organizers of civil rights campaigns in the United States). Gandhi himself used them again in his successful efforts to help free India from British colonialism.

India became independent in 1947, the first colony to join the international community as a sovereign state. In the two decades that followed, other colonies also gained independence, with indigenous leaders taking the reins of government. Ghana became the first black African state in 1957. Most transitions took place with remarkably little violence. Exhaustion and increasing colonial costs, together with the power of ideals such as nationalism, sovereignty, self-determination, and human rights (often articulated through methods of passive resistance by their subjects), proved to be convincing to the colonial masters. As table 2.1 demonstrates, in southern Africa Botswana, Lesotho, Swaziland, Malawi, and Zambia became part of the global tendency to sever formal colonial ties. All these countries attained independence in the 1960s. The Portuguese colonies and the white-settler societies in Zimbabwe (Rhodesia), South Africa, and its occupied territory, Namibia (South-West Africa), however, defied the trend, holding fast to their political, economic, and military control.[45]

Although white minority rule gripped much of the region, cultural globalization's powerful diffusion of ideas and ideologies that envisioned a better world for the majority profoundly affected those living in southern Africa. Furthermore, whites and blacks alike witnessed the political globalization of newly independent states growing in number and influence, and just as black organizations were determined to demand the same, white settlers were determined to deny such possibilities.

The Regionalization of White Intransigence

Not only did the region's colonial and white regimes defy world trends, they systematically instituted a number of measures to tighten their control to ensure African subordination. Demographic factors were crucial to this process. Large numbers of European émigrés poured into the region. Whites in Zimbabwe numbered about 34,000 in 1921, 69,000 in 1941, and 222,000 in the early 1960s. They came from Britain and South Africa in roughly even proportions. In 1940, Angola had 44,000 whites, and Mozambique had about 27,000. By the early 1970s, Angola's white population had jumped to about 335,000 and Mozambique's whites rose to 200,000. South Africa's white population grew from 1.3 million in 1911 to 2 million in 1936, expanding to 3.1 million in 1960. Most of these immigrants came from Britain. Across these decades, Africans constituted about 70 percent of the population in South Africa. Their proportion of the population relative to whites was always higher in other countries.[46]

Therefore, although the white population grew dramatically after the war, Africans continued to be the large majority.

Europeans came to the region in part to seek their fortune. The southern African economies offered bountiful opportunities for new settlers and foreign investment. Mining expanded through mechanization made possible by massive infusions of capital from abroad. Manufacturing took hold in South Africa due in part to investment by multinational corporations from the United States and Britain. The United States became South Africa's second-largest trading partner. The agricultural sector grew significantly in Zimbabwe (tobacco) and northern Angola (coffee). Mozambique continued to depend largely on the export of labor to the mines in South Africa as well as to the mines and farms in Zimbabwe. Infrastructure to serve these industries across the region also grew. Although whites enjoyed prosperity and new economic possibilities, Africans continued to see their opportunities dwindle.

Building on a foundation of policies put in place by previous governments, the Afrikaner-led government elected in South Africa in 1948 introduced a series of measures that formalized the system called apartheid, an Afrikaner word meaning "separate development." The concept of apartheid envisioned a country where Africans, mixed-race people, Indians, and whites would live separately in carefully designated areas. The system of influx control meant that people of color would be allowed to travel and lodge temporarily in white areas for work, but only if they had a work permit stamped in their passbook issued by the government. Africans were confined to ten homelands, formerly the reserves that together constituted a total of 13 percent of the land. Eventually deprived of South African citizenship, Africans held citizenship in their designated homeland instead. The regime envisioned granting all the homelands "independence" in due time. The passbook, carried by all adult Africans, contained their racial, ethnic, and homeland designation, tax records, work permits, and permission to be in white areas for purposes of work. If caught without the passbook or in the wrong place, Africans could be jailed or sent back to their homelands, which on the whole were economically destitute sections of the country with very little potential for development. Most of the homelands came to be repositories for women, children, and old people who had no permission to be elsewhere—"superfluous appendages," as one

South African prime minister called them. Thus, one significant consequence of apartheid was the separation of many families for all but one
or two weeks a year, with husbands working near the cities and living
"temporarily" in black townships such as Soweto, while their families
stayed behind in the homeland.

The policies instituted by the Afrikaners' National Party after its 1948
electoral victory also included an aggressive program of promoting and
supporting Afrikaner businesses, professionals, and workers. The government appointed Afrikaners to all levels of the civil service, awarded
state contracts to Afrikaner businesses, and channeled government
monies through Afrikaner banks. By the 1970s, the English-speaking
whites in the country no longer dominated the country's economy as
they had done historically, and many of the ethnic divisions between
whites began to fade.

Although South Africa exhibited a more formal and extreme pattern of
increased racial subjugation and tightened controls, the other four territories with significant numbers of white settlers adopted somewhat similar
policies. Furthermore, in attempts to resist international pressure for
change, whites across the region dug in their heels, sometimes mixing violent mechanisms of control with limited openness to change. For example,
Portugal formally declared its colonies to be the nation's overseas
provinces in 1951. After putting down an uprising in Angola, the Portuguese government extended citizenship to all people in the colonies, established limited local self-rule for Africans, and put concessions
companies under greater regulation.[47]

Fearful that their continued link with Britain would necessitate concessions to Africans as had occurred in nearby Malawi and Zambia (then
Northern Rhodesia), whites in Zimbabwe (then Southern Rhodesia) re-
belled and issued the Unilateral Declaration of Independence (UDI) in
1965. Britain and the world community responded with moral condemnation and economic sanctions (topics to be covered in more depth in
chapter 4). South Africa continued to institute apartheid-like policies in
Namibia. With a number of newly independent nations now in its membership, the United Nations revoked South Africa's trusteeship mandate
over the former German colony in 1966. In 1971, the International Court
of Justice declared South Africa's presence in Namibia to be illegal, a find-
ing largely ignored by the apartheid regime.

The region readied itself to address threats to colonial and white minority rule both internally and externally. As will be seen in the next chapter, civil unrest escalated in South Africa in the 1950s, and the war for independence in Angola began in 1961, but guerrilla warfare had begun more than a decade earlier in Zimbabwe and Namibia. The South African, Rhodesian, and Portuguese governments began to cooperate to apprehend political activists and guerrilla leaders in the region. Geographically strong, white-ruled territories stood between the apartheid state and the black-ruled nations to the north, and South Africa was determined to keep it that way. At this point, whites in South Africa felt quite confident that they could survive whatever challenges arose to their dominance in the region. Yet globally, bucking the currents of world opinion as well as the aspirations of the majority put the nations of the region on course for becoming the center of attention as international pariahs. As chapter 4 will demonstrate in more depth, the cultural globalization of ideas joined in a powerful partnership with the political globalization of networks and organizations determined to end white minority rule.

Africans in southern Africa campaigned for their freedom, just as did others subjected to colonialism. Some, for example the African National Congress (ANC), founded in 1912 in South Africa, had for many years been making formal, legal appeals to government leaders for greater democracy. This approach contrasted with the open rebellions that occasionally arose in scattered places across the region. In the 1950s, some protesters adopted a third strategy, the Gandhian approach of passive resistance. Frustration and impatience with all these tactics grew, however, as colonialism and white minority rule became more entrenched after World War II. Furthermore, the most frequent reaction to African resistance entailed massive repression and violence against armed rebellions and nonviolent direct action campaigns alike.

CONCLUSION

Since the earliest days of human interaction, southern Africa has played a significant role in world affairs. Modern globalization, however, brought coherence to the region as an economically significant and politically peculiar place and thrust it onto the world stage with prominence unequaled in most other parts of the globe. White minority rule in much of the region instituted structures and patterns of racial domination that would make an indelible impact far into the future, not only on the countries governed by these regimes but on their neighbors as well. Inevitably, world trends in the political and cultural domains began to penetrate southern Africa in the contemporary period, but in the end white minority rule proved remarkably resistant to change. Addressing the wars, civil strife, and some of the international dynamics that finally brought a formal end to apartheid and other forms of white minority government in the region is the task of the next chapter on military globalization.

Notes

1. Rick Gore, "The Dawn of Humans: Tracking the First of Our Kind," *National Geographic* 192, no. 3 (September 1997): 92–100; and Bruce Bower, "Ancient Human Saunters into Limelight," *Science News* 152, no. 8 (August 23, 1997): 117.

2. Kevin MacDonald, "Ancient African Civilizations," in Kwame A. Appiah and Henry Louis Gates Jr., eds., *Africana: The Encyclopedia of the African and African American Experience* (New York: Basic Civitas, 1999), pp. 91–100.

3. William Minter, *King Solomon's Mines Revisited* (New York: Basic Books, 1986), pp. 3–4.

4. David Sweetman, *Women Leaders in African History* (London: Heinemann, 1984), p. 39.

5. The Portuguese mistook the title of the ruler *(ngola)* for the name of the country and called the land of the Mbundu people Angola, the name by which it is known today.

6. Inge Tvedten, *Angola: Struggle for Peace and Reconstruction* (Boulder, CO: Westview Press, 1997), p. 20.

7. James Ciment, *Angola and Mozambique: Postcolonial Wars in Southern Africa* (New York: Facts on File, 1997), p. 27.

8. Minter, *King Solomon's Mines Revisited*, p. 4.

9. T. R. H. Davenport, *South Africa: A Modern History*, 4th ed. (Toronto: University of Toronto Press, 1991), p. 12.

10. Leonard Thompson, *A History of South Africa*, rev. ed. (New Haven, CT: Yale University Press, 1995), p. 87.

11. Appiah and Gates, *Africana*, p. 1697.

12. John Laband, "Shaka," http://encarta.msn.com, 1997–2003.

13. Thompson, *A History of South Africa*, pp. 108–109.

14. Benjamin J. Cohen, *The Question of Imperialism: The Political Economy of Dominance and Dependence* (New York: Basic Books, 1973), pp. 23–31; and Michael W. Doyle, *Empires* (Ithaca: Cornell University Press, 1986), pp. 232–256.

15. Thompson, *A History of South Africa*, pp. 142–143.

16. Appiah and Gates, *Africana*, p. 1614.

17. Malyn Newitt, *Portugal in Africa: The Last Hundred Years* (London: C. Hurst, 1981), pp. 24–40; Ciment, *Angola and Mozambique*, pp. 28–31.

18. Eric Young, "Namibia," in Appiah and Gates, *Africana*, pp. 1381–1382.

19. Doyle, *Empires*, pp. 170–171.

20. Interestingly, the largest growth in adherents to Christianity is now in Africa.

21. John Reader, *Africa: A Biography of the Continent* (New York: Vintage, 1997), pp. 528–529.

22. Doyle, *Empires*, p. 172.

23. Andrew Hacker, *Two Nations: Black and White, Separate, Hostile, Unequal* (New York: Scribner's, 1992), pp. 19–30.

24. A similar phenomenon, ethnocentrism, occurs when people make and act upon limited impressions of another person based on the other person's language, culture, customs, or history, or some combination of these.

25. "Protest and Confrontation over Zimbabwe Land Issue," *New York Times*, April 2, 2000; and Rachel L. Swarns, "Mugabe's Real Foes Aren't the Ones He Denounces," *New York Times*, April 30, 2000.

26. Hacker, *Two Nations*, p. 23.

27. Arthur Jensen, "How Much Can We Boost IQ and Scholastic Achievement?" *Harvard Educational Review* (February 1969). For a recent, more subtle scholarly expression of this ideology, see Richard J. Herrnstein and Charles Murray, *The Bell Curve: Intelligence and Class Structure in American Life* (New York: Free Press, 1994). For a scholarly refutation of such arguments, see Stephen Jay Gould, *The Mismeasure of Man* (New York: W. W. Norton, 1981).

28. See Louis L. Snyder, ed., *The Imperialism Reader: Documents and Readings on Modern Expansionism* (Princeton: D. Van Nostrand, 1962), pp. 87–88, for Rudyard Kipling's famous poem, "White Man's Burden," as well as a number of other interesting texts on imperialism in the nineteenth and twentieth centuries.

29. Hacker, *Two Nations*, pp. 23–27; George M. Fredrickson, *White Supremacy: A Comparative Study in American and South African History* (New York: Oxford University Press, 1981), pp. 188–190; and Pierre L. van den Berghe, *Race and Racism: A Comparative Perspective* (New York: John Wiley and Sons, 1967), pp. 11–18.

30. Van den Berghe, *Race and Racism*, p. 13.

31. Newitt, *Portugal in Africa*, pp. 167–168.

32. Ibid., pp. 138–142.

33. Ibid., p. 164.

34. Ibid., pp. 163–165; and Davenport, *South Africa*, pp. 207–208.

35. Newitt, *Portugal in Africa*, pp. 102–103, 135.

36. Ibid., pp. 106–112.

37. Ibid., p. 114.

38. For an introduction to the evolution of the concept of human rights, see Jack Donnelly, *International Human Rights*, 2nd ed. (Boulder, CO: Westview Press, 1998). For a discussion of the relationship between African American organizations in the United States and African independence movements, see chap. 5 of this book.

39. Kwame Anthony Appiah, "Pan-Africanism," in Appiah and Gates, *Africana*, pp. 1484–1486; and Kate Tuttle, "Du Bois, William Edward Burghardt," in ibid., pp. 635–636.

40. See Gail Gerhart, *Black Power in South Africa: The Evolution of an Ideology* (Berkeley: University of California Press, 1978); and George M. Fredrickson, *Black Liberation: A Comparative History of Black Ideologies in the United States and South Africa* (New York: Oxford University Press, 1995).

41. George Dalton, *Economic Systems and Society: Capitalism, Communism, and the Third World* (Middlesex, England: Penguin, 1977).

42. See Cohen, *The Question of Imperialism;* and Doyle, *Empires.*

43. See Julius K. Nyerere, *Ujamaa: Essays on Socialism* (Oxford: Oxford University Press, 1968) and *Freedom and Socialism: Uhuru na Ujamaa: A Selection from Writings and Speeches, 1965–1967* (Oxford: Oxford University Press, 1968); and Kwame Nkrumah, *Class Struggle in Africa* (New York: International Publishers, 1970), *Neo-Colonialism: The Last Stage of Imperialism* (New York: International Publishers, 1965), and *I Speak of Freedom: A Statement of African Ideology* (London: Heinemann, 1961).

44. Davenport, *South Africa,* pp. 211, 239–242; see also Fredrickson, *Black Liberation.*

45. Two other major exceptions are the French colonies of Algeria in North Africa and Vietnam in Southeast Asia, where long wars for independence were fought.

46. Minter, *King Solomon's Mines Revisited,* p. 77; Newitt, *Portugal in Africa,* p. 164; Thompson, *A History of South Africa,* p. 278.

47. Ciment, *Angola and Mozambique,* p. 41.

3

Old Wars Made New: Military Globalization

A NUMBER OF NEW, HIGHLY VISIBLE CONFLICTS ERUPTED IN THE WAKE of the end of the Cold War. Some burst forth in Eastern Europe and the Balkans as the Soviet Union and Yugoslavia fell apart, but others, notably the Rwandan genocide and prolonged war in the Democratic Republic of the Congo, arose in Africa. Many analysts attributed such conflicts to a revival of "tribalism" the world over. An old type of enmity appeared to have found new opportunities to emerge in more vicious ways, catching policymakers in many places off guard.[1] Localization in the form of strong attachments to very narrow identities seemed to be as formidable as globalization.

The end of the Cold War indeed had profound impact on conflicts and wars in many places, including southern Africa. Upon closer inspection, however, rather than signaling a resurgence of tribalism, the conflicts that erupted in the 1990s vividly demonstrate the changing dynamic of how global, regional, and local forces interact to work toward resolving or, alternatively, perpetuating armed conflict during the contemporary era of globalization.[2] Violent confrontations in southern Africa provide particularly good cases for investigating changes in warfare that accompanied dramatic shifts in world politics.

This chapter explores the impact of military globalization in the contemporary period in southern Africa, with particular emphasis on Angola and Mozambique. The chapter also briefly traces the history of black resistance to white rule, civil strife, and wars among blacks themselves.

When other colonies across the continent were becoming independent states in the early 1960s, white minority rule appeared to be fully entrenched in five southern African territories. Thirty years later, however, white rule ended. In their efforts to cling to power, these white minority regimes aligned themselves with local, regional, and global forces to fight for the preservation of their privileged way of life and authoritarian control. Black groups determined to end white rule also found willing assistance across the region and internationally. In the end, southern Africa as a whole remained wracked by strife until the Cold War ended and apartheid fell.

For a decade after conflicts in other parts of the region abated, however, civil strife in Angola continued. Then, both Angola and Zimbabwe got drawn into what had become by 2001 Africa's first nearly continent-wide war. The changing nature of these local-to-global dynamics in part reflects significant shifts in military globalization during the last half of the twentieth century, and demonstrates the dilemmas facing the region in this domain. If the interaction of global, regional, and local military trends played a significant role in creating and perpetuating war in southern Africa, how might global and regional forces be used to increase the chances of local settlements and contribute to the reconstruction of war-torn societies?

CONTEMPORARY MILITARY GLOBALIZATION AND SOUTHERN AFRICA

Chapter 1 summarized military globalization as the network of worldwide military ties and relations, in combination with key military technological innovations. According to David Held et al., this "expanding reach of organized violence" can be characterized by three interrelated factors: first, the war system, defined as the geopolitical order, including great power rivalry, conflict, and security relations; second, the arms dynamic, defined as the diffusion of military production and trade in arms; and third, the expanding geographic reach of agreements governing organized violence, defined as "the formal and informal international regulation of the acquisition, deployment and use of military power."[3]

During the contemporary era, the war system driven by the two competing superpowers spread quickly across the entire globe, as did the expanse of military production and trade. Military globalization thus became widely extended through channels that functioned at relatively high speeds. The unprecedented connections among military arenas and processes all over the world resulted in much greater intensity of globalization in this domain and, across time, increasingly high impact. In addition, global and regional efforts to institutionalize security arrangements grew dramatically. Yet within these overall trends, important changes can be discerned in military globalization during the decades following World War II.

For example, when the wars in southern Africa began in the 1960s, they could be characterized as wars of independence against imperial powers. After Portugal granted Angola and Mozambique independence in 1975, however, the armed strife continued, primarily for two reasons, one regional and one global. Coordinating their security arrangements and military efforts, the apartheid regime in South Africa and white settlers in Zimbabwe (then Rhodesia) demonstrated a deadly resolve to prevent black rule from fully taking hold in neighboring states. This had particularly devastating consequences for the former Portuguese colonies. Globally, the United States and the Soviet Union contributed to the conflict by transforming their Cold War standoff into a "hot" war, especially in Angola. As Held and his colleagues put it, the nuclear arms race made war between the superpowers almost unthinkable (but not necessarily improbable). Therefore, "East-West rivalry was displaced into Africa, Asia and Latin America. In turn, the process of decolonization and the struggle for national liberation became imbued with a Cold War military dynamic. Where direct intervention was eschewed, war by proxy ensued."[4]

When apartheid began to wither, so did the war in Mozambique. Similarly, the end of both apartheid and superpower competition brought a great opportunity for peaceful resolution in Angola. Having played such a crucial role in perpetuating the war, however, the United States and Russia (successor to the Soviet Union) had little interest in guaranteeing peace. Meanwhile, South Africa was preoccupied with its own uneasy transition. Driven by a somewhat new, and in some respects less organized, interaction of local, regional, and global military dynamics, the war in Angola continued with increasing ferocity until 2002 and became a part of a much larger set of armed confrontations in central Africa.

Post–Cold War conflicts like the ones in Angola and Central Africa appear to have several common characteristics that analysts argue represent new developments in military globalization at the turn of the century.[5] First, they revolve around disputes within nations with weak political institutions and occur in places where a combination of political instability and militarism provide almost "no effective deterrent to war as a rational instrument of state policy."[6] These local conflicts often spill over to become regional. Occasionally, they also become more widely international, but less often than during the Cold War.

Second, contrary to historic tactics of guerrilla warfare and against all institutionalized norms of engagement, warring parties *target* civilians by expelling them from territory desired by the combatants or by looting to gain profits and fuel the war. Civilian targeting includes such actions as conscripting children into fighting forces and systematic raping of women.

Third, a globalized war economy sustains the armed conflicts much as it did during the Cold War. Then, as now, arms producers faced tremendous pressure to export their wares in order to recoup their substantial investments in research and development. This has made for an intensive arms trade that can rapidly penetrate almost anywhere. The number of suppliers expanded considerably after 1970, however, as more governments, including that of South Africa, encouraged the growth of arms industries not only for defense but also as a key component of their industrial and trade policies. Rather than obtaining arms transfers from the superpowers, as happened frequently during the Cold War, now conflicting parties rely on the global market for armaments, glutted in the early 1990s with massive amounts left over from the U.S.-Soviet conflict. Governments and groups at war in Africa now finance their purchases through the export of valuable commodities such as oil or diamonds and through plunder of local resources and humanitarian aid provided by external agencies.[7] Thus, at the turn of the century, the arms dynamic within military globalization had more players with less centralized control than earlier in the contemporary period.

When post–Cold War conflicts erupted in Central and Eastern Europe in the 1990s, international media and governments alike closely monitored the unfolding events and debated how to respond. Likewise, news reporters attentively chronicled a contrasting situation in South Africa, the remarkable and relatively peaceful transition from an authoritarian apartheid state to democratic governance. When in 1990 Prime Minister F.

W. de Klerk released Nelson Mandela from prison, where he had served more than twenty-seven years, he saw television cameras for the first time in his life. Later, as many others stared at their TVs, both de Klerk and Mandela were jointly awarded Nobel Peace Prizes in 1993 for negotiating a plan for a new democracy in their country. Most observers expected apartheid to end in a bloodbath, but the transition to democracy proceeded more smoothly than had been predicted. And the whole world was watching with great interest as these events unfolded.

In contrast, international media largely ignored the gruesome and devastating wars in Angola and Mozambique. Somehow, they seemed more remote and complex when compared to what appeared to be a fairly clear white versus black contest in South Africa, that is, between apartheid, which had become an internationally vilified system, and its opponents. Yet despite this inattention, global forces had a profound impact on the seeming perpetuity of war as well as on the possibilities for peace in these former Portuguese colonies. So did the changing nature of regional dynamics.

Overstating the extent of devastation caused by these wars would be difficult. For example, across thirty years in Mozambique, about 1 million people died, somewhere between one-third and one-half of the population was uprooted from their homes and families, and at least 10,000 amputees had to cope with a new way of life. Across forty years in Angola, 1 million people died there, too, and about 100,000 amputees lost one or more limbs. Angola has at least 2 million internal or external refugees, and aid agencies that seek to provide them with assistance inside the country sometimes face attack by renegade forces.

Across these decades, the changing characterization of war raises several dilemmas. If global and regional military trends played a significant role in creating and perpetuating wars in Mozambique and Angola, how might global and regional forces be used to reconstruct these war-torn societies? How can the national governments that have been party to devastating conflicts regain the loyalty and productive participation of their citizens who fought on the other side? Can populations mobilized for war for generations rediscover and re-create social patterns that deemphasize and delegitimate the use of violence as a normal way of life? This chapter will begin to explore these dilemmas, which are addressed as well throughout the remainder of the book.

Although this chapter on military globalization in the contemporary era features a discussion of the wars in Angola and Mozambique, demonstrating the interaction of local, regional, and global dynamics will necessarily involve some examination of struggles in the other formerly white-ruled territories as well. The nature of the global war system changes across time. The next sections of this chapter analyze the causes and consequences of conflicts in Angola, Mozambique, and other parts of the region in three periods since World War II: before independence, after independence during the Cold War, and after the Cold War ended.

WARS OF INDEPENDENCE AGAINST WHITE RULE

The factors that initially gave rise to violence, civil unrest, and eventual warfare grew out of local reactions to centuries of colonial occupation. As with independence movements elsewhere, African nationalists in southern Africa made very predictable demands. They wanted access to land, freedom to grow the crops they chose, an end to forced labor, an end to discrimination based on race, access to basic services such as education, shared political power, and so on. As discussed in chapter 2, the Portuguese and other white-settler regimes in the region had imposed a more authoritarian system of government than was the case with most colonial powers in other parts of the continent, where authorities were at times somewhat responsive to African petitions. Moreover, the Portuguese territories mirrored the reality of a harsh dictatorship back in Portugal, with whites (along with blacks) having no right to organize political parties of their own. In almost every case, Portuguese colonial rulers and the white settler regimes elsewhere in the region met blacks' early public protests and demands for change with overwhelming military response, killing large numbers of unarmed civilians.

For example, in South Africa in March 1960, in a famous incident in Sharpeville, police killed sixty-nine and wounded about 186 unarmed Africans protesting pass laws. Seventy percent were shot in the back while trying to flee.[8] In Angola, Portuguese authorities killed thirty and injured 200 when they fired on unarmed demonstrators in June 1960. Later that year, the military killed 7,000 Africans after cotton farmers in the north attacked Portuguese livestock and property, but notably not the white settlers themselves. When African peasants in the northeast of Mozambique petitioned Portuguese administrators for some relief in 1960, soldiers fired on the unarmed crowds, killing more than 500.[9]

Putting aside for the moment the situation with other white minority regimes (in South Africa, Zimbabwe, and Namibia), why was Portugal so out of step with other colonial powers that had begun relinquishing their hold on imperial territories? Besides dramatic growth in the numbers of white settlers and their recalcitrance, the Portuguese government believed that it needed its colonies for economic and political gain. In the 1960s, Portugal remained a small, poor country without the benefits of widespread industrialization or the growing economic base shared by most of its West European neighbors. Furthermore, in contrast to the Portuguese dictatorship, much of the rest of Western Europe had well-established democracies.

The colonies provided a number of benefits. Unemployed and discontented Portuguese could be sent from home to settle there. Portugal forced black Mozambican migrants working in South African mines to remit half their earnings and (with help from the apartheid regime) deposited them (in gold) directly into the Portuguese treasury. Oil was discovered in Angola in 1960, and Portugal benefited enormously from other colonial imports, too. Furthermore, if Portugal agreed to withdraw from Africa, the government feared that businesses from other European states would easily replace their own enterprises in the colonies. Therefore, like the other white-settler regimes in the region, Portuguese colonial authorities dug in their heels, refused African demands, and responded to political opposition with extreme violence and repression.

Regionally, white intransigence and fear was met with black impatience and rage, particularly over the brutal killing of protesters. Although each territory had its own local dynamics, these circumstances produced the conditions for the wars and civil strife across the region that occurred in various places from 1961 until democracy dawned in South Africa in the early 1990s. The war in Angola, however, did not end until 2002 and continued to be shaped by trends in military globalization.

To understand how the interaction of local, regional, and global dynamics shaped the contest for power in the region across several decades of the contemporary era, the next section begins at the local level with an analysis of the black guerrilla groups and their allies.

Black Guerrillas and the Weak Link of Ethnically Based Localism

In all of the white settler territories of southern Africa, localism in the form of accentuated ethnic identity and competition among blacks sooner or later played some role in the region's wars. Overall, however, this role was fairly weak in comparison to ethnic strife in other parts of the continent and the world in the 1990s. As indicated in chapter 2, colonialism drew boundaries in Africa that disregarded where Africans themselves considered their own territories to be. This split some ethnic groups and combined others that were unaccustomed to living under the same governing authority. Then, through fairly rigid classification schemes, European powers in many places and the white-settler regimes in Southern Africa in particular constructed and imposed rigid ethnic categories on Africans who in earlier times had experienced more fluid understandings of themselves and their neighbors.[10] Furthermore, colonial and settler governments frequently discriminated in favor of or against particular ethnic groups.

Obviously, African groups had occasionally warred against one another prior to their encounters with European imperialism, but the political systems instituted by white regimes accentuated ethnic identity and often promoted conflict among African groups, a strategy of divide and conquer. Thus, at times ethnic identities and differences sometimes divided those hoping to achieve black rule, as will be explained below. Other differences, however, proved to be more powerful. Furthermore, in the face of rising black resistance, whites found themselves less divided along ethnic lines than had been the case prior to World War II. Race increasingly united them despite any historic enmities or cultural, linguistic, economic, and political differences.

As with many Africans organizing movements for independence across the continent, the concepts of nationalism and self-determination inspired southern African leaders as well. As shown earlier in chapter 2, these ideas spread worldwide through processes of cultural globalization as Africans and blacks from other continents wrote books and sponsored international gatherings to promote their causes. Within this overall context of nationalist aspirations, however, ideological differences divided some groups from others, and this, in turn, had profound consequences for localism.

Some black leaders and their small number of white allies found the ideology of multiracialism very appealing. It offered the opportunity to forge a future that turned away from the rigid classification and stratification of racial and ethnic identity they all found so debilitating. In contrast, groups using the ideology of ethnonationalism emphasized ethnicity and eagerly anticipated the chance to regain the lost cohesion and glory of their own particular people. Still others, the Africanists, believed that ethnic differences between Africans must be overcome, but they saw no future for whites in the region and no room for working with whites who also sought profound change.

In addition, as discussed earlier in the book, another global ideology that had very significant local manifestation in the region was socialism. Most of those who subscribed to multiracialism or Africanism also rejected capitalism as an integral part of the imperialism that they considered so devastating for their countries. Although not necessarily enamored of the Soviet model, these groups found great appeal in the efforts of poor countries such as Cuba, China, and (at the time) North Vietnam to find a different path, one that seemed to offer the chance to redistribute economic gains to those from whom so much had been stolen. Due to a number of factors that will be discussed later, however, none of the guerrilla organizations that became governments actually implemented or sustained socialist policies. Ethnonationalists, in contrast to the other two, pragmatically had no attachment to socialism.

Although none of the black political organizations seeking change in southern Africa began as guerrilla groups, across time and in the face of extreme violence they all took up arms and military campaigns. Table 3.1 lists those groups that fought in the wars for independence and identifies their significant leaders, ideologies, and ethnic or geographic base. The table displays the organizations in the order of their country's independence or achievement of majority rule, but this discussion will proceed in roughly the reverse order, ending with a focus on Angola and Mozambique. A brief examination of these groups' origins helps shed light on later analysis, especially in that some of these groups became the founders of new governments.

South Africa, Namibia, and Zimbabwe. As indicated in chapter 2, the apartheid government of South Africa illegally occupied South-West

TABLE 3.1 Southern Africa Guerrilla Groups

Country	Group	Date Founded	Significant Leaders	Ideology	Geographic or Ethnic Base	Guerilla Allies	African Allies	Primary International Allies
Mozambique 1975	FRELIMO Front for the Liberation of Mozambique	1962	Eduardo Mondlane Samora Machel Joachim Chissano	Multiracialism Socialism Nationalism	Northern Province	PAC ZANU	Algeria Tanzania	Cuba China E. Europe USSR
Angola 1975	FNLA Frente de Libertacao de Angola (founded as UPNA)	1957	Holden Roberto	Ethno-Nationalism	Bakongo		Algeria Zaire	USA China Romania
	MPLA Movimento Popular de Libertacao de Angola	1956	Agostinho Neto Eduardo dos Santos	Multiracialism Socialism Nationalism	Urban Mbundu Mestizos Whites	SWAPO ANC FRELIMO ZAPU	Nigeria; Katanga (province of Zaire); Tanzania; Zambia; Congo/Brazzaville	Cuba USSR E. Europe Sweden Denmark Gulf Oil Co.
	UNITA Uniao Nacional para a Independencia Total de Angola	1966	Jonas Savimbi	Ethno-Nationalism	Rural Ovimbundu		South Africa Zambia (intermittent)	USA France Britain China N. Korea Romania

(continues)

TABLE 3.1 (*continued*)

	Party	Founded	Leaders	Ideology	Ethnic	Allies	Regional support	Foreign support
Zimbabwe 1980	ZANU Zimbabwe African National Union → united as PF (Patriotic Front) briefly ↑ ZAPU Zimbabwe African People's Union	1963 1978 1961	Herbert Chitepo Robert Mugabe	Nationalism Socialism	Shona	PAC FRELIMO	Zambia Tanzania Mozambique	China
		1961	Joshua Nkomo	Multiracialism Nationalism Socialism	Ndebele	ANC SWAPO MPLA	Zambia Botswana Angola	USSR
Namibia 1990	SWAPO South West Africa People's Organization	1960	Toivoja Toivo Sam Nujoma	Multiracialism Nationalism Socialism	Ovambo	MPLA ANC ZAPU	Tanzania Zambia	China USSR N. Korea
South Africa 1994	ANC African National Congress	1912, as guerillas since 1961	Albert Luthuli Oliver Tambo Nelson Mandela Thabo Mbeki Winnie Mandela Walter Sisulu Joe Slovo	Multiracialism Nationalism Socialism		ZAPU SWAPO MPLA	Tanzania Zambia Angola Mozambique Namibia	USSR
	PAC Pan Africanist Congress	1959	Robert Sobukwe	Africanism Nationalism		ZANU FRELIMO	Tanzania Mozambique	China

Africa (now Namibia) during this time period. Furthermore, not far away, whites in Rhodesia (now Zimbabwe) issued their Unilateral Declaration of Independence (UDI) from Great Britain in 1965. The UDI, they hoped, would prevent any decolonization effort in their country whereby whites would have to share power with blacks. Yet despite their efforts to maintain the status quo, white-settler regimes in all three places increasingly faced formidable pressures for change.

Although blacks in South Africa were the last to achieve black majority rule, they were the first to organize. The African National Congress (ANC) dates back to 1912 and was founded by teachers, lawyers, Christian ministers, and other professionals. One of its most famous leaders, Zulu chief Albert John Luthuli, won the 1960 Nobel Peace Prize. The ANC embraced multiracialism, and by 1956, upon the adoption of a document entitled the Freedom Charter, socialism. After the Sharpeville massacre in 1960, the government outlawed the ANC and other resistance groups, and they went underground. The ANC military wing, Umkonto we Sizwe (Spear of the Nation) committed its first act of sabotage in December 1961. By 1963, most of its key leaders were in prison, including Nelson Mandela, a young lawyer rising in prominence in the organization. Until very late in its years of operation, Umkonto honored its pledge to avoid killing people and instead directed its violent activities against such targets as electric pylons, post offices, administrative offices, jails, and railways.[11]

The founders of the Pan Africanist Congress (PAC) were bold activists who had become frustrated with what they considered to be the inaction of the ANC. Led by Robert Sobukwe, they broke away in 1959 and embraced Africanist ideology. They had grown impatient with the ANC insistence on multiracialism and its openness to working with the Communist Party of South Africa, composed at the time primarily of white people. The PAC is noted for organizing the protests at Sharpeville.

Both the ANC and the PAC rejected any concept of ethnonationalism, and neither organization was closely associated with a particular ethnic group. Although at times the ANC seemed to have a disproportionate number of African leaders from the Xhosa, the organization recruited leaders and followers alike from all ethnic groups and all races.

In Namibia, about 50 percent of the population are Ovambo, with the remaining population distributed across a number of ethnic groups, as shown in table 2.1 in the previous chapter. The South-West Africa Peoples'

Organization (SWAPO) began its work in the 1950s as the Ovamboland Peoples' Organization but adopted the name change to SWAPO in 1960 in an effort to broaden its ethnic base and become a more nationalist organization. From the point of view of some other ethnic groups in the country, however, the organization never quite succeeded in its goal. Like the ANC, SWAPO articulated a socialist vision for Namibia's future.

SWAPO used the word *Namibia* deliberately as its name for the independent country the group aspired to achieve. The term comes from the Nama word *namib*, meaning shield, and had earlier been coined by a nationalist leader. The military wing launched its guerrilla war in 1966, and the country eventually won its independence from South Africa in 1990 after having been used by the apartheid regime as a base from which to wage war in Angola. When elections were finally held, the head of SWAPO, Sam Nujoma, became Namibia's first president.

Zimbabwe (then Rhodesia) presents a more complicated story. Two guerrilla groups formed there. Like SWAPO, both had primary ethnic bases, but neither actively promoted ethnonationalism. Table 2.1 shows the ethnic composition of present-day Zimbabwe, where the Shona compose a large majority. A Ndebele labor organizer who had been involved in previously banned black political organizations, Joshua Nkomo, founded the first guerrilla group in 1961, the Zimbabwe African Peoples Union (ZAPU).

In 1963, claiming that the Ndebele dominated ZAPU, Shona members left to form the Zimbabwe African National Union (ZANU) under the leadership of Ndabaningi Sithole. In 1964, guerrilla attacks primarily operated by ZANU began. Robert Mugabe, a teacher who had served a number of years in prison for his political activities, became the leader of ZANU in the mid-1970s. It was not surprising that after independence, Mugabe, a member of the Shona majority, was elected prime minister, and the country was renamed after the ancient civilization of Zimbabwe.

The increased war effort sustained by ZANU and ZAPU in the mid- to late-1970s, combined with international pressure on Rhodesian whites, both figured importantly in a negotiated settlement that brought independence in 1980. The organizations' capacity to step up military pressure came largely as a result of Angola and Mozambique reaching independence in 1975 and then harboring guerrillas. Like these new governments, both ZANU and ZAPU articulated ideologies of nationalism and socialism.

As noted earlier, the end of Portuguese colonialism in Africa had profound consequences for the three remaining nations dominated by white settlers.

Angola and Mozambique. Of all the black guerrilla organizations in southern Africa, only two had some form of ethnonationalist ideology that asserted this form of localism from the outset, and both came from Angola: the National Front for the Liberation of Angola (FNLA) and the Union for the Total Independence of Angola (UNITA). Holden Roberto headed the FNLA, and unlike most other guerrilla groups, he championed anti-Communist rhetoric. Some of the FNLA leaders came from groups other than the Bakongo, but the organization's mode of operation and base of followers reflected a vision of Bakongo pride and unity. In addition to being in Angola, the Bakongo live in neighboring states, including the Congo Republic (renamed Zaire for many years). Roberto's brother-in-law, Colonel Joseph Mobutu led a U.S.-backed coup d'état in 1965 to become head of the newly independent Congo and gave considerable support to the FNLA. Although in 1960 the FNLA was the first to use guerrilla strategies, the group proved unable to sustain its efforts after the war for independence and collapsed in 1976.

The Bakongo constitute a fairly small proportion of Angola's population. In contrast, the Ovimbundu constitute a much larger ethnic group, 37 percent of present-day Angola. An Ovimbundu charismatic orator who served as a leader in the FNLA, Jonas Savimbi, broke away in 1966 to found UNITA. UNITA had little coherent ideology and shifted its message regularly across the years, at times espousing socialist principles, at times capitalist ones. Although it frequently stated its openness to all ethnic groups and occasionally drew leaders from outside the Ovimbundu, UNITA located its headquarters and operations in the heart of Ovimbundu territory and resorted to ethnonationalist ideology.

The first to actually get organized, the third guerrilla group in Angola called itself the Popular Movement for the Liberation of Angola (MPLA). It was founded in Luanda by white Portuguese dissidents, mestizos, and *assimilados* from the colonies, and the group immediately became a strong advocate of multiracialism. The organization also espoused nationalism and socialism, and some of its early leaders, including Agostinho Neto, actively participated in Communist Party activities. Because the MPLA had a strong urban and multiracial base, it avoided being overidentified with any ethnic group, although among its African members, more leaders came from the Mbundu. Factionalism among various leaders became evident during the war for independence and continued to cause difficulty in the organization for many years.

From early on in their efforts to oust the Portuguese, the three guerrilla organizations fought each other as well. Indeed, UNITA colluded with the Portuguese in attacks on the MPLA in the late 1960s and agreed not to target the Portuguese military. In exchange, UNITA got permission from the Portuguese to exercise control over Ovimbunduland. The MPLA shouldered much of the burden of prosecuting the war for independence, with the FNLA making a sizable contribution.

In contrast, only one black guerrilla organization waged the war for independence in Mozambique. Students in Lisbon, Portugal, and Paris, together with exiles living in Rhodesia, Malawi, and Tanzania, gathered in 1962 in Dar es Salaam, Tanzania, to forge the Mozambique Liberation Front (FRELIMO). The group began military attacks in 1964. Led in its early years by U.S.-educated Eduardo Mondlane, FRELIMO advocated nationalism, multiracialism, and socialism. Its leadership included mestizos and a disproportionate number of Africans from southern provinces, even though the war was eventually fought primarily in the north. Portuguese agents assassinated Mondlane in 1969, and leadership passed to Samora Machel. Determined to remain close to ordinary peasants and demonstrate their socialist commitment, FRELIMO members provided model educational and social services in "liberated zones" in the north where they could maintain some confidence of military control.

The African wars took a toll on Portugal. Eventually, the government committed half its budget and nearly 200,000 troops to colonial combat.[12] In the meantime, the Portuguese military and population grew wearier of a brutal dictatorship at home. Fed up with the toll of war, an anti-imperialist faction of the military overthrew the Portuguese dictatorship in April 1974. Ironically, as the colonies fought for their own independence, their wars made a significant contribution to progress toward parliamentary democracy in Portugal.

Unlike the departing colonial governments in other parts of the continent, the new Portuguese regime made no preparations for independence. As one author put it, "Empires may be born in glory, but they always die of embarrassment."[13] The transitions came quickly nonetheless, with the new

Portuguese regime turning the reins of government over to the guerrillas in 1975. Many whites in the colonies felt bitter and angry over these surprising events. Over 160,000 of the 200,000 Portuguese in Mozambique left for Portugal or South Africa, taking their assets with them. Many sabotaged property as they departed, but more important, with the absence of educational opportunities for Africans over the centuries of colonialism, white flight meant the loss of the majority of skilled technicians, administrators, and professionals, including those operating crucial port and railway facilities. Nonetheless, in contrast to Angola, the transition to a black independent government in Mozambique went fairly smoothly.

The new government in Portugal negotiated an uneasy arrangement for sharing power among the three guerrilla groups in Angola. Nonetheless, fighting immediately ensued, with substantial intervention by outsiders, including the South African and Cuban militaries. This massive outside intervention marked the turning point of the war. Rather than continuing as a war for national independence, the new goals became internal control of the new Angolan government and white control of the region, the subject of later sections of this chapter. The immediate outcomes, however, were the following: The Organization of African Unity (OAU, now called the African Union, or AU) recognized the MPLA as the legitimate government of Angola in January 1976 because it held the most territory and occupied the capital, Luanda. The head of the MPLA, Agostinho Neto, became the new president. Over 100,000 Angolans died, and about the same number fled as refugees to Zambia and Zaire (now Congo). By one estimate, the war cost $6.7 billion in weapons and lost property. Over 300,000 whites took flight, with the same economic consequences as in Mozambique.[14]

These terrible costs of the contest for power in Angola as the Portuguese departed, however, pale in comparison to those that were still to come. Prior to an examination of the globalized and regionalized civil wars that plagued Angola and Mozambique, the regional and global entangling alliances of both black guerrilla groups and white regimes in the pre-independence period warrant discussion.

The Persuasive Power of Ideas: The Cold War Context

As the previous discussion demonstrates, on the whole ideology rather than ethnicity was more powerful in defining the guerrilla groups of southern Africa and their affiliations. Their attachments to various forms of socialist ideologies grew out of their analyses and convictions about how to confront the oppression around them and how to build new societies. The local context in which the guerrilla groups framed their ideological attachments,[15] however, was at the same time the global context of the Cold War. Furthermore, the regional context of white against black compounded the Cold War dynamic. The apartheid regime articulated the threat of black rule as a threat of communism. This framing of the issue obviously reflected in part the rhetoric the guerrilla organizations themselves espoused. Yet just as important to white settlers, it also served to attract the attention of those in the West who feared that in the aftermath of decolonization, communism would spread from Eastern Europe to the countries of Africa, Asia, and Latin America. Moreover, the regional context of race relations also had a global dimension, as discussed earlier. Many leaders in Western governments continued to believe that Africans, especially in southern Africa, had not yet reached the stage of readiness to govern themselves, an attitude described in chapter 2 as institutional racism. The confrontation between East and West and between socialism and capitalism, along with the domestic and international dynamics of race relations, played key roles in regionalizing and globalizing the wars for independence. In other words, as Held et al. have put it, the region's prospects for peace would be "increasingly contingent on the complex dynamics of global power relations and developments across interconnected sites of military and political decision-making."[16]

In general, the United States paid little attention to Africa in the 1960s, although the Kennedy and Johnson administrations condemned colonialism and racism. From an economic standpoint, however, relations between the United States and southern Africa expanded throughout the decade. U.S.-based multinational corporations and banks helped supply the capital for substantial economic growth in the region and profited from it, particularly in South Africa. Military supplies from the West, including the United States, flowed to the white regimes despite a military embargo in place since the 1960 Sharpeville massacre. During this period, military globalization grew with intensity and speed worldwide, including in southern Africa.

Under the Nixon administration, the U.S. government's diplomatic tone shifted and became more consistent with the perspective of U.S. business. On the recommendation of his national security adviser, Henry Kissinger, the Nixon regime adopted a more conciliatory stance toward the region's white settlers, concluding in 1970 that

[t]he whites are here to stay and the only way that constructive change can come about is through them. There is no hope for the blacks to gain the political rights they seek through violence, which will only lead to chaos and increased opportunities for the communists.[17]

The U.S. government leased land from Portugal for an air base in the Azores, and through more friendly relations wanted to ensure continued use of this strategic asset. Four short years later, however, to the surprise of analysts predicting long-term white rule in the region, the Portuguese coup occurred and progress toward independence for its colonies began.

In contrast to the United States, the Soviet Union warmly embraced black groups' attraction to socialism. Moreover, white rule in southern Africa represented one of the last vestiges of Western imperialism, which the Soviets had condemned for decades. With little indication that Western governments would lend support to their cause, black leaders cultivated relations with socialist countries such as the Soviet Union and Cuba to augment the aid and training they received from their African neighbors. The Soviets approached African affairs in quite pragmatic terms, however, and at times took sides with governments or groups on the basis of strategic rather than ideological concerns. The Chinese government, communist only since 1949, severely criticized the Soviet Union for taking such considerations into account, and rivalries within the communist camp became as evident in southern Africa as in other parts of the world.

With more countries in Africa, Asia, and the Caribbean gaining independence, some support for change emerged in the West. For example, the Commonwealth, the organization of former British colonies, placed demands on Britain to put some pressure on white minority regimes. Scandinavian governments began to provide important support for guerrilla movements in the region. With larger numbers of newly independent nations gaining membership, the United Nations, whose activities will be covered in more detail in the next chapter, increasingly sought to end colonialism and to isolate white minority rule.

Table 3.1 displays the international allies of each black guerrilla organization. In part because U.S. support had been key to bringing the anti-Communist colonel Joseph Mobutu to power in Zaire (now Congo), the United States also supported Roberto's FNLA. With the demise of the FNLA and the growing anti-Communist rhetoric of UNITA, the United

States soon switched its support to Savimbi's group. The United States backed no other guerrilla organizations in the region, however. In contrast, the Soviet Union had close ties with the MPLA in Angola, as well as with ZAPU, SWAPO, and the ANC. Cuba sent massive support to the MPLA. China allied itself with FRELIMO, ZANU, and the PAC. Thus, as in many places, military globalization found its way into southern Africa through superpower rivalry.

In addition to the global connections, ties to newly independent African countries had proven pivotal to the guerrilla organizations and remained so throughout the decades of struggle. Through various alliances and meetings across the continent and worldwide, leaders of black guerrilla groups across the region came to know each other. Founded in 1963, the Organization of African Unity organized a Liberation Committee to support those countries still under colonial or white minority rule and gave official recognition to all the groups except UNITA (excluded because of its South African backing). A number of African states gave significant, long-term support to guerrillas, including the provision of headquarters for their operations and bases for military maneuvers. Tanzania hosted all those recognized by the OAU and frequently teamed up with Zambia to confront white minority rule in various ways. Black-ruled governments that harbored guerrillas fighting against white minority regimes came to be known as the Frontline States (FLS). Table 3.1 lists the African allies of each guerrilla group and demonstrates the still unfolding, shaky regional coalitions they aspired to use to confront entrenched white-settler regimes, which had already forged a strong regionalism some time ago, as shown in chapter 2.

REGIONALIZED AND GLOBALIZED CIVIL WARS: INDEPENDENCE AND THE COLD WAR

On the day of Angola's formal independence, November 11, 1975, the impact of fairly extensive and intensive military globalization was clearly evident. The three guerrilla groups vying for power fought one another on many fronts across the country, each backed by potent allies from outside. Although the South African military had provided supplies to UNITA for some time, troops from the South African Defense Forces (SADF) launched a massive invasion from bases in Namibia (then South-West

Africa) in mid-October. Previously, in August, the U.S. Central Intelligence Agency (CIA) had shipped large quantities of arms to the FNLA. Cuban troops arrived in early October, and Soviet military supplies continued to flow into the country to bolster the MPLA. Therefore, although the MPLA held the capital and gained some international recognition as the government of Angola, power in the country remained very much contested. With brief pauses for negotiations, including an eventual end to superpower support for the war, the armed conflict continued until 2002, more than a decade after the democratic transition began in South Africa.

Mozambique had a bit of a reprieve after its independence in 1975 prior to plunging back into war. By 1976, the Rhodesian military and its freshly created mercenary organization (see below) had already begun attacks of sabotage, particularly in central Mozambique, to punish the newly independent government for its support of guerrilla groups fighting for Zimbabwean (then Rhodesian) independence. Mozambique continued to suffer a devastating war until a 1992 negotiated settlement charted a course for the cessation of military conflict.

Post-independence wars in Angola and Mozambique invite an examination of the interaction of local, regional, and global forces in the perpetuation and cessation of armed conflict, and raise important questions. Why did regional and global powers take such an interest in these countries and their internal disputes? Would these wars have lasted so long and caused such devastation if they had remained local? The analysis below demonstrates that primary responsibility for perpetuating armed conflict lay with regional and global players, although local forces played more of a role in Angola than in Mozambique. Just as important, the discussion reveals the changing nature of local wars when contexts and dynamics of military globalization and regionalism shift dramatically. Furthermore, if analysts basically agree about what caused decades of war and destruction in Angola and Mozambique, what does that imply about who holds responsibility for reconstruction after the shooting stops? The discussion below begins with local and regional factors related to these wars and then moves to examine the global dynamics that helped perpetuate widespread death and destruction.

Regional and Local Dynamics

Mozambique. The aggressive defense of white minority rule in the region had a profound impact on escalating and perpetuating war in Angola

and Mozambique. Just as important, Angolan and Mozambican independence galvanized the efforts of black guerrillas to bring an end to racial
domination in the region. The consequences soon became evident when,
from Mozambique, ZANU intensified its attacks on the Rhodesian
regime. During the war, however, the Rhodesian regime not only regularly
attacked ZANU bases and other targets in Mozambique, it also created a
mercenary organization, the Mozambican National Resistance, known at
first by its English acronym, MNR, but later by its Portuguese acronym,
RENAMO. Its primary purpose consisted of destabilizing the Mozambican government, punishing it for its strict enforcement of economic sanctions against Rhodesia, and for aiding ZANU. RENAMO also drew
funding from former Portuguese industrialists and plantation owners. At
this point, most of its troops were white, and the only Mozambicans involved in the group were a few disaffected FRELIMO officials, most notably André Matsangaissa, the first leader, and Afonso Dhlakama, the
leader who took over when Matsangaissa died in action. Both men had become regime critics after being arrested for theft.

At first RENAMO effectively destroyed Mozambican infrastructure and
killed and maimed its citizens primarily in the central provinces. The organization proved that FRELIMO, under repeated attacks in the area, could
not protect its citizens or deliver services. When Zimbabwe approached its
independence under black rule, however, the former white government
could no longer support RENAMO. Instead, South Africa sponsored REN-
AMO, giving the organization substantially greater resources and the military capacity to destroy targets more widely across the country.

By 1982, RENAMO had increased its war effort considerably, had con-
scripted a number of troops, and had strategically divided the country
into three zones. The first zone included areas where it maintained control, many of which were in regions near Zimbabwe where many Ndau
people lived. Dhlakama was a Ndau, as were many of RENAMO's leaders.
Ndau became the functional language for RENAMO. In the areas of control, the rebel group forcibly resettled peasants around its bases. REN-
AMO set up a few clinics and schools, and the farmers reestablished a
basic peasant economy that fed the group's troops. Life became relatively
stable in these parts of the country.

The second zone included the areas of taxation where neither REN-
AMO nor FRELIMO had effective control. These parts of the country

largely became a free fire zone. RENAMO periodically raided these areas to expropriate food and other goods.

> Finally, there were the areas of destruction, under FRELIMO control. Here, RENAMO employed its strategy of terror. To undermine the government, RENAMO committed a host of brutal atrocities to demonstrate to Mozambicans FRELIMO's inability to protect them. It also forcibly recruited soldiers, some as young as twelve years old, and then trained them in the most brutal forms of aggression.[18]

The apartheid regime's sponsorship of RENAMO developed within the context of significant changes occurring within the South African government, one of which was a comprehensive reevaluation of the threats it faced. The white minority regime perceived a "total onslaught" aimed at apartheid, an overwhelming threat "orchestrated by the Soviet Union, involving South African exiles, internal demonstrators, African states, and their collaborators among Western churches, lobbies and even governments."[19] During the Soweto massacre in 1976, apartheid brutality erupted again for the world to see, and South Africa came under increasing pressure from abroad. The United Nations instituted an arms embargo in 1977, and anti-apartheid activists lobbied Western governments much more intensely (see chapter 4).

In its evaluation of a "total onslaught," the apartheid regime underestimated the strength and determination of its own internal black opposition, as well as that in Zimbabwe (then Rhodesia) and Namibia (then South-West Africa). The government also overestimated the degree of collaboration among external opponents. Nonetheless, significant threats to the perpetuation of white rule existed. In three of the four neighboring states, the protective buffer of minority rule that had existed only a few years earlier no longer held. Furthermore, the ANC gained new recruits and vigor after Soweto. For example, the ANC succeeded in blowing up coal-to-oil plants near Johannesburg in 1980, its first successful large-scale attack.

The South African regime named its new vision for protecting white minority rule the "total strategy" and in 1978 elected a new prime minister to implement it, P. W. Botha, the head of the Defence Ministry since 1973. "Total strategy" involved a mix of domestic repression and reform, together with a similar strategy aimed abroad. The plan gained inspiration and momentum with the election of a conservative "cold warrior" in the United States, Ronald Reagan (discussed below). For Mozambique, this shift in the South African government, especially after Zimbabwean independence, meant significantly escalated SADF attacks on infrastructure and refugees and systematic assaults against other civilian populations by RENAMO. Such devastation, coupled with a severe drought, brought Mozambique to the verge of collapse.

Although the FRELIMO government, like many newly independent regimes, had made significant mistakes in its early years, one of its strengths had always been a group of urbane, multilingual leaders who knew how to cultivate close diplomatic relations internationally with a wide variety of governments. With catastrophe facing the country, FRELIMO began a series of bold diplomatic initiatives. Cold War military globalization had always been less intense and extensive in Mozambique, due in part to the superpowers' having fewer strategic interests there. In this context, President Samora Machel met with and charmed both President Reagan and Prime Minister Margaret Thatcher, and in turn, their governments put increasing pressure on South Africa to end its war on Mozambique. As a consequence, in 1984, South Africa and Mozambique signed the Nkomati Accords, an agreement whereby the Mozambican government would oust the ANC from its territories and the South African government would end its support for RENAMO.

Mozambique honored its pledge to expel the ANC, and in order to help provide security, Zimbabwe and Tanzania together sent several thousand troops to guard transportation routes and civilians in the north. The United States began to send aid and helped Mozambique reschedule its debt with the International Monetary Fund. Then, despite its previous commitment to socialism, the Mozambican government adopted structural adjustment policies (SAPs), IMF-mandated prescriptions intended to remove government services from the economy (see chapter 5).

The apartheid regime did not honor its side of the Nkomati Accords, however. Aided by Malawi and Kenya, the SADF renewed its support for RENAMO military campaigns after 1984. Thus, South Africa undermined the peace so desperately sought by Machel, and the SAPs required by the country's economic partners compounded the destructive effects of the war by depriving citizens of services. A renewed drought made everything worse. Greater devastation alienated more people from the FRELIMO government and drove them into the arms of RENAMO. Furthermore, a mysterious airplane crash that some blame on the SADF killed Machel in 1986. Joaquim Chissano became the country's new leader.

By 1990, Mozambique held the distinction of being the world's poorest country and the one most dependent on external aid. "Fully two-thirds of its national income by 1990 was provided by aid from other governments and non-governmental organizations (NGOs)."[20] The government whose war of independence had been backed by the Chinese and whose connection to the Soviet Union had been strengthened with a friendship treaty in 1977 evolved by 1990 into a national leadership supported primarily by the United States, Britain, and the former colonial master, Portugal.

Meanwhile, another significant regime change occurred in South Africa, a country whose white population had become weary of far-flung wars, troop causalities, and the militaristic emphasis of "total strategy." F. W. de Klerk replaced Botha as prime minister in 1989 and undertook a series of dramatic changes domestically and regionally that brought new possibilities for a negotiated settlement in Mozambique and elsewhere. A Roman Catholic order, the Sant'Edigio community in Rome, played a key role in negotiations (see chapter 4) that, after many delays and tortured processes, brought about a cease-fire in 1992 and official recognition of RENAMO as a political party. The United Nations provided oversight for these transitions, including elections in 1994. FRELIMO won a slight majority of the 250 seats in the new parliament, and Chissano won 53 percent of the vote (compared to 34 percent for Dhlakama) to become the president in a multiparty republic.

Angola.   Unlike the case in Mozambique, when the Portuguese left Angola in 1975, the Rhodesian and South African military did not need to create a mercenary group. A black guerrilla organization willing to align itself with white minority rulers in the region already existed: UNITA. Backed by Cuban troops, the MPLA had defeated UNITA militarily and forced its withdrawal into the interior of the country in 1976, whence UNITA attacked railways and other transportation routes. By 1979, UNITA had retreated and regrouped further in the south, near the border with Namibia. Besides giving arms and training to UNITA, the SADF directly attacked SWAPO bases and refugee camps in southern Angola in the late 1970s. The apartheid regime wanted to clear the border of SWAPO guerrillas, whom the MPLA harbored in its effort to help end the illegal South African occupation of Namibia.

During the late 1970s, the MPLA transformed its guerrilla operations into a national conventional military capability. Although Soviet and Cuban aid provided an important basis of support for this buildup, government revenue from oil also paid for a substantial part of it. Throughout its decades of war, the MPLA, a self-declared Marxist-Leninist regime, maintained excellent relations with Western oil companies, an irony demonstrating that economic and military globalization do not always converge. (In other words, the U.S. government backed UNITA while U.S. oil companies backed MPLA.) As the war continued, Angolan oil revenues got increasingly diverted into military spending rather than economic development. From the MPLA's point of view, this strong conventional force proved to be worth the price when confronting South Africa's "total strategy" and the escalation of hostilities after 1980.

Through a number of massive assaults, the SADF repeatedly invaded southern Angola during the early 1980s and helped UNITA take large portions of territory in the south and east. The costs for all sides were mounting, and just as pressure from the U.S. and British governments pushed South Africa into negotiating the Nkomati Accords with Mozambique, the apartheid regime entered into a similar agreement with Angola in 1984. The SADF and UNITA had suffered a significant defeat in 1983, when South Africa invaded to try to capture the capital and permanently oust the MPLA.

The agreements stipulated that South African troops would be withdrawn from Angola in return for more limited support by MPLA for SWAPO guerrillas. Again, however, just as with Mozambique, South Africa failed to honor its promises, and the war in Angola escalated. Ironically, having played a somewhat constructive role in the Mozambican Nkomati negotiations, the U.S. government pursued a different tactic in Angola and became an active sponsor of UNITA (discussed below). Determined to defend itself, the MPLA launched a major offensive in 1987, and a series of massive land battles lasted through much of 1988. The SADF and UNITA forces fought the MPLA soldiers backed by Cuban troops. All took heavy losses, with South Africa and UNITA suffering the worst defeats. Under these circumstances, South Africa again agreed to a cease-fire, a move that

Savimbi considered a betrayal. The South African government's abandonment of Savimbi and "total strategy" demonstrated one of the apartheid regime's extraordinary failures and contributed to the change in leaders from Botha to de Klerk in 1989.

War weary and again under pressure from the two superpowers, South Africa, Angola, and Cuba entered negotiations culminating in agreements signed in New York in late 1988. South Africa agreed to UN-supervised elections in Namibia (then South-West Africa) and to end its support for UNITA. Cuban troops would leave Angola in stages timed to coordinate with Namibian independence. The talks deliberately excluded UNITA. The United States and the Soviet Union participated as observers. This left each superpower free to support its ally. For its part, the Soviet Union signaled its interest in withdrawing from regional conflicts around the world (thereby putting pressure on the MPLA to negotiate), but significant U.S. aid to UNITA continued.

The MPLA and UNITA began peace talks in 1990, after Namibian independence. The two signed the Bicesse Accord in 1991. It provided for UN-monitored demobilization of military forces, the creation of a new Angolan army made up of both UNITA and MPLA soldiers, and elections to be held within eighteen months. Implementation of the Bicesse Accord largely failed, however, due to poorly funded and staffed UN monitoring and MPLA resistance to a strong international presence, with the group citing concerns about sovereignty. In addition, UNITA regularly violated the accord.

Nonetheless, notable success came with voter registration of 4.8 million people, 92 percent of the eligible voters. Voting went smoothly, although the population's discontent over their choice of candidates became evident with the appearance of a frequent graffiti slogan, "MPLA Steals, UNITA Kills." Continual war, which citizens generally blamed on UNITA, caused severe deterioration in the economy, also generally blamed on the government.

The UN and other international observers declared the elections to be generally free and fair. The MPLA won 129 of the 220 seats in the assembly (and majorities in every region except the Ovimbundu heartland), whereas UNITA took seventy seats. MPLA president José Eduardo dos Santos won 49.6 percent to Jonas Savimbi's 40.1 percent of the vote for president. Deeply disappointed with the elections, UNITA resorted to war again in late 1992 and immediately made substantial gains. By 1993, Savimbi's army controlled Angola's second-largest city as well as about 70 percent of the countryside. Most important, UNITA controlled access to oil and diamonds bringing the group much-needed revenue, now that its South African and U.S. aid had ended, but the consequence was to cripple the Angolan economy further.

With Western states now ready to abandon UNITA and recognize the MPLA as the legitimate government of the country (discussed below), the Angolan military rearmed yet again. By 1994, UNITA had been pushed back to its old stronghold in the south, but more significant, it held onto the diamond-rich pockets of the northeast, near Zaire. International pressure, through measures like the 1993 UN Security Council sanctions against UNITA, once again pressured Savimbi into another set of negotiations that decreased hostilities, resulting in a 1994 agreement called the Lusaka Protocol. This document embraced many of the same principles as the previous agreement, namely that UNITA would return territory to state control, demobilize its troops, and surrender its weapons.

Yet the war that had already lasted thirty years escalated once again when it became one of several conflicts that reignited central Africa in the mid- and late 1990s. Before describing this third phase of the war, however, the discussion contemplates why, unlike in Mozambique, the seemingly endless war in Angola remained so immune to resolution. Although up to this point regional and global forces undoubtedly perpetuated and prolonged the war, local factors also played a key role.

Analysts agree that UNITA's survival across time depended on South African and U.S. support, but there was one other essential supporting factor: the leadership of Jonas Savimbi. Born in 1934, Savimbi developed into a brilliant, charismatic, and ruthless leader. He was reared by an African American missionary mother and an Ovimbundu *assimilado* father in a Protestant evangelical environment and in a family with long-standing nationalist aspirations. Well educated in Europe and linguistically gifted, Savimbi has long been noted for his oratorical skills, including holding his audiences spellbound with speeches full of proverb and allegory in the classical Ovimbundu tradition. Although described as an ideological "chameleon" because of his eager willingness to change rhetoric to suit those sponsoring him, he gained key military skills in China early in the Angolan war for independence. He also seemed devoted to rural people, among whom he frequently operated as a guerrilla. He demonstrated his considerable charm and diplomatic acumen by repeatedly wooing support from a diverse group of governments, almost all of which, like the United States, wanted to counter Soviet support for the MPLA.

Savimbi's reputation for ruthlessness arose from his ordering the execution of political rivals within UNITA and those who did not perform up to his standards. As with RENAMO in Mozambique, his tactics and troops repeatedly subjected civilians to brutal treatment, frequently attempting to make government-controlled territories unlivable through robbing, burning, maiming, and killing. The group regularly took children into its territory as trainable fighters. Over the years, UNITA continually earned far more condemnation for its extreme abuses from the UN and international human rights organizations than did the MPLA.[21]

Savimbi and his followers could not win the war, but they prevented peace for almost three decades, until he died in battle in 2002. Across numerous series of negotiations, a variety of foreign supporters, and horrific levels of death and destruction, one goal became obvious. Savimbi wanted to be the head of state in Angola. Nothing less would satisfy the man who broke virtually every formal agreement he made with his opponents. Under these circumstances, some UNITA loyalists abandoned the military cause and openly disagreed with Savimbi, returning to Luanda to function under the 1994 Lusaka Protocol within the political system.

Although it has more credibility as a partner in negotiations and a much better reputation for the treatment of civilians, the MPLA became more militarized across time and its abuse of the Angolan people became more common. Historically a faction-ridden movement, for many years the MPLA had difficulty governing itself and the country, even during periods of relative calm. Challengers and rivals to established leaders met harsh fates in this organization as well. As the internationally recognized government of Angola, however, the MPLA hardly had a chance to succeed, first in the face of extreme economic hardship after the Portuguese departed and then under the continual challenge of a war that would not end. Because of its many difficulties, the MPLA vested a great deal of power in its leader, first Agostinho Neto, and after his death in 1979, Jose Eduardo dos Santos, who was known for his ability to unite various groups within the party. In contrast to Savimbi and the leadership of

FRELIMO in Mozambique, however, Neto and, later, dos Santos lacked diplomatic acumen and the ability to charm foreign diplomats and heads of state.

Besides war and economic hardship, the government encountered chronic problems in implementing policies and programs because of its weak and inefficient bureaucracy. Thus, the MPLA rarely succeeded for any great length of time in effectively delivering badly needed goods and services to the Angolan people. This resulted in part from an acute shortage of trained personnel as well as from a highly centralized system in which midlevel personnel had little freedom and no incentive to make decisions. Again, in contrast to FRELIMO, MPLA officials did not place a priority on vigilance against corruption, and beginning in the 1980s, as the war took its toll on the economy, corruption became commonplace. The 1992 election graffiti slogan mentioned earlier stated, "MPLA Steals, UNITA Kills." Under MPLA governance, Angolans could legitimately ask: If the killing stops, will the stealing stop, too?

Thus, unlike the Mozambique situation, significant local dynamics in Angola helped to fuel and prolong military regionalism and globalization during the Cold War era. Without outside help, UNITA would have had much more difficulty maintaining its aggressive military campaigns. Yet with or without outside help, Savimbi refused to adhere to any agreement to share power with the MPLA. After he once again resorted to war in the late 1990s, the MPLA decided not to give him another chance to negotiate, a set of developments that are discussed below. First, however, the dynamics of military globalization and the keen interest the superpowers took in the region deserve further attention.

Global Dynamics: The Impact of the War System During the Cold War

Although the United States and the Soviet Union remained locked in a global war system that accentuated competition for more than forty years, the degree of hostility between the superpowers changed across time. These fluctuations affected the superpowers' policies toward the various countries of southern Africa.

The 1970s represented a time of relative easing of tensions, or détente, led on the U.S. side by President Richard Nixon and his chief foreign policy adviser, Henry Kissinger, from 1969 to 1976. The Nixon administration sought greater cooperation in a number of arenas, including some assistance from both the People's Republic of China and the Soviet Union in extricating the United States from its war in Vietnam. This long, costly, and difficult conflict eventually had little support among the American people and, across time, few consistent goals. Together with the Watergate scandal that rocked the U.S. government, the Vietnam War eroded domestic support for prolonged, distant military engagements. Beginning in 1977, Jimmy Carter's presidency placed even more emphasis on improving economic relations and arms control.

For his part, the Soviet leader, Leonid Brezhnev, wanted to reduce the level of hostility in the 1970s in order to get access to the Western technology and goods necessary for improving the Soviet economy. Even in the context of better relations, however, superpower competition continued in various conflicts in Asia, Latin America, the Middle East, and Africa. For example, as already indicated, the U.S. CIA had supported the FNLA and UNITA in Angola, whereas the Soviets and Cubans backed the MPLA. Nonetheless, within the United States, the "Vietnam syndrome" reflected a growing weariness of entanglements in distant conflicts, and, as a consequence, Congress initiated important legislative restrictions in foreign policy. One such was the Clark Amendment, a 1976 law forbidding covert aid to the guerrilla groups in Angola.

Any possibility of further progress on superpower détente changed in 1979 when a number of unanticipated international events shook both parties' confidence in cooperation. That year an Islamic fundamentalist revolution overthrew a long-standing ally of the United States, the shah of Iran. Then a socialist revolution occurred in Nicaragua, when the Sandinista guerrillas overthrew the forty-year right-wing dictatorship of the Somoza family, a regime long supported by the United States. The most disturbing events, however, occurred that December. The Soviet Union invaded Afghanistan with 80,000 troops to overthrow an unstable Marxist regime and replace it with one more responsive to Moscow. Governments the world over denounced this act of aggression but failed to secure Soviet withdrawal.

Cold War tensions dramatically accelerated even further when, in 1980, the leadership of the United States changed. Ronald Reagan, who had called the Soviet Union the evil empire, became president. His administration instituted the Reagan Doctrine, a policy of supporting anti-

Communist guerrillas and governments involved in civil conflicts in many parts of the world with supplies, training, and other material resources. This included Cambodia, Central America (where the U.S. government covertly assisted counterrevolutionary guerrillas, even though Congress outlawed such aid), and most important for this discussion, Angola. In 1986, the Reagan administration persuaded Congress to repeal the 1976 Clark Amendment, and within two years, the United States replaced South Africa as the principal supplier for UNITA. Although the SADF generally viewed Reagan's policies as a "green light" for its aggression against both countries, the more military approach the United States chose for its Cold War competition in Angola contrasted with the economic strategies it employed with Mozambique. During the 1980s, U.S. economic aid became a key tool in convincing FRELIMO to abandon its commitment to socialism.

In a quickening pace of change, military globalization took another significant turn in the mid-1980s when Mikhail Gorbachev became the leader of the Soviet Union. Recognizing the increasingly vulnerable state of its withering economic and political institutions as well as its inability to maintain a fairly far-flung sphere of influence, Gorbachev instituted a number of domestic and international reforms. When East European regimes began giving way to peaceful revolutions in the late 1980s, the Soviet Union did not step in to save its Communist allies. They all fell. In 1989, citizens from East and West Germany peacefully dismantled the Berlin Wall, a powerful Cold War symbol of the division between East and West, capitalism and communism.

There is vigorous debate over what caused the end of the Cold War. For purposes of the analysis here, however, the consequences matter more. The Soviet Union signaled its unwillingness to continue supporting Cuban troops and massive amounts of military supplies to the Angolan government, despite the Cuban government's deep and long-standing commitment to MPLA. Too poor and dependent on Soviet aid, Cuba could not sustain its support unilaterally. Along with helping to strengthen UNITA, foreign policy in the Reagan and George H. W. Bush (1988–1992) administrations began to emphasize a negotiated settlement in both Angola and Namibia (then South-West Africa), linking the withdrawal of Cuban troops in the former with the withdrawal of South Africa from the latter. By the time of Namibian independence in 1990, the U.S. government had also used substantial economic aid to entice RENAMO into negotiations to end the war, while threatening to cut off economic assistance to FRELIMO unless it recognized RENAMO as a negotiating partner.

As chapter 4 will demonstrate in more detail, the UN supervision of elections in Angola and Mozambique illustrates a significant change in both the political and military domains of globalization that accompanied the decline and end of the Cold War. For four decades, the superpowers had blocked the regular, active involvement of the UN in helping to bring resolution to disputes within and between countries.

While emphasizing diplomacy and the involvement of the UN, however, the Reagan and Bush (1988–1992) administrations continued to grant significant material support to UNITA. This, in effect, placed considerably less pressure on Savimbi to find a negotiated solution to its conflict with the MPLA, which many analysts expected to lose the elections. Moreover, despite the MPLA victory in the 1992 elections, the Bush administration still harbored anti-Communist sentiment and refused to recognize the new government of Angola. Significant change in U.S. foreign policy came, however, when Bill Clinton became president. In 1993, the United States established formal diplomatic relations with the official government of Angola (thereby recognizing MPLA), ended its trade sanctions against the country, and began allowing U.S. companies to sell nonlethal military equipment to Angola. Furthermore, Britain ended its arms embargo against MPLA, and the UN Security Council imposed global sanctions on the export of arms and oil to UNITA. By this time, however, UNITA had its own internal source of support—diamonds.

Although the change in administration from Bush to Clinton in 1993 finally ended the extension of the Cold War to Angola, the deadly standoff between MPLA and UNITA continued. By the late 1990s, a decade after the end of the Cold War, analysts and foreign policy makers alike agreed that although both parties to the violence brutally attempted to crush the opposition, UNITA alone stands to blame for perpetuating the armed conflict. It continued for two reasons: Savimbi's preference for war over abiding by negotiated agreements, and his ability to underwrite the costs of his military capability through the export of Angolan diamonds. Yet the United States, the superpower so eager in earlier decades to prevent a socialist state in Angola by insuring Savimbi's war-fighting capability, now placed little priority on helping to finish what had been started. Margaret Anstee, the head of the UN mission to oversee the 1992 demobilization and elections, characterized Angola as an "orphan of the Cold War." When headlines the world over featured wars in Yugoslavia, Somalia, and Cambodia, she described events in Angola in the early 1990s as "a tragedy that left the world unmoved and unaware."[22] The carnage continued until Savimbi's death in 2002.

Costs of Thirty- and Forty-Year Wars

Massive costs accumulated over the decades of violent conflict in both countries as well as in the neighboring states. Although the entire region has felt the impact, this discussion will be limited to illustrating some of the more immediate consequences for Mozambique and Angola. By the end of the war in Mozambique, as already indicated, the World Bank had declared the country one of the poorest in the world, with a per capita GDP of about $80 and two-thirds of the population living in "absolute poverty." A child mortality rate (death before the age of five) of 280 per 1,000 demonstrated one of the consequences of such deprivation. Out of a total population of 17 million at the time, the war uprooted between 6 and 8 million Mozambicans, including 2 million who took refuge in neighboring countries. The others were displaced within the country. They crowded into cities and along transportation corridors where they overwhelmed available roads, water and sewage facilities, electric power, and other basic social services.

Most analysts estimate that during the war about 1 million people lost their lives directly because of the fighting or indirectly from starvation and disease. Many of these indirect victims were children. Another 200,000 lost their parents. The war destroyed half the primary schools and many of the health clinics. Much industry lay in ruins, as did the transportation system. In 1992, at least 10,000 amputees who had been injured by land mines or maimed by RENAMO had survived the war. The country still had to cope with the over 2 million largely unmapped land mines still likely to cause more injury and death to an estimated 2 percent of the population in some areas.

Prolonged wars and the uprooted people that accompany them inflict severe ecological damage and other costs difficult to calculate. For example, Mozambique lost about 90 percent of its elephant population, meaning

50,000 elephants (calculated from the time of independence). About one-half of the country's coastal mangrove forest was cut down, and no trees live within about 100 kilometers of the capital, Maputo. At the end of the war, about one-half the population was under twenty years old. They became adults knowing only war as a normal way of life. With many children forcibly recruited as soldiers and many others also traumatized by violence, the social and psychological costs of recovery will be felt for some time to come but will also be difficult to measure. Large numbers of unemployed, armed soldiers for example, engage in theft and raids on villages and rural businesses.[23]

By the late 1990s the costs of Angola's war were already staggering. Across almost forty years, more than 1 million people died. About 2 million had to flee their homes and, as uprooted persons, lack basic amenities. For most of the 1990s, humanitarian agencies have had no access to another 3 million in areas of active combat and presumed to be in similar conditions. Internationally, among countries receiving emergency food assistance at the turn of the century, the UN Food and Agricultural Organization rated Angola as having the worst conditions, including periodic attacks by UNITA on aid agencies.

Angola qualifies as one of the most extremely militarized countries worldwide. Until 2002, normal economic life had largely ceased, and a country rich in mineral resources and agricultural potential ranked as one of the fifteen poorest. The UN and other international agencies rate Angola among the most at-risk nations for child malnutrition, death, and abuse. The country also hosts one of the highest numbers of amputees, about 100,000. Around 10 million land mines scattered throughout the country threaten further loss of life and limb. Billions of dollars earned in the sale of oil and diamonds by both the government and UNITA went to pay for the war, but its costs have nonetheless placed the government in deep debt. International humanitarian aid intended to help victims often further exacerbates the corruption already entrenched in the economy. As with Mozambique, Angola faces severe ecological consequences. For example, more than 100,000 elephants were slaughtered, primarily by UNITA, in order to use ivory to pay for the war.[24]

For both countries, prolonged war brought humanitarian disasters. Mozambique began the process of recovery in the early 1990s, but Angola began only in 2002. Indeed, new developments in central Africa in the late

1990s escalated both the immediate conflict in Angola and the long-term prospects for war in the region.

REGIONALIZED AND GLOBALIZED CIVIL WARS: AFTER THE COLD WAR

The end of the Cold War changed military globalization considerably, just as the end of apartheid changed the regional military dynamics. Local forces had to find ways to adjust to the new situation. Only one superpower remained, an important change in the nature of the war system. Whereas both the United States and the Soviet Union had previously given assistance for armed conflict to their allies in southern Africa, these sources dried up. The various sources of weapons, however, did not. The Cold War represented the largest military buildup in history, and when the superpower standoff ended, a huge stockpile of weapons became available to the global market from both the East and West. Other sources, such as those from the military buildup in South Africa under apartheid, also added to what had already been a flourishing global arms dynamic. Small arms used effectively by unskilled soldiers—that is, rifles, machine guns, hand grenades, land mines, low-caliber artillery and short-range rockets—play a prominent role in this trade. With no outside governmental donors available, local forces in Angola had to rely almost exclusively on revenue from the export of diamonds, oil, and other minerals to pay for arms imports, and such reliance increased the determination of each group to control territories rich in raw materials. Troops took provisions in part from looting or "taxing" humanitarian assistance from outside the country and through confiscating the few goods locally produced.

With no Cubans to support the MPLA and no SADF to support UNITA, these warring parties turned to new partners, both governmental and private; in other words, mercenaries. Executive Outcomes, a company in South Africa that employed soldiers who used to defend apartheid, for example, provided training and strategic advice to the Angolan government and defended some of the country's diamond mines against UNITA attacks. Modern communications technology dramatically increased the efficiency of communication for these and other fighting forces.

Rather than attempting to nurture loyalty among local populations or appealing to ideological or other justifications for their cause, the military group occupying any particular area simply displaced those people it could not control, resulting in massive numbers of refugees. Revenue left over from arms purchased with the sale of minerals went primarily to line the pockets of those waging the war rather than to developing services for the citizens.

Some of these changes in the interaction of global, regional, and local forces in armed conflict had become evident even before the end of the Cold War and apartheid. But these monumental shifts in military globalization and regionalism significantly affected the war in Angola. Eventually, they had effects elsewhere in central Africa, an area that exhibits all the post–Cold War trends listed above. This chapter concludes with a brief description below of the somewhat complex events that drew both Angola and Zimbabwe into Africa's largest war ever, the conflict waged primarily in the Democratic Republic of the Congo (DRC) that promotes what some analysts call warlord politics.[25]

In 1998, under the umbrella of the Southern Africa Development Community (SADC), an organization to be discussed in chapter 4, Angola, Namibia, and Zimbabwe sent troops into the DRC, formerly known as Zaire. In 1997, the rebels who ousted the long-standing dictator, Mobutu, gave the country its new name. During the Cold War, as noted earlier, Mobutu had been a key ally of the United States. Angola and Zimbabwe invaded to support the new DRC government, now headed by the rebel movement leader, Laurent Kabila. Kabila's regime, a weak government plagued by instability and militarism, faced a critical threat from a variety of other rebel forces backed by an invasion from Rwanda and Uganda. UNITA had also received crucial support from the old Mobutu regime, as discussed earlier, and now sided with some of the new anti-Kabila forces as well as with the invading troops from Rwanda and Uganda. Troops from these countries reportedly engaged in combat alongside UNITA in Angola. By helping to prop up the Kabila regime, the Angolan government seized the opportunity to accomplish several goals. It wanted to save its new ally in the DRC; to crush UNITA's military capacity, supply routes, and bases historically associated with the previous regime in Zaire; and to demonstrate to the governments of Rwanda and Uganda that aiding UNITA carried a heavy price.

With the downfall of apartheid and no help from South Africa, Savimbi's military capacity depended on bases and supply routes in Zaire more than ever. Furthermore, Zaire had backed another more recently organized rebel group fighting for the independence of Cabinda, Angola's oil-rich enclave territorially situated on the Atlantic Coast and wedged between Congo Brazzaville and Zaire. To protect Cabinda and destroy bases supporting rebels there, Angola also invaded Congo Brazzaville twice in the late 1990s.

Angola's interventions in its neighbors' affairs succeeded in routing the rebels, and by 2000, only a few thousand government troops remain deployed outside of the country. UNITA's conventional military capacity had been destroyed. The group still maintained an ability to sabotage facilities and ambush government troops within Angola, however, financed in part by the sale of diamonds exported through Rwanda. Besides inflicting significant damage on UNITA, Angola's interventions also yielded considerable economic gain. In return for saving its government, the DRC granted Angola's national oil company, Sonangol, control of the DRC's oil production and distribution networks as well as rights to explore for offshore oil. This represented a remarkable concession of sovereignty and revenue from one government to another and demonstrated an interesting and unusual security agreement between the two governments.

Zimbabwe and Namibia had much less incentive than Angola to intervene in the DRC to help save the Kabila regime, yet these governments also sent in troops in 1998, with Zimbabwe's 11,000 soldiers far outnumbering those from Namibia. The war contributed to bankrupting Zimbabwe. Mugabe's government, which faces increasing political challenges from opposition movements within the country, is increasingly weak and unstable. He has responded to these domestic challenges with heightened repression and human rights abuses, including the apparent assassination of critics. His reward from the DRC has been huge mining concessions from the Kabila regime, including copper, cobalt, diamonds, and gold, as well as other potentially profitable contracts for Zimbabwean companies. So far, however, during the war, these concessions have yielded little revenue.

Various governments and leaders in southern and eastern Africa have attempted to bring the numerous parties to the war in the DRC together to try to find some way to stop the fighting. However, the United States

and Russia (the core of the old Soviet Union), those that previously played
key roles in the region, have shown little interest in Africa at all. In the
United States, the Clinton administration had demonstrated some concern about resolving Angola's forty-year-old war and the unfolding wider
conflagration, but the George W. Bush (2000–) administration has not.

CONCLUSION

The global war system and regional defense of apartheid played significant roles in creating and perpetuating wars in southern Africa in the
contemporary era. Angola is the only case in which local factors prolonged violent confrontation significantly, giving it the character of warlord politics. Angolans lived with this organized violence as the normal
state of affairs for two generations, and recovery may take as long or
longer. Periodically, global powers used their influence to promote peace,
but these efforts, together with various contributions for postwar reconstruction, pale in comparison to the material and ideological fuel poured
on the flames of violent confrontation. The UN, reinvigorated at the end
of the Cold War, played important, positive roles, as will be shown in the
next chapter, but it, too, often contributed too little, too late. Humanitarian INGOs administered aid to those uprooted by the war and, on occasion, contributed to conflict resolution. In the end, military globalization
during the Cold War, together with a vigorous defense of apartheid,
crushed the aspirations of southern Africa's people and governments
alike to address basic needs by building socialist societies and using other
mechanisms. Such commitments became victim not only to prolonged
war and militarism but also in some cases to the forms of corruption
such violent confrontations always breed. Then structural adjustment
policies imposed by global financial institutions subsequently insured
that government social services could not be resurrected to address basic
needs. Chapter 5 discusses local, regional, and global economic dynamics, but these cannot be fully comprehended outside the context of the region's history of sustained violent conflict.

Since the end of the Cold War, new conflicts driven by local factors but
prolonged by global and regional dynamics have taken root in central
Africa and threaten to draw in neighbors to the south. This quite bleak

picture on military globalization in southern Africa, however, is offset in part by considerably more life-affirming efforts in the domain of political globalization, which also have a long history and a powerful presence in the region. Chapter 4 turns now to analyzing these dynamics in the interplay of global, regional, and local arenas.

Notes

1. See, for example, Robert Kaplan, *Balkan Ghosts: A Journey Through History* (London: Vintage, 1994).

2. Ted Robert Gurr, "Ethnic Warfare on the Wane," *Foreign Affairs* 79, no. 3 (May-June 2000).

3. David Held et al., *Global Transformations: Politics, Economics, and Culture* (Stanford: Stanford University Press, 1999), pp. 87–148.

4. Held et al., *Global Transformations*, p. 97.

5. Ibid., pp. 99–102; and Mary Kaldor, *New and Old Wars: Organized Violence in a Global Era* (Stanford: Stanford University Press, 1999). See also David Keen, "When War Itself Is Privatized," *Times Literary Supplement* (December 1995); Mark Duffield, "Post-Modern Conflict: Warlords, Post-Adjustment States and Private Protection," *Journal of Civil Wars* (April 1998); Michael Ignatieff, *The Warrior's Honor: Ethnic War and the Modern Conscience* (London: Chatto and Windus, 1998); and Chris Hables Gray, *Post-Modern War: The New Politics of Conflicts* (New York: Routledge, 1997).

6. Held et al., *Global Transformations*, p. 101.

7. Kaldor, *New and Old Wars.*

8. William Minter, *King Solomon's Mines Revisited: Western Interests and the Burdened History of Southern Africa* (New York: Basic Books, 1986), p. 182; and Rodney Davenport and Christopher Saunders, *South Africa: A Modern History* (New York: St. Martin's, 2000), p. 413.

9. James Ciment, *Angola and Mozambique: Postcolonial Wars in Southern Africa* (New York: Facts on File, 1997), pp. 38, 42.

10. For a historical analysis of how fairly fluid ethnic ties became more rigid, see Linda Heywood, *Contested Power in Angola: 1840s to the Present* (Rochester, NY: University of Rochester Press, 2000).

11. T. R. H. Davenport, *South Africa: A Modern History*, 4th ed. (Toronto: University of Toronto Press, 1991), pp. 349–365.

12. Crawford Young, *The African Colonial State in Comparative Perspective* (New Haven, CT: Yale University Press, 1994), p. 191.

13. Daniel Spikes, *Angola and the Politics of Intervention* (Jefferson, NC: McFarland, 1993), p. xiii.

14. Ciment, *Angola and Mozambique*, pp. 45–54; and William Minter, *Apartheid's Contras: An Inquiry into the Roots of War in Angola* (London: Zed, 1994), p. 99.

15. See chap. 4 for a discussion of "framing" issues.

16. Held et al., *Global Transformations*, p. 95.

17. Mohamed A. El-Khawas and Barry Cohen, eds., *National Security Study Memorandum 39: The Kissinger Study of Southern Africa* (Westport, CT: Lawrence Hill), p. 105.

18. Ciment, *Angola and Mozambique*, p. 79.

19. Minter, *Apartheid's Contras*, p. 37.

20. Ciment, *Angola and Mozambique*, p. 84.

21. Ibid., pp. 70–76, 98–102; Inge Tvedten, *Angola: Struggle for Peace and Reconstruction* (Boulder: Westview Press, 1997), pp. 50–51; and Eric Young, "Jonas Malheiro Savimbi," in Kwame A. Appiah and Henry Louis Gates Jr., eds., *Africana: The Encyclopedia of the African and African American Experience* (New York: Basic Civitas, 1999), p. 1676.

22. Margaret J. Anstee, *Orphan of the Cold War: The Inside Story of the Collapse of the Angolan Peace Process, 1992–93* (New York: St. Martin's, 1996), p. xi.

23. Ciment, *Angola and Mozambique*, pp. 90, 226; Thomas Ohlson, Stephen J. Stedman, and Robert Davies, *The New Is Not Yet Born: Conflict Resolution in Southern Africa* (Washington, D.C.: Brookings Institution, 1994), pp. 194–200, 296–298; Rachel Waterhouse, *Mozambique: Rising from the Ashes* (Oxford: Oxfam, 1996), p. 14.

24. Ciment, *Angola and Mozambique*, pp. 218–220; Heywood, *Contested Power*, p. 229–230; Ohlson, Stedman, and Davies, *The New Is Not Yet Born*, pp. 296–298; John Prendergast, *Angola's Deadly War: Dealing with Savimbi's Hell on Earth* (Washington, D.C.: United States Institute of Peace, 1999), pp. 2–3.

25. William Reno, *Warlord Politics and African States* (Boulder, CO: Lynne Rienner, 1998).

4

Political Globalization

FEW ACROSS THE GLOBE WHO WITNESSED THE SCENES BROADCAST from South Africa in April 1994 will forget the long queues of thousands of black citizens standing in line, sometimes for more than a day, to cast their first vote in the history of the country. Later that year, Nelson Mandela was sworn in as the nation's first democratically elected president. Despite his twenty-seven years in prison, his inaugural address emphasized reconciliation, stating:

> Out of the experience of an extraordinary human disaster that lasted too long, must be born a society of which all humanity will be proud. . . . Never, never, and never again shall it be that this beautiful land will again experience the oppression of one by another.[1]

Across decades, in repeated cycles of black civil unrest met with forceful violent responses by the apartheid regime, the people of South Africa paid a high price for their political freedom. Once it was gained, they were determined to use it. An estimated 86 percent of the electorate participated across the four days allowed for voting, and the whole world was watching. Such riveted attention was due in part to the thousands of activists in dozens of countries who had devoted time, energy, and for some, entire careers to an international movement whose primary goal consisted of bringing democracy to South Africa. The global anti-apartheid movement developed across decades and came to illustrate a powerful new tool for social change that helped to shape contemporary political globalization.

Activists advocating racial justice demonstrate only one aspect of the global reach of politics. Other forms of political globalization can be found in southern Africa, too, beginning with its history of colonization. During the early modern and modern periods, as shown in chapter 2, various European imperial powers extended their control over the region. Independence from colonial rule in the contemporary period institutionalized the European form of political rule, the nation-state, and solidified many arbitrary borders in southern Africa and across the continent. More recently, governments in the region find themselves sharing political power with global institutions such as the United Nations and the International Monetary Fund, or such regional ones as the Southern Africa Development Community (SADC). Moreover, in a reversal of the flow of influence, many across the world seek to emulate practical political models developed in the region, for example the South African Truth and Reconciliation Commission (TRC), to test their applicability in addressing difficult problems elsewhere.

This chapter examines various contemporary manifestations of the interaction of local, regional, and global politics in shaping events and institutions in the region and explores regional models of political leadership that offer potential for the rest of the world. If phenomena as varied as empires, nation-states, the United Nations, activists, leaders, and others all fit under the rubric of political globalization, however, the first task must be to examine this domain more carefully for the ideas that make it an analytic whole. In doing so, we will begin the process of addressing a number of dilemmas.

The dilemmas facing southern Africa in the arena of political globalization bear a striking similarity to those in the military and economic domains. If global and regional powers, authority, and forms of rule have had in the past and continue to have such profound impact on politics in southern Africa, what are the possibilities that the people of the region can govern their own future? What obstacles and opportunities do these nations face, and what partnerships might they want to forge, since governing a country involves coping with multiple layers of powerful political actors across the world and the region? Can a government be locally, regionally, and globally accountable to sometimes crosscutting pressures all at the same time?

CONTEMPORARY POLITICAL GLOBALIZATION AND SOUTHERN AFRICA

Chapter 1 summarized political globalization as "the reach of political power, authority and forms of rule."[2] The concept of power lies at the heart of the study of politics and can be defined as the ability of one actor to convince another to do what it normally would not do. Similarly, power can be understood as the ability to control outcomes. Persuasion, influence, the threat of force, and coercion can all be means of exercising power. Individuals, groups, nation-states, and organizations that play a role in world politics are all actors that can use power, and clearly, different actors have different capabilities for exercising power.

For example, nation-states that draw on the resources of a substantial and well-educated population, a robust economy, a heritage of technological innovation, and a military suited to the challenges they face are likely to be powerful. Those with a small, relatively uneducated population, a poor economy, an aversion to change, and an unprepared military will probably not be able to exercise much power. Actors other than nation-states, however, also possess the ability to influence others. Leaders such as Nelson Mandela who possess the charisma and organizational skills to persuade people to work together toward a common vision have power beyond what one might expect from simply analyzing the resources of their base organization, especially, for example, in the case of South Africa, when the African National Congress was still an outlawed group. As demonstrated in chapter 3, leaders with diplomatic acumen, such as Jonas Savimbi or Samora Machel, have power to achieve goals through forging relationships with unusual and more powerful partners. In other arenas, nongovernmental organizations (NGOs) exercise power when they effectively campaign to convince the public or policymakers that the NGOs' preferred solutions to various problems are the best ones available. These illustrations demonstrate a reality that will be examined in more depth below: Power comes in many forms and is exercised by a number of actors in the world arena, with profound consequences for particular locales.

Authority, the second concept in the definition of political globalization, has to do with the acceptance of a person's or institution's right to make rules or issue commands and to expect compliance. Authority "denotes power that is viewed as proper and is voluntarily accepted. . . . [A]uthority involves the sense that those who rule do so rightfully and should be obeyed." This term is closely linked to legitimacy, which means that "the governed not only acknowledge the power of their governors but the ruled feel the power wielders ought to have power and they ought to be obeyed."[3] Across the modern and contemporary eras, legitimacy has increasingly become linked with the observance of democratic principles, no matter who or what the governing body is.[4] Therefore, an NGO that operates through democratic processes exercises more legitimate authority than an NGO that operates through authoritarian rule. The same is true of governments or intergovernmental organizations (IGOs). Historically, one of the features of international relations among sovereign nation-states, however, has been the absence of a legitimate authority that can wield power over national governments. Yet more recent trends in globalization have changed this situation considerably, an issue that will be discussed in more depth below.

Across time, the world has witnessed a number of different forms of political rule, the last concept in the definition of political globalization. Examples include empires, nation-states, and IGOs such as the European Union, SADC, or more globally, the United Nations and the World Trade Organization. As noted above, the willingness of governments to cede their own authority and, indeed, their sovereignty to institutions outside of their national boundaries demonstrates one of the hallmarks of the contemporary period of political globalization. Scholars of world politics assert that such interwoven political authority "challenges the traditional distinctions between domestic/international, inside/outside, territorial/non-territorial politics, as embedded in conventional conceptions of 'the political.'"[5]

Global governance, a concept closely related to political globalization, demonstrates why sharply distinguishing the domestic arena of politics from the global is no longer analytically useful. Global governance refers to "a process of political co-ordination in which the tasks of making and implementing global or transnational rules, or managing trans-border issues, are shared among governments and international and transnational agencies (both public and private), with the object of realizing a common purpose or collectively agreed goals."[6] The actors participating in global governance have proliferated, particularly since World War II, and they spring up from a variety of places. They interact to create a "multilayered" system that emerges both within and across formal political boundaries. As Held et al. have described global politics in the new century, "political communities . . . can no longer be characterized simply as 'discrete worlds'; they are enmeshed and entrenched in complex structures of overlapping forces, relations and, movements."[7] Although inequality and hierarchy often infuse these structures, even the most powerful political actors, including nation-states such as the United States, experience the impact of these changing conditions.

The complexity of contemporary political globalization and global governance results in part from rapid growth in the number of IGOs and INGOs. Governments create IGOs through treaties designed to establish institutions that will manage particular problems. With the expansion in commerce and technological innovations of the 1800s, governments, especially in Europe, began to see a need for cooperation and regulation across national borders. Nation-states faced practical issues most easily tackled through IGOs, for example the International Telegraphic Union, founded in 1865, and the Universal Postal Union, established in 1874. Earlier in the century (1815–1878), European governments used the Concert of Europe to address matters of common concern. This body established precedents and procedures that would later carry over into the founding of the League of Nations in 1919 and the United Nations in 1945.[8] The number of IGOs grew from fewer than forty in 1900 to more than 250 in 2000. However, only thirty-six of these have universal membership, meaning they garner participation from virtually all the states in the world. Others such as SADC are regional.[9]

Private citizens create nongovernmental organizations to address common concerns and international problems. They may be professional associations, foundations, activists, or other types of groups. They vary widely and span almost every imaginable activity. When their formal membership comes from more than one country, they can be called INGOs. Like IGOs, INGOs began in the 1800s. For example, activists in the United States and Britain formed transnational advocacy networks to conduct international campaigns against slavery in the late 1700s and early 1800s. Religious groups sought to cooperate across boundaries, founding, for example, the Young Men's Christian Association (YMCA) in 1844, and in 1894 the Young Women's Christian Association (YWCA). In 1900, fewer than 175 INGOs existed, but the number had grown to almost 6,000 by 2000. Of these, less than 10 percent qualify as having universal membership. Most have a regional membership or cross a few continents, with much higher concentrations in the North than the South. Growth in NGOs is associated with countries that have higher socioeconomic status and more democratic political systems.[10] Most analysts agree that, on the whole, the rise in the number of NGOs constitutes a democratizing trend in globalization, but the larger issue of the relationship between democracy and globalization involves considerable debate, a matter to which we now turn.

The word *democracy* derives from the Greek words *demos* (people) and *kratos* (rule). Held has stated, "Democracy means a form of government in which, in contradistinction to monarchies and aristocracies, the people rule."[11] Jan Scholte elaborated by asserting that "democracy is understood to prevail when members of a polity determine—collectively, equally and without arbitrarily imposed constraints—the policies that shape their destinies." Democratic decisionmaking can take many forms, the kind practiced in most of the Western nation-states being just one of many. Scholte has said that whatever form it takes, "in one way or another democratic governance is participatory, consultative, transparent and publicly accountable."[12]

In analyzing the connection between democracy and globalization, an important question arises: In the contemporary era of multilayered global governance, is decisionmaking about the various policies that profoundly affect people's lives participatory, consultative, transparent, and publicly accountable? The answer, as one might expect, is mixed, but the question provides a good yardstick for judging political globalization in southern Africa. For example, by supporting forces for democratic change inside South Africa, the global anti-apartheid movement had an important impact on ending white rule and ushering in universal suffrage. In another illustration, the international community helped put an end to Mozambique's civil war by having the United Nations supervise elections. Yet, in contrast, the global networks of governments, corporations, and other private organizations that funneled aid to Jonas Savimbi and UNITA perpetuated a civil war in Angola for decades beyond what these rebels could have fought on their own resources and momentum.

Events and organizations at work in southern Africa demonstrate some of the complexities of a large number of actors participating in the multilayered governance of contemporary political globalization and illustrate the dilemmas stated earlier. All the countries of southern Africa claim to be democratic. How can these governments cope with the powerful assertions of multiple global and regional actors, while at the same time ensuring participation, consultation, transparency, and public accountability at home? How do global and regional institutions and processes enhance local governance, and how do they undermine it? By examining a number of specific connections among local, regional, and global politics, the remainder of this chapter examines these dilemmas and carries the issues into the next chapter, whose subject, economic globalization, is intimately related to political globalization.

The discussion below is divided into three categories: governmental and intergovernmental politics, nongovernmental politics, and the influence of individual leaders. Chapter 5 addresses the issue of the impact of economic IGOs and multinational corporations.

GLOBAL, REGIONAL, AND LOCAL GOVERNANCE

The United Nations, particularly in its peacekeeping missions, and the Southern African Development Community illustrate the multilayered nature of governance and the impact of global and regional institutions on national politics. Both will be examined here. Due in part to the efforts of both IGOs and INGOs, southern Africa can be counted in what some analysts call one of the most significant aspects of political globalization, the "third wave of democracy" (the first two waves being in the early 1800s and the mid-1900s).[13] In the late twentieth century, an increasing number of countries worldwide adopted democratic processes of governance, and this tendency will also be examined here. The last section in this part of the chapter focuses on the South African Truth and Reconciliation Commission and demonstrates a reversal of the flow of influence, that is, ways in which local governance in the region can have substantial impact on global trends.

United Nations Peacekeeping Missions

The Charter of the United Nations, ratified in 1945, envisions a primary role for the organization in maintaining peace and security, and places the Security Council in charge of making decisions about most of these matters. Chapter VI of the charter outlines ways the Security Council can promote the peaceful settlement of disputes in order to try to avoid the outbreak of armed conflict. Chapter VII details actions the Security Council and the organization as a whole can pursue (including the use of military force) in response to threats to the peace, breaches of the peace, and acts of aggression. Chapter VIII promotes the role of regional organizations in maintaining peace and security, and provides a mechanism whereby the Security Council may authorize such a group to conduct enforcement action on behalf of the international community.

Because the United States and Russia (previously the Soviet Union) are two of the five permanent members of the Security Council, tensions from these superpowers' Cold War standoff prevented the UN from engaging actively and regularly in peacekeeping activities, even though the charter encouraged such a role. A dramatic foreign policy change initiated in 1987 by the Soviet leader Mikhail Gorbachev, however, gave the UN an opportunity to reverse course in this arena. Beginning in 1989, the UN undertook a number of peacekeeping missions all over the world, including in Angola, Mozambique, and Namibia. Because they are all related to the region's wars, some of this UN work has been briefly noted in chapter 3. This discussion will compare the missions and their implications for political globalization.

UN peacekeepers, often referred to as the Blue Helmets because of the color of their headgear, carry out a variety of tasks and in doing so may use military force as a last resort in self-defense. They may observe cease-fires, troop withdrawals, arms control agreements, elections, and the implementation of human rights standards. Peacekeepers may separate armed forces and establish buffer zones. They may be called on to restore peace, maintain law and order, rebuild and train police forces, and establish civil administration. Peacekeepers may open supply lines and may guard supplies, as well as protect aid workers and refugees in the delivery of humanitarian aid.[14] In southern Africa, peacekeepers performed most of these tasks during one or more missions.

The New York Accords signed in late 1988 by Angola, Cuba, and South Africa to address the long-standing war in Angola and Namibia initiated two UN peacekeeping operations there. A small group of military observers, the UN Angola Verification Mission (UNVEM), oversaw the withdrawal of Cuban troops from Angola from 1989 to 1991. A much larger contingent of about 4,500 UN troops from 109 countries was deployed to Namibia from 1989 to 1990 as the UN Transition Assistance Group (UNTAG).

Although at the time this was the most ambitious peacekeeping operation the UN had ever undertaken, the number of personnel and the budget for UNTAG were about half what many observers thought was necessary to complete the assignment. The tasks were many, all in an effort to end the war in Namibia between SWAPO and the South African Defense Forces and to provide for the election of an independent government. To those ends, UNTAG supervised the cease-fire; monitored the withdrawal of the SADF; confined SWAPO forces to their bases; oversaw the civil police force; repealed discriminatory and restrictive legislation; arranged for the release of political prisoners and the return of exiles; and created conditions for free and fair elections. Most observers hail the UNTAG mission as very successful, despite early difficulties in the implementation of the cease-fire and the lack of funds to provide safe housing for all those seeking to return.[15] UNTAG demonstrated that the UN could, from a global level, play a crucial role in building the conditions for peace and democracy at a local level, a prime illustration of political globalization producing positive outcomes. The same cannot be said of the UN missions in Angola.

Altogether the United Nations sponsored four peacekeeping missions in Angola from 1989 to 1999, only one of which was a success. The first UN-VEM operation worked well to oversee the withdrawal of Cuban troops from Angola (1989–1991), but UNVEM II (1991–1995) initiated by the Bicesse Accord of 1991, UNVEM III (1995–1997) organized under the Lusaka Protocol of 1994, and the UN Observer Mission in Angola (MONUA, 1997–1999) failed to help the country move toward sustained cessation of the war. By 1999, the Angolan government had decided to end its participation in the Lusaka Protocol, requested that the peacekeepers associated with MONUA leave the country, and then launched a new offensive to try to crush UNITA, as discussed in chapter 3.

A number of factors account for the failure of these four peacekeeping missions in Angola. The two parties had depended on external help to wage their war since 1975, but in 1991 neither party wanted a strong international presence within the country to help secure the peace. By design, UNVEM II had only 550 peacekeepers and an extremely limited mission that basically required its personnel to remain as detached observers. The Lusaka Protocol and UNVEM III corrected many of the mistakes of the previous mission by empowering the UN operation with enforcement mechanisms and supplying, at its height, 7,000 troops. The provisions required, for example, that power be shared between the warring parties. Elections could not be held until after the military had demobilized, and the UN had direct supervision of both the peace process and the elections. The process achieved some success, with UNITA's members being seated in the legislature in 1992 and UNITA's minister appointed to a Government of Unity and National Reconciliation in 1997.

Yet when UNITA demonstrated repeatedly its unwillingness to abide by those aspects of the Lusaka agreement that would require the discharge of all troops or the ceding of territory, the UN responded with appeasement more than coercion, as well as "premature optimism" about the eventual outcomes of the peace process.[16] In 1997, a new mission, the MONUA, took over the peacekeeping role of UNVEM III but downsized to only 1,500 troops. Then, as the peacekeeping mission was reduced, the Security Council initiated a renewed strategy of sanctions to try to cut off UNITA's contacts and resources. In 1997 and 1998, the Security Council banned UNITA officials from international travel, closed UNITA's overseas offices, and prohibited all aircraft from flying to or from UNITA-controlled territory. The Security Council also froze UNITA bank accounts and banned the purchase of Angolan diamonds, the organization's means of paying for its military might, unless the gems were accompanied by a government certificate of origin.[17]

Still the war continued, and a few months after the leader of MONUA died in an airliner crash the Angolan government asked MONUA to leave. Yet even with all the sanctions and the government's more powerful and effective military offensive begun in 1999, UNITA remained strong enough to deny government troops a victory. The war ended only when Jonas Savimbi was killed in action in 2002.

Although the UN might have done more to create successful peacekeeping missions in Angola, most analysts agree that the UN is not primarily responsible for their failure. On the whole, the war was sustained by the unwillingness of both parties to find mutually agreeable means for addressing their differences. Under such circumstances, efforts by those in the international community to create the conditions for peace lose their effectiveness. Like Namibia, however, Mozambique's experience of UN peacekeeping had a more positive outcome, in part because both sides of the conflict were more war weary and ready to settle, and because those in the international arena were well aware of the failures of UNVEM II.

In Mozambique, after sustained negotiations driven in large part by a nongovernmental organization, the Sant'Egidio Community (discussed below), the Mozambican government, led by FRELIMO, and the insurgent organization, RENAMO, signed the Rome Accord in 1992. It outlined a process whereby the country would move from war to peace with help from a large, impartial force of UN peacekeepers. The 7,500 member UN Operation in Mozambique (ONUMOZ) lasted from 1992 to 1994 and had a mandate to enforce a cease-fire, disarm the two armies, and supervise elections. In setting up ONUMOZ, the Security Council also provided for immediate aid to distressed areas and the reconstruction of damaged infrastructure. Upon implementation of the cease-fire, a number of international NGOs rushed into the country with so much aid that some referred to the country as the "Donor Republic of Mozambique."[18] The presence of more than 250 NGOs gave rise to an alternative, nonstate source of power and authority. Furthermore, as is often the case in civil conflicts, another UN agency, the office of the UN High Commissioner for Refugees (UNHCR), also played a vital role in providing help and repatriation for those who fled the fighting.

In combination with the willingness of the conflicting parties to settle their disputes, these many efforts on the part of the international community helped to bring about a free and fair election in 1994 that provided a substantial political victory for FRELIMO, as described in chapter 3. Throughout the peacekeeping process in Mozambique, a number of problems arose. Yet the contrast between this mission's success and others' failure in Angola can be attributed to three factors: the various parties' willingness to contest their differences by means other than war; the eagerness of the UN repeatedly to adjust its mission to the needs of the local circumstances; and substantial resources to undergird the presence and work of those from the international community.[19] Once again, Mozambique provided another illustration of the powerful positive potential of political globalization.

UN involvement in the region extends far beyond its peacekeeping missions to work related to refugees and other humanitarian assistance, economic development, health, education, and more. As will be seen in chapter 5, economic-oriented IGOs related to the UN also have a profound impact on the region. Within this wide range of activities, however, the UN peacekeeping missions vividly illustrate political globalization and the multilayered nature of governance.

The Southern Africa Development Community

Significant regional implications have infused politics in southern Africa for centuries. Regional dynamics permeated many precolonial African societies, as well as colonial regimes and businesses. In the twentieth century (as discussed in chapter 3), the struggles to end white minority rule engaged the region's Frontline States (FLS), the nearby black-majority-ruled nations. They made the greatest and costliest contributions to these efforts. This political alliance gave birth to the Southern Africa Development Community (SADC), initially named the Southern African Development Coordination Conference (SADCC). Its goals were to promote black majority rule and resistance to apartheid destabilization campaigns, to reduce dependence on South Africa and the global economy, and to achieve balanced and sustained development as a region. By 2002, the goal of black majority rule had been reached, but the other objectives proved more elusive. Furthermore, it is important that SADC shifted from its initial commitments to resist the kind of regionalism that would complement the penetration of global economic forces, as had the member states.

In economic terms, regions can be described as "closed" or "open." A closed region, like the European Union, partially or fully insulates its markets from the rest of the world through customs unions or other mechanisms. Such relations foster more contact and flows within the region but may obstruct more global transactions outside of the protected area. In open regions such as the North American Free Trade Agreement (NAFTA) and the Asia-Pacific Economic Cooperation (APEC), member governments simply reduce economic barriers against each other without taking a common stance against outsiders. Therefore, a closed area provides a potential countervailing tendency to globalization, whereas an open one complements worldwide interactions.[20] These economic choices and the dilemmas they pose will be discussed in chapter 5. The section that follows places more emphasis on SADC's political contributions to regional ties among governments.

Two heads of state, Kenneth Kuanda of Zambia and Julius Nyerere of Tanzania, played crucial roles in organizing the FLS in 1974. They envisioned a "transcontinental belt of independent and economically powerful nations from Dar es Salaam and Maputo on the Indian Ocean to Luanda on the Atlantic."[21] The political commitments of the FLS to end white minority rule through support of guerrilla organizations and other strategies, combined with persistent aggression against them by the apartheid state, led to a search for regional economic cooperation that excluded South Africa. Founded in 1980 in Lusaka, SADCC consisted of nine countries: Angola, Botswana, Lesotho, Malawi, Mozambique, Swaziland, Tanzania, Zambia, and newly independent Zimbabwe. This original group included one of South Africa's close collaborators, Malawi, but not another, Zaire under the Mobutu regime (now the DRC), which was giving strong support to UNITA in Angola. Namibia joined in 1990 immediately following its independence. The organization shortened its name to SADC in 1992. South Africa joined as a new democracy in 1994, with Mauritius, the Seychelles, and the DRC (after Mobutu's fall) joining in the next three years. Now SADC has fourteen members.

Well aware of failed experiments in regional cooperation in Africa (such as the East African Community), founders of the original organization, SADCC, deliberately designed a limited and flexible organization. They emphasized sectoral coordination, national decisionmaking, and compensation to weaker members for any monetary or trade decisions that might adversely affect them. SADCC placed a priority on industrial planning that would mobilize resources across the region within the context of the goal of sustained development, and envisioned increases in trade to be of secondary importance. Taking into account various resource endowments, in 1981 SADCC assigned each state its own sector. For example, as the logical alternative to the rail routes that ran through South Africa, Mozambique assumed responsibility for transport and communications. As the region's largest oil producer, Angola led the energy sector. As the region's largest food producer, Zimbabwe took charge of food security. Botswana housed the secretariat.

Donor countries and multilateral development agencies responded with some enthusiasm, particularly to large infrastructure projects such as integrating the transport systems in Tanzania, Angola, and Mozambique (with substantial benefits for Malawi, Zambia, and Zimbabwe) as alternatives to those routed through South Africa. A centerpiece of this work was the 170-mile Beira corridor, a crucial road, rail, and oil pipeline from eastern Zimbabwe to Beira, Mozambique, the closest access port for Zimbabwe. Demonstrating the close link between economic, political, and military policies in the region, Zimbabwe and Mozambique cooperated closely on military protection for the corridor in the face of RENAMO's assaults on rail lines and other infrastructure. SADCC also established the Beira Corridor Group (BCG) to help develop strategic business projects built on a consortium of private and public companies from the affected states.[22] The amount of transit traffic from the landlocked states through SADC ports demonstrates the success of the emphasis on transportation infrastructure. Traffic dramatically rose from 20 percent in 1980 to 60 percent by 1991. Other accomplishments were the linking of all SADC capitals by air and for all members, direct satellite telecommunications connections (rather than being routed through South Africa).[23]

Among other initiatives, SADCC attempted to coordinate food security and to promote comprehensive strategies for attracting foreign direct investment. These efforts achieved less success, in part because national interests began to take precedence over regional ones, although at points the group implemented significant improvements related to food production. Despite SADCC's efforts, Botswana and Zimbabwe, the two more industrially developed countries (prior to the admission of South Africa), continued to attract disproportionate amounts of foreign investment. Furthermore, a number of countries had to place a priority on national structural adjustment programs required by the IMF and the World Bank that ran counter to SADCC's economic goals.

Across the 1980s, the regional organization managed to convince European donor agencies in Scandinavia and the European Economic Community (which later became the European Union) to support SADCC's work, and eventually the United States and Britain followed suit. By the end of the 1980s, the organization had secured $2.7 billion in financing from such sources.[24] SADCC's hopes of using its regional unity to persuade Western governments to disengage economically from South Africa or to prevent the apartheid regime's aggressive destabilization efforts during this decade, however, largely failed. The organization had only modest success in achieving its goals of balanced and sustained development across the region and reduced dependence on South Africa and the global economy.

For several reasons, SADCC also largely reversed course on attempting to use the organization as a counterpoint to the larger trends of market forces within economic globalization. Many of the countries in the region responded to pressure from the IMF, the World Bank, and other Western donors to reform their economies in the direction of allowing more integration with global economic forces and market incentives (to be discussed in chapter 5). South Africa's membership as a new democracy also brought a completely new dynamic, since lessening dependence on apartheid had been a primary goal. Furthermore, another free trade organization, COMESA, the Common Market for Eastern and Southern Africa, became a significant rival. The new name, SADC, in 1992 signaled a new vision of economic integration that promotes a single regional market for the free movement of goods, labor, capital, and services, and eventually a single currency. By 2002, further changes in SADC structure consolidated its previously decentralized sectoral approach into a considerably more centralized mechanism of four directorates located at the Gaborone headquarters to manage the sectors formerly dispersed across all member states. In 2004, economic and political stresses at the national level continue to hamper regional economic integration, however, as will be discussed further in chapter 5.

The same is true for COMESA. Formed originally as the Preferential Trade Area (PTA) in 1981, COMESA replaced the PTA in 1994. It stretches primarily along the eastern side of the whole African continent, overlapping substantially with SADC. Egypt is a member of COMESA, but South Africa is not. Unlike SADC, strengthening intraregional free trade and settling accounts with national (as distinct from global) currencies formed the goals of PTA/COMESA from the beginning as a more traditional organization. SADC has at times pressured its members not to join COMESA, and the political ties among states within SADC continue to be considerably stronger.[25]

Two other organizations that bind governments in the region are substantially smaller and older than both COMESA and SADC, and both depend on South Africa. The Southern African Customs Union (SACU), which includes Botswana, Lesotho, Namibia, South Africa, and Swaziland, has its roots in British colonialism. Nonagricultural goods move within SACU duty free, and members exercise a common external tariff and share the combined customs union revenues. The Southern Africa Multilateral Monetary Area (MMA) also dates back to colonial times and gives South Africa overall control of the issue of rand currency and over the foreign reserves of the other members, which include Lesotho, Namibia, and Swaziland. These two organizations reign as the most successful examples of economic and political cooperation in the region, largely because one partner, South Africa, has always dominated the rest and gains the most economically from both groups.[26]

When noting the noneconomic character of regionalism, however, unlike the other organizations, SADC continues to be a significant arena for coordination of political and military matters. This builds on SADC's tradition of being founded by the FLS. In early 1993, SADC offered military assistance to the Angolan government when Savimbi and UNITA again took up arms after their disappointing showing in the 1992 elections. SADC also took an active role in trying to address the conflict between the African National Congress and the Zulu-based Inkatha organization in the period leading up to the South African elections in 1994.

By 1996, SADC created an Organ on Defence, Politics, and Security to continue this FLS legacy in security matters. Under this organ, SADC members are allowed militarily to assist a member state at the request of its government, if they are able. As discussed in chapter 3, in 1998, under the umbrella of SADC, Angola, Namibia, and Zimbabwe sent troops into the DRC to help save the government of Laurent Kabila. South Africa and Botswana intervened in Lesotho in 1998 to avert a military coup d'état against a democratically elected government there.

In the political sphere, using its Parliamentary Forum Norms and Standards, the SADC tried to pressure President Mugabe into holding free and fair elections in 2002 and then documented systemic and large-scale problems in the electoral process. In 2001, SADC had expressed concern about Zimbabwe's economic collapse and its implications for the region. Yet, in part due to the decades-old ties among former guerrilla fighters who became heads of state, leaders in South Africa, Mozambique, and Namibia accepted Mugabe's victory as "legitimate." This action was condemned internally by some of their own citizens and stood in sharp contrast to virtually all other governmental and nongovernmental organizations inside and outside the region that monitored the Zimbabwe elections. For example, former archbishop Desmond Tutu harshly and publicly criticized his own government for accepting Mugabe's election.

So far, political and military cooperation seems to be at least as significant as economic integration within SADC. What the future holds for this regional organization remains unclear, particularly as a democratic South Africa carves out its economic relations across the region and continent, and the aging former leaders of the FLS and various guerrilla organizations get replaced by a new generation. SADC has endured, however, for more than twenty years as a significant actor in the region and currently stands as the only viable organization for pursuing larger issues of economic regionalism among all the governments in the area.

When analyzing multilayered governance in southern Africa, however, SADC does not yet play the same prominent role in affecting decisions of national governments, particularly in the domain of economics, that global IGOs do, the influence of which will be discussed in more detail in the next chapter. When choosing to whom to cede their sovereignty, as in most regions of the world, the national governments in southern Africa have not yet given much authority to regional organizations, other than the few who give South Africa control over their trade and monetary matters in SACU and MMA.

Black Majority Rule

Most of the people and organizations (more of them will be discussed below) that committed themselves to the cause of eliminating white minority rule from southern Africa assumed that racially based authoritarianism within each nation-state would be replaced by multiracial democracies. The end of the Cold War, as shown in chapter 3, accelerated the move to black rule. Now that black rule has been achieved, however, is majority rule secure?

A significant aspect of political globalization in the late twentieth century has been the spread of democracy to countries previously under dictatorships. The last twenty-five years of the century witnessed transitions to more democratic forms of governance in dozens of countries in Africa, Asia, Latin America, and Europe. In southern Africa, for example, Botswana, Namibia, and Zimbabwe held their first genuinely competitive elections in the 1980s. Angola, Lesotho, Malawi, Mozambique, Namibia, and South Africa joined their ranks in the 1990s. As discussed earlier, however, the election results in Angola did not lead to peace, and only military intervention by South Africa and Botswana, on behalf of SADC, averted an attempted coup d'état by the military in Lesotho after elections in 1998. Furthermore, Zimbabwe resorted to harsh authoritarian rule that resulted in a widely condemned "election" in 2002. Nonetheless, across the region, Swaziland stands alone as the only country never willing to undergo multiparty elections.

Democracy cannot be defined by elections alone, but having governmental authorities subjected to regular electoral accountability clearly helps citizens collectively determine the policies that matter most in their lives. As discussed earlier in this chapter, democratic decisionmaking can take many forms, only one being the kind practiced in most of the Western nation-states. But whatever form it takes, democracy must be participatory, consultative, transparent, and publicly accountable. Besides elections, a number of other factors matter a great deal. For example, the protection of civil and political liberties makes a big difference. In this regard, South Africa's new constitution goes further than most others in the world to protect human rights regardless of race, religion, gender, and sexual orientation. It also abolishes the death penalty, in accordance with international law. Having a decently nourished and more educated population helps considerably in such a process. Extreme and sustained poverty undermines the conditions conducive to sustaining democracy, and unfortunately, at the beginning of the new century many in the region are politically freer but economically poorer than they have been in decades.

Given the history of long-standing warfare and economic deprivation in southern Africa, will these new experiments in democracy survive, or will they give way to more familiar patterns of elites charting the country's course while the masses remain excluded from meaningful political participation? The economic issues will be discussed in more detail in the next chapter. This following section addresses two troublesome cases, Zimbabwe and Zambia.

The story of politics in Zimbabwe in recent years portrays a disheartening case for those who hope to see regular free and fair elections as well as other processes that uphold the possibility of democracy. A number of problems plagued Zimbabwe's economy in the 1990s, including the need for land reform, which spurred war veterans to occupy a few white-owned farms in 1998. The promises of genuine land redistribution at the time of independence in 1980 had never been fulfilled. Although these particular illegal occupations ended by 2000, Mugabe's government began to encourage war veterans (many of whom were not genuine veterans) to occupy virtually all the white-owned farms. White-owned commercial farms dominate Zimbabwe's agricultural sector. The massive destruction accompanying the occupations meant that food production declined dramatically. As the food supply deteriorated, the government's decision to intervene in the war in Congo in 1998 ushered in a period of almost complete economic collapse.

These events, in concert with increasing discontent with the domination of Zimbabwe politics for twenty years by Mugabe's party (ZANU-PF), spurred the rise of an opposition group, the Movement for Democratic Change (MDC). Beginning in 1999, the government responded to increasingly critical voices by arresting journalists, both foreign and domestic, and destroying press properties, removing judges from office when they ruled against Mugabe's government, verbally assaulting

NGOs, including church authorities, that dared to criticize the government, and more recently imprisoning and torturing thousands of people and killing dozens. In 2000, however, despite government-instigated intimidation and violence, voters defeated a constitutional referendum endorsed by the government and gave over one-third of the seats in parliament, historically dominated by ZANU-PF, to the MDC.

With the escalation of violence against governmental opponents, independent observers of the March 2002 elections agree that they were neither free nor fair. Having judged that nothing could redeem an exercise that was already so corrupt, the EU pulled out its election monitors weeks prior to the voting. Soon after the results were announced, the Commonwealth, together with a number of other organizations, condemned the process and its outcome, the election of Robert Mugabe. As mentioned earlier, SADC found the election process deeply flawed but did not join in the chorus of Western governments, IGOs, and INGOs condemning the outcome. The Commonwealth formally suspended Zimbabwe in late March 2002, a move reluctantly affirmed by other African governments.

Although Zimbabwe was economically and politically very isolated as of 2003 as indicated above, heads of state in the region have been very hesitant to criticize Mugabe's government out of respect for his past leadership in ending white minority rule. They also worry that Western governments have overreacted to the illegal seizure of white farms. Since 1980, the West has shown little concern about genuine land and other reforms that would challenge the legacy of colonialism in the region and perhaps establish better economic conditions conducive to developing a strong democracy. This legacy includes not only white minority control of Zimbabwe's agricultural sector but also white control of this and other sectors in other countries. Despite these differences, however, almost all parties agree that the government of President Mugabe moved his country radically away from political globalization's third wave of democracy.

Zambia's story offers more hope than that of Zimbabwe. President Frederick Chiluba, elected in 1991 as the country's second president since independence in 1964, stood for reelection in 1996. Not content to allow voters simply to choose between him and his primary rival, former President Kenneth Kuanda, Chiluba manipulated changes to the constitution that would bar Kuanda and his deputy from running for office. Chiluba also charged some of his opponents with treason and placed substantial restrictions on freedom of the press. After winning the election in 1996, President Chiluba tried in 2001 to amend the constitution further, this time to end presidential term limits, but he failed when Zambians took to the streets in protest. (A similar effort in Malawi met the same result.) Then, in January 2002, after elections that some in the country claimed were not conducted fairly, Zambia installed a new president, who was a former vice president and Chiluba's handpicked successor, Ley Mwanawasa.

These cases illustrate that democracy has not yet established deep roots across the whole region. Yet with all the obstacles to freedom that these nations have endured, few expect that one or two decades can completely overturn generations of authoritarian rule. At this point, any verdict about southern Africa's long-term contribution to rule by and for the people would be premature.

The South African Truth and Reconciliation Commission

Most commentators and analysts repeatedly expressed surprise at how little violence occurred in South Africa's transition to democracy. Many expected a long and bloody struggle. Although civil unrest continued up through the election in 1994, the apartheid regime relinquished the reins of government to new democratically elected officials in an atmosphere of remarkable calm. Such success was due in part to magnanimous leadership by both white and black politicians. Another reason, however, was that white officials had extracted a major concession as the price of a peaceful departure: some form of amnesty from prosecution for apartheid security forces, most of whom were still well organized and well armed. These forces, frequently under orders from the highest political authorities, had committed horrendous atrocities in the name of defending the state. The particular form and mechanisms for reprieve were left to the newly elected parliament, but without the promise of some kind of amnesty, the new government risked an insurrection or coup d'état, a danger a number of other fledgling democracies had already faced.

How should governments respond to atrocities and those who commit them? Unfortunately, too many governments have faced this question in the contemporary period of globalization, and they have chosen a variety of routes to try to cope with the consequences of whole societies being subjected to collective violence. How do such societies move into the future constructively, learning from but not repeating the horrific pain of the past, a process often characterized as "transitional justice"?[27]

The famous Nuremberg trials at the end of World War II offer one model. The victory of the Allies over the Nazis gave the winners a chance to put the losers on trial, thereby exposing the horrors of the Holocaust and holding some of the leaders responsible for their crimes. The Holocaust was deemed to be a "crime against humanity," a label applied officially by the international community to apartheid as well.

In an effort to hold accountable numerous others perpetrating crimes against humanity—and giving more evidence of growing political globalization—the members of the United Nations concluded a treaty in 1998 to establish the International Criminal Court (ICC). Although the U.S. government voted against establishing the ICC (in contrast to 120 states in favor), founders hoped to address in a more permanent institution some of the difficulties that arose in ad hoc war crimes tribunals such as those held for the former Yugoslavia and Rwanda. But South Africa chose a different path to cope with its long history of collective violence.

The new South African parliament, under the leadership of justice minister Dullah Omar, chose to address the crimes of the past by establishing a truth commission. The hope was to expose as much information as possible about South Africa's traumatic history. Other countries (e.g., El Salvador, Argentina) had used truth commissions to cope with similar circumstances,[28] and the new South African government conducted research to learn from previous models. Parliament then established the Truth and Reconciliation Commission (TRC) and forged a new path. The TRC tied the possibility of amnesty for perpetrators of gross human rights violations to their willingness to make full disclosure of their crimes:

> Amnesty would be available but only conditionally: to individuals who personally applied for it and who disclosed fully the facts of misdeeds that could be fairly characterized as having a political objective. Trading truth for amnesty, and amnesty for truth, the commission was intended to promote the gathering of facts and the basis for the society to move on toward a strong democratic future.[29]

Furthermore, the government provided substantial funding, staffing, and legal authority in order for the TRC to do its job well. Emphasizing the role of the commission in beginning the process of reconciliation and healing in the country, President Mandela appointed Anglican archbishop Desmond Tutu to head the TRC. Alex Boraine, a former white member of parliament (who had resigned in 1986) and a leader in the Methodist Church, was appointed deputy chair.[30] From the beginning, these men and others from the religious community played key roles in conceptualizing the TRC around Christian theological and ethical principles such as that of restorative justice.

> Unlike punishment, which imposes a penalty or injury for a violation, restorative justice seeks to repair the injustice, to make up for it, and to effect corrective changes in the record, in relationships, and in future behavior. Offenders have responsibility in the resolution. The harmful act, rather than the offender, is to be renounced. Repentance and forgiveness are encouraged.[31]

R. Scott Appleby has asserted that two factors made the TRC's model of restorative justice possible. First, South Africa is a predominantly Christian country where "citizens accord theological discourse on political matters a significant measure of respect." Shaping a legal process around a Christian concept, therefore, seemed natural. Second,

> [t]raditional African thought, which places great emphasis on rehabilitating rather than punishing evildoers, reinforces Christian sensibilities on the issue of forgiveness. The concept of *ubuntu*, which derives from the Xhosa expression *Umuntu ngumuntu ngabanye bantu* ("People are people through other people"), holds that humanity, the common possession of the entire people, is diminished when even one individual is lost to inhumanity. African jurisprudence is restorative rather than retributive . . . because *ubuntu* teaches that the dignity of one is linked to the dignity of all.[32]

In a five-volume, 3,500 page document, the TRC published findings from its more than two years of work in 1996–1998. More than 21,000 victims came forward to testify about their experiences and those of their family members who had been killed or disappeared. The commission also listened to politicians, military officials, those who bombed and tortured, those who spied and sabotaged, extremist Afrikaners, and extremist Africanists. The TRC investigated vigilante groups, township youth who victimized suspected collaborators, chemical and biological warfare projects, and secret burial grounds. Leaders from business, the church, the media, and the law were asked to testify in hearings that examined their complicity with apartheid. The apartheid government, however, destroyed documents related to the police, defense forces, and other government bodies, leaving the full picture painfully incomplete.[33]

No group escaped scrutiny, including the National Party and its current leader, F. W. de Klerk (who had released Nelson Mandela from prison), the African National Congress (which had designed and authorized the TRC), Chief Buthelezi and the Inkatha Freedom Party (which was responsible for the death of thousands of people in the period leading up to the elections), and the Pan Africanist Congress (which, like the ANC, had engaged in guerrilla warfare against apartheid). The black community sharply criticized the TRC's determination to examine the violent excesses of any and all groups. Compounding this criticism, a number of individuals who committed horrible atrocities and gave a full account of their deeds received the promised amnesty, thereby removing themselves from future prosecution or punishment.

Despite the controversies and its own acknowledged shortcomings, the commission stood by its findings, which included repeated condemnations of the system of apartheid as a whole as well as the security policies that upheld it. The TRC noted that in general the whites who testified showed little remorse for their actions. The commission stated in its report: "With rare exceptions, the response of the former state, its leaders, institutions and the predominant organs of civil society of that era, was to hedge and obfuscate. Few grasped the olive branch of full disclosure."[34]

With so little responsiveness on the part of those who instituted a system deemed to be a crime against humanity, was the TRC successful? Furthermore, with such systematic discrimination against poor black people still in place in South Africa, did the TRC succeed in contributing to genuine racial reconciliation in the country? With the somewhat unique circumstances that gave it birth, does the TRC serve as a model for other nations torn by mass violence? The answers to such questions are complex, mixed, and not yet clear, according to most analysts. Yet in spite of this ambiguity, the TRC findings accomplish at least two goals. One is that no one will be able to claim with credibility, as so many had for so many decades, that apartheid was justified or good for the country.

This can never again be stated as the truth. Furthermore, analysts argue that the long-term restorative benefits of the TRC should not be underestimated for building a democratic future for the country. Official recognition and reporting of individuals' stories helps to "create a framework for the nation to deal with its past. Echoing the assumptions of psychotherapy, religious confession, and journalistic muckraking, truth commissions presume that telling and hearing the truth is healing."[35] Invoking the work of psychotherapist Judith Herman with victims of trauma, Martha Minow argued:

> "The fundamental premise of the psychotherapeutic work is a belief in the restorative power of truth-telling," reports Herman. The same premise undergirds a truth commission that affords opportunities for victims to tell their stories. In both settings, the story of trauma becomes testimony. Know the truth and it will set you free; expose the terrible secrets of a sick society and heal that society. . . . Coming to know that one's suffering is not solely a private experience, best forgotten, but instead an indictment of a social cataclysm, can permit individuals to move beyond trauma, hopelessness, numbness, and preoccupation with loss and injury. . . . Treating those who testify . . . as persons to be believed, rather than troublemakers or even people with a burden to prove their story, the TRC offers a stark contrast with adversarial hearings and inquests. . . . [I]ts truth value lies in its capacity to elicit acknowledgment and to build the general picture of apartheid's violations.[36]

The ultimate utility of this rather extraordinary exercise, however, and its applicability to similar circumstances in other places, awaits a final verdict that only time can bring.

This overview of how political globalization gets exercised through governmental institutions at the global, regional, and local level in southern Africa would be incomplete without a similar examination of the work of nongovernmental organizations. The next section tackles this task.

TRANSNATIONAL ADVOCACY NETWORKS

Since the 1800s and the international antislavery campaigns, NGOs have focused considerable attention on southern Africa. Among other issues, they have sought to address white minority governments' gross violations of human rights, the region's long and complex civil conflicts, repeated debt crises, elections monitoring, and the AIDS pandemic. This section examines three sets of campaigns: the anti-apartheid movement, the campaign against land mines, and the conflict resolution work of a Catholic lay community. These were all conducted by groups that Margaret Keck and Kathryn Sikkink call transnational advocacy networks (TANs).

TANs take shape when activists in various countries develop working relationships with one another and combine forces to tackle significant value-laden debates (such as race and human rights). These networks thus participate in international and domestic politics at the same time. TANs hold values and principled ideas at the center of their work, and their participants believe that individuals can make a difference in the world. Activists are "people who care enough about some issue that they are prepared to incur significant costs and act to achieve their goals."[37] Visionary leaders among them propose "strategies for political action around apparently intractable problems," and they often succeed in whole or part.[38]

Keck and Sikkink have defined networks as "forms of organization characterized by voluntary, reciprocal, and horizontal patterns of communication and exchange." This concept "stresses fluid and open relations among committed and knowledgeable actors working in specialized issue areas. . . . Advocacy captures what is unique about these transnational networks: they are organized to promote causes, principled ideas, and norms, and they often involve individuals advocating policy changes that cannot be easily linked to a rationalist understanding of their 'interests.'"[39] A wide variety of NGOs may participate in such networks. Some might be called private voluntary organizations (e.g., churches and aid organizations), others might specialize in research or funding research (e.g., foundations), and others might be professional associations (e.g., trade unions and academic groups). Furthermore, NGOs are not the only actors in these networks. They may also include parts of IGOs at the regional or global levels (e.g., the UN General Assembly) and parts of some governments (e.g., the legislature or a particular agency in a country).

Keck and Sikkink asserted that a "boomerang" pattern of network influence often develops (see figure 4.1) when nation-states violate norms or values held dear by the activists and when channels between national governments and domestic NGOs are blocked: "[D]omestic NGOs bypass

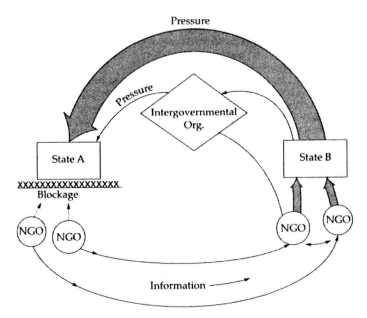

FIGURE 4.1   Boomerang Pattern
SOURCE: Margaret E. Keck and Kathryn Sikkink, *Activists Beyond Borders: Advocacy Networks in International Politics* (Ithaca, NY: Cornell University Press, 1998), p. 13.

their state and directly search out international allies to try to bring pressure on their states from outside . . . Linkages are important for both sides: for the less powerful, third world actors, networks provide access, leverage, and information (and often money) they could not expect to have on their own." For the more powerful groups that often originate in the North, the networks "make credible the assertion that they are struggling with, and not only for, their southern partners." The significance of NGOs having contacts outside national boundaries lies in their ability to "amplify the demands of domestic groups, pry open space for new issues, and then echo back these demands into the domestic arena."

The power of TANs comes primarily from framing international and domestic debates on issues so as "to make possible the previously unimaginable."[40] Framing means "conscious strategic efforts by groups of people to fashion shared understandings of the world and of themselves that legitimate and motivate collective action."[41] Networks succeed in reframing debates in a variety of ways: (1) through generating attention to new issues and placing them on the agendas of institutions that had previously ignored such issues; (2) by changing the terms of debate and discussion through persuading governments and international organizations to support international declarations or to change their stated policy positions; (3) by convincing institutions to change their procedures such that activists have more access to and contact with other key actors in an issue area; and (4) by convincing governments or international organizations to change their policies and shift to the desired direction.[42] Networks achieve such outcomes by strategically producing and using reliable, well-documented information in a timely and dramatic way; by calling on symbols, actions, or stories that enliven the information the TAN wants to use; by using leverage with key actors more powerful than the network itself; and by holding powerful actors accountable for their previously stated policies or principles.[43] Governments often value the good opinion of others, and through the "mobilization of shame," networks "can demonstrate that a state is violating international obligations or is not living up to its own claims," thereby jeopardizing the government's standing with others and possibly motivating a change in policy or behavior.[44]

The three network campaigns described below demonstrate in different issue areas and with somewhat different combinations of tactics, how TANs sometimes achieve powerful outcomes in political globalization.

The U.S. Anti-Apartheid Movement

Many who labored to end white minority rule in southern Africa, pouring their energy into one campaign after another across a number of years, did not imagine that apartheid, so deeply entrenched over so many centuries, would actually end in their lifetime—or even that Nelson Mandela would ever be released from prison. Nonetheless, they pressed their cause anyway, because they believed that what they were doing was right, regardless of whether or when change would eventually come. A Zulu proverb says that when a thorn gets stuck in the toe, the whole body bends over to take it out. Apartheid represented such a thorn, and at times it seemed like the whole world was stooping to pull it out. Not literally everyone across the globe wanted to end apartheid, because some profited from it. Sustained black resistance within the country, however, buttressed by international support finally made the unimaginable possible. White minority rule in South Africa finally ended in 1994.

As discussed in chapter 2, cultural globalization in the modern era brought with it the power of ideas in world politics and, in turn, had an impact on political globalization. As proponents of early articulations of Pan-Africanism, African Americans and others in the African diaspora had personal and organizational ties to southern Africa. For example, the National Association for the Advancement of Colored People (NAACP) played a role in organizing the African National Congress in 1912. As mentioned earlier, the NAACP was cofounded by W. E. B. Du Bois, the father of Pan-Africanism.

After World War II, in the contemporary era, however, several catalysts emerged for more widespread and sustained attention to the region by TANs. The founding of the United Nations brought renewed attention to human rights issues. Decolonization across Africa outside of southern Africa, new African leadership, and the birth of the Organization for African Unity (OAU, now the African Union) ushered in new initiatives for change. African resistance to apartheid and other forms of white minority rule increased inside the region, particularly in the 1950s, through campaigns such as those against pass laws in South Africa. A number of organizations across the world—for instance, the American Committee on Africa (1953), the British Anti-Apartheid Movement (1959), and others—organized specifically for the purpose of supporting black resistance. Worldwide attention to civil rights and black power struggles in the United States thrust race to the forefront of human rights issues internationally.

As noted in chapter 3, the Sharpeville massacre of 1960 and other similar incidents drew attention to the region and inflamed world opinion. Subsequently, when white minority regimes outlawed black resistance groups and drove a number of activists out of their countries, these exiles often provided direct links between groups inside and outside the region.[45]

Anti-apartheid work caught on quickly, and organizers began to coordinate their efforts with a wide range of people and organizations. For example, in less than a year from its founding, the British Anti-Apartheid Movement organized a mass rally of over 20,000 people addressed by leading public figures in London's Trafalgar Square in 1960. Soon thereafter, "In virtually every town and city throughout Britain there existed a voluntary group to promote the Movement's campaign."[46]

Across four decades of sustained activity, the anti-apartheid movement spread to dozens of countries and thousands of cities, campuses, churches, union halls, and other places where concerned people gathered, including international NGOs. It also involved IGOs, however, such as the United Nations, the Organization for African Unity, the Commonwealth (an informal organization of Britain and its former colonies), and the European Economic Community. Some state and local governments (e.g., in Alabama, Connecticut, Michigan, New York City) as well as some national ones also got involved. Frontline States and Scandinavian governments in particular gave considerable sustained support.

In bold challenges to the foreign policies of most Western governments, the global movement focused its campaigns in four areas: direct aid to black resistance groups within the region, the complete isolation of white minority governments, education about racial oppression, and the generation of credible research and documentation to support all these activities.[47] Direct aid consisted of military and nonmilitary assistance to groups in the region. As discussed in chapter 3, military supplies for guerrillas came primarily from governments in Eastern Europe. Other forms of aid, however, came from numerous governmental and nongovernmental sources and included assistance to refugees, legal defense for political prisoners and their families, scholarships for black students inside the region and in exile, and refuge and relocation of deserters from the regimes' armed forces. Scandinavian governments' aid stands above all the rest in both volume and consistency.

Attempts to isolate white minority governments occurred in military, economic, political, and cultural arenas. The UN General Assembly first called for sanctions against South Africa in 1962, and the Security Council adopted a resolution for a voluntary embargo on military sales to South Africa the next year. In 1977, after the Soweto uprisings and the death in detention of resistance leader Steve Biko, the Security Council made the embargo mandatory. Table 4.1 shows the range of multilateral and bilateral governmental sanctions imposed against South Africa from 1960 to 1989, but other white minority regimes were also targeted for isolation. Great Britain, for example, imposed sanctions against Rhodesia (now Zimbabwe) after its government issued the Unilateral Declaration of Independence in 1965. The Security Council followed suit and adopted comprehensive mandatory sanctions against Rhodesia in 1968.

The most effective sanctions against trade and finance in South Africa only came in the 1980s, however, partially in response to sustained civil unrest inside the apartheid state and its unwillingness to change. In the United States, for example, the Congressional Black Caucus (CBC) and an organization closely linked to it, Transafrica, proved to be key players in

TABLE 4.1   Sanctions Against South Africa, 1960–1989

	Military[1]	Trade[2]	Finance[3]
Multilateral			
UN General Assembly	1962-63, 1983	1962, 1965	1966, 1969
UN Security Council	1977, 1984	1985 voluntary	1985 voluntary
Commonwealth	1971	1985-86	1985-86
European Community	1985	1986	1986
Nordic countries	1977, 1985	1985-87	1979, 1985-86
Organization of African Unity	1963	1963	1963
Bilateral			
United States	1963, 1977, 1985, 1986	1978, 1985-86	1985-86
Britain	1985	1986	1985-87
West Germany	1986	1977	1977 informal
France	1985-86	1986	1985
Japan	1986	1986 informal	1969, 1985-86

SOURCE: Audie Klotz, *Norms in International Relations: The Struggle Against Apartheid* (Ithaca, NY: Cornell University Press, 1995), p. 5.

NOTE: Dates indicate only initiation of substantive new measures.
[1]Including oil and technology in addition to arms.
[2]Including airline landing rights in addition to imports and exports.
[3]Including Krugerrands in addition to investments, loans, and credits.

1986 in leading the House (313 to 83) and the Senate (78–21) to override the veto of sanctions by President Ronald Reagan.[48] Earlier, in 1985, major world banks called in their loans to the South African government, demanding the repayment of about $23.7 billion. For more than two decades prior to this time, however, activists had pressured banks and corporations to divest their holdings in South Africa and other white-minority-controlled countries. The early work gained substantial momentum in the 1970s, when various public and private organizations began to remove from their pension fund investments those corporations that continued to do business with apartheid. These divestment efforts laid the groundwork for eventual imposition of bilateral and multilateral governmental sanctions, as well as business decisions by banks and corporations to withdraw.

In a movement whose work stretched across more than four decades and involved thousands of small and large organizations across the world, disputes over analysis, strategy, and goals inevitably arose. Some of the debates within anti-apartheid networks reflected contention over some of the same issues debated by activists in the region. For example, these TANs discussed multiracialism versus Africanism, socialist futures for the countries of the region versus capitalist choices, and guerrilla warfare versus nonviolent active resistance. Yet despite such contention, the movement gained momentum and considerable power across time.

The research and information provided by the TANs succeeded in reframing the debate about the region, moving it away from characterizations preferred by most Western governments and the white minority regimes to those preferred by black resistance groups and their allies in anti-apartheid work. Many Western governments, for example, preferred to believe the South African claim that it remained the last bastion of capitalist democracy[49] in the continent, especially true in a region increasingly devoted to socialist authoritarianism. Apartheid produced considerable profits for international business based primarily in Europe and the United States. Furthermore, those reluctant to condemn white minority rule argued that the West needed South Africa as a strategic ally against Communist encroachment as well as a source of key minerals vital to military preparedness.

In contrast, the global anti-apartheid movement claimed that the best way to ensure peace and democracy in the region was to support a key principle at the heart of Western democracy: majority rule, the basis of which in the contemporary era had come to be racial equality. Strategic access and economic profits, activists claimed, could only be assured in the long run if white minority rule gave way to political freedom for all, and in the short run, the pursuit of stability and profits was immoral in the face of such extreme racial oppression.

Across about three decades, the number of successful campaigns by anti-apartheid TANs against a wide variety of targets began to add up. More and more IGOs, governments, multinational corporations, and other institutions wanted to be counted on the side of change. Some were shamed into change. Others changed for more noble reasons. Activists relentlessly and creatively reframed the debate and steadily improved their access to decisionmakers, common strategies used by TANs to achieve outcomes, according to Keck and Sikkink. When one target proved difficult to penetrate, activists employed the boomerang mechanism to come at it from a different angle, through others in the networks. Together with mounting domestic pressures for change within the region, these anti-apartheid networks helped to bring an end to white minority rule. The international anti-apartheid movement stands as a frequently cited illustration of the power of TANs in political globalization.

Leaders from the region such as now retired archbishop Desmond Tutu and Nelson Mandela, both recipients of the Nobel Peace Prize, repeatedly thanked those in other countries for their work in solidarity with activists in the region, as did the South African government itself. For example, the South African government bestowed the Order of the Companions of O. R. Tambo, the highest honor given to foreigners, on a former staff leader of the World Council of Churches' Programme to Combat Racism, Baldwin Sjollema from the Netherlands. Created in 2002 to honor Oliver Tambo, the ANC president in 1967 to 1991, the order is conferred annually. The decision to honor Sjollema served as a formal recognition of the WCC efforts to end apartheid.

In 1994, thousands flocked from across the globe to witness the inauguration of the first democratically elected government in South Africa, and in his inaugural address Mandela acknowledged their decades of dedication, their presence, and by implication, the crucial links between the global and the local.

> We, who were outlaws not so long ago, have today been given the rare privilege to be host to the nations of the world on our own soil. We thank all of our distinguished international guests for having come to take possession with the people of our country of what is, after all, a common victory for justice, for peace, for human dignity.[50]

The Land Mines Campaigns

There is a path to the Kavungo River in eastern Angola, and the people of the village of Kavungo learned to walk along the path in fear. For generations, the rich soil, abundant game, and fish from the river provided residents of surrounding villages with a secure livelihood. But in 1983 rebel forces attacked government troops and the path to the river became a raging battlefield. The battle was brief, but intense enough to cause the villagers to flee, and it left in its wake the usual detritus of war: spent cartridges, burnt hamlets, abandoned livestock and a more enduring and dangerous legacy—

innumerable anti-personnel (AP) mines, buried along the war-path, ever alert and ready to strike.

AP mines provided no decisive advantage to either side in the battle along the Kavungo River. . . . Strewn haphazardly to provide momentary perimeter security for units in a highly mobile and irregular conflict, live mines were simply left in the ground as the soldiers moved on—a modern version of salting the enemy's soil in order to poison the land. . . . When the fighting ended, the visible scars of war along the path to the river healed quickly, vegetation covering what rot and rust failed to consume. Beneath the path, however, the mines remained untouched by the passage of time. . . . Government forces retook the area the next year, allowing the local population to begin to drift back to their land. . . .

The villagers knew that the path to the river was mined, but remaining confined to their hamlets meant a slow death by starvation. Thousands of random footsteps, heavy with loads of water, firewood, and food, beat back nature's intrusions upon the path to the river. Miraculously, not a single foot fell on the detonator of a mine for many years. But on a cool summer morning in 1990, two village women were struck by a small blast mine. That the footstep detonating the mine was that of a civilian, not a soldier, was not a subtlety that the mine was designed to appreciate. In fact, the mine performed exactly as intended.[51]

Stories like this one are common in Angola, Mozambique, and a number of other countries plagued by AP land mines. The land mines crisis escalated dramatically in the 1970s and 1980s, and a transnational advocacy network sprang up to address the issue in the 1990s. Founded in 1992, the International Campaign to Ban Land Mines (ICBL) led a vigorous and effective activist network determined to eliminate the use of AP land mines. By 1997, 122 states had signed on to a comprehensive ban, which by 1999 became a new international law, the Land Mines Treaty (LMT). This treaty prohibits the use, development, production, stockpiling, and transfer of AP land mines. It also provides mechanisms to support the removal of mines and to verify compliance. In recognition of this remarkable achievement, which had eluded governments and intergovernmental organizations for decades, the ICBL and Jody Williams of Vermont, its coordinator, were awarded the Nobel Peace Prize in 1997.

Notably missing from the list of governments that signed and ratified the LMT are the United States and China. Both argued that land mines continue to provide an essential element in their arsenals of national defense. In particular, the United States wanted to continue using land mines in the border areas between North and South Korea. Yet even some nonsignatories shifted their policies and practices in order to respond at least in part to the ICBL campaign and the inauguration of the LMT.

Land mines in Angola and Mozambique remain as one of the enduring and horrific legacies of war. More than 100,000 people are estimated to have endured amputations in Angola alone. In similar kinds of conflicts during the Cold War, other countries such as Cambodia and Afghanistan inherited comparable burdens. These sites of surrogate superpower struggle contain the highest concentrations of buried AP mines, but the problem looms larger. During the contemporary era of globalization, tens of millions of AP mines made in nineteen countries (including the United States, Italy, Germany, France, and Sweden) proliferated to about seventy countries. Mines are cheap, costing as little as $3–$5 each, and many were provided free. During the Cold War, for example, both superpowers supplied tens of thousands to their allies in more localized conflicts. In contrast to the cost of production and deployment, safely removing a single land mine costs thousands of dollars in equipment and trained personnel. Moreover, in the mid-1990s, the International Committee of the Red Cross (ICRC) estimated that for every 100,000 mines removed, another 2 million were being planted.[52]

A U.S. State Department study claimed in 1994 that land mines killed or maimed about 500 people per week worldwide. In their campaign, activists in the ICBL frequently cited the shocking statistic that "1 in every 236 Cambodians is an amputee, compared with one in every 22,000 Americans."[53] As illustrated in the Angolan story, land mines cause frequent noncombatant casualties because unsuspecting people go into mined areas to carry out ordinary and necessary daily tasks. They come out, however, with extraordinary injuries, if they come out at all. Civilians represent more than 80 percent of all victims of AP land mines.

In contrast to the anti-apartheid movement, the TANs advocating the elimination of land mines succeeded in achieving their goals in less than a decade. How did this happen, especially in arms control, an area where governments seem less vulnerable to activists' pressure? One of the factors contributing to activists' success was the narrow focus on a single issue. The ICRC had begun already in the 1970s to pressure governments to address the issue of indiscriminate weapons that caused excessive injury and needless suffering. Others came to understand the effects of land mines a decade or so later and contributed their efforts to those of the ICRC, forming the ICBL. These NGOs included some concerned with providing prosthetic limbs to mine victims (i.e., Handicap International), some focusing on human rights (i.e., Human Rights Watch), some coping with war recovery (i.e., Vietnam Veterans of America Foundation), some hindered from implementing agricultural development programs (because AP mines got in the way), and so on. NGOs of this kind came together to form a TAN, the ICLM, and began their work to reframe the global discussion and debate on land mines.

Using such relatively new technology at the time as fax machines and the Internet, the ICBL generated and disseminated considerable reliable research on the extent of the problem and the horrific consequences. Using "moral proselytism,"[54] the campaign sought and garnered the public support of such luminaries as the UN secretary-general, Pope John Paul II, Archbishop Desmond Tutu, the Dalai Lama, and Princess Diana. The campaign got institutional support from organizations such as the European Parliament and the OAU. This provided the basis for launching considerable efforts aimed at international media, and it had at least two effects. It placed the issue on the agenda of governments and IGOs, creating the perception of a crisis; and it conveyed basic information about the extent and severity of the problem as well as some practical means of addressing it.

Previously accepted norms of international law provided the foundation for activists' arguments against land mines. The laws of war and international humanitarian law have long established two concepts of how combat should be conducted: with civilian discrimination, and with avoidance of unnecessary suffering. "Discrimination (or noncombatant immunity) is one of the oldest notions of the just war doctrine. According to this norm, civilians are not to be the intentional objects of attack during conflict. 'Unnecessary suffering' refers to the principle that means of warfare that cause 'superfluous injury' are prohibited."[55] The TANs focused their efforts on shaming governments for using or tolerating the use of land mines and thus deviating from their own long-standing articulations of what is allowed and disallowed in situations of warfare. Some activists even equated AP mines with chemical and biological weapons, a category long reviled by the world.

By reframing the issue within the context of well-established international norms and principles advocated by most governments, activists managed fairly quickly to put on the defensive any state claiming to need land mines as a legitimate weapon for national security. These governments were shamed and forced to prove why they should retain or possibly use such hideous weapons. Such mobilization of shame demonstrated that states such as the United States violate international obligations, which they have willingly ratified, and do not live up to their own claims. The government of Canada became a key ally in the transnational advocacy network providing NGOs with access to conferences and documentation they otherwise would have difficulty obtaining. Additionally, activists repeatedly used the boomerang pattern of network influence to effect change in reluctant governments.

Thus, the ICBL employed a number of mechanisms of political globalization to convince governmental, intergovernmental, and nongovernmental actors worldwide to address the humanitarian disaster that various warring parties had created in numerous countries. The outcome of the campaign, the addition of a treaty to a growing body of international law, contributed to the increasing volume of regulations that themselves intensify political globalization.

The Community of Sant'Egidio

The Catholic INGO, Sant'Egidio, played a key role in ending Mozambique's civil war and subsequently came to be one of the most powerful conflict mediators in the 1990s. Begun in 1968 by a group of students at Virgil High School in Rome, Sant'Egidio grew by 1999 to have approximately 18,000 members worldwide in about 300 local groups. About half are in Italy, with the other half spread across northern Europe, Africa, the United States, and elsewhere. Augmenting these permanent members are thousands of volunteers who work in various services that the lay community provides in its various locales.[56]

Two key leaders are a layman, Andrea Riccardi, who was eighteen years old when he became Sant'Egidio's first president, and Matteo Zuppi, who joined in 1971 and became a priest thereafter. Both these men and the community have close ties to the Vatican and with Pope John Paul II. The pope granted Sant'Egidio special status in 1986, "specifying a vocation that focuses on bringing Christianity to those furthest from the experience of a practicing religion, on ecumenical dialogue with other religions, and on service to the poor."[57] As reflected in its vocation to serve the "neediest of the needy," the community originally took its inspiration from the spirit of the Second Vatican Council (1962–1965). Soon after its founding, the Vatican donated the convent of Sant'Egidio in Rome for its headquarters, the place from which the group takes its name.

The community quickly established an impressive record in several arenas: social services to the poor, to addicts, orphans, AIDs victims, the disabled, and others in the group's various locales; ecumenical networks with other Christian churches as well as other faith communities; and excellent networking among political leaders, beginning with the Italian government. Sant'Egidio first gained international attention when it helped to negotiate an end to fighting between factions in the Lebanese civil war in 1982. Its work in Mozambique began in 1976.[58]

Historically, the Catholic Church in Mozambique maintained close relations with the Portuguese colonial authorities. The church held primary authority for educating Africans, and the colonial administration had the right to review the appointment of bishops. Having criticized the church throughout the war for independence, FRELIMO's new government nationalized some church property, closed church clinics and schools, and severely restricted religious leaders and church outreach. Meanwhile, a young Mozambican priest, Don Jaime Goncalves, became archbishop. He had joined Sant'Egidio in 1976 while in school in Rome and called on the group for help in Mozambique.[59]

Although the country's religious community was divided by the civil war, its Protestant ecumenical association (the Mozambican Council of Churches) and others condemned the group responsible for most of the atrocities—RENAMO. The Catholic bishops condemned violence committed by both sides and called for negotiations. Opportunities for such arose after the United States began its programs of assistance to the country in 1981, with the Mozambican government subsequently allowing a number of NGOs to help distribute the aid and provide essential services that FRELIMO was no longer able to provide. The NGOs included church groups such as Sant'Egidio, which delivered more than 10,000 tons of aid, sent in church workers to help victims in war zones, and eventually convinced the Italian government to send additional massive shipments of food and medicine. At about the same time, the community put Archbishop Goncalves in touch with Italian Communist Party leaders who made two key connections. They helped to convince the FRELIMO government to remove some of the restrictions against the church and introduced leaders of Sant'Egidio to political leaders in Mozambique. Meanwhile, through Archbishop Goncalves, who came from the same area as the head of RENAMO, Dhlakama, the community negotiated the release of some of its members being held by the rebels and began to establish a credible relationship of trust with RENAMO. By 1985 Sant'Egidio had sufficient authority with all parties to arrange a crucial meeting between Pope John Paul II and President Machel. After Machel's death, the pope visited Mozambique and its new President Chissano in 1987.[60]

The Mozambican Christian Council, together with Goncalves and other Catholic leaders in the country, made the initial overtures for peace talks with RENAMO, but the first face-to-face contact between RENAMO leaders and the Mozambican government took place at the headquarters of Sant'Egidio in Rome in 1990. Goncalves, Riccardi, and Zuppi were all on the mediation team, together with a representative of the Italian government. Pressed by the UN, the U.S. government, NGOs giving assistance to the country, and others, over the next two years the two warring parties held ten rounds of talks hosted by Sant'Egidio. These culminated in a formal peace accord in 1992.

How did Sant'Egidio come to play such a significant role? Besides its access to powerful international actors in the Vatican and the Italian government, other factors also contributed to the group's success. Sant'Egidio initiated transnational advocacy networks among key governmental and nongovernmental actors. The community also focused its work with TANs to specialize in conflict mediation, actively helping to forge negotiations in a number of seemingly intractable wars in the 1990s, such as those in Uganda, Burundi, Algeria, Kosovo, and Guatemala. One of the group's key assets is its nonpartisanship and its "unimpeachable record for integrity and good offices in the societies it comes to serve"; that is, the community treats all parties to a conflict with equal dignity and respect.[61] One scholar characterized the community as militants for peace, stating:

Lest one take the gentle demeanor of Sant'Egidio's operatives for passivity or nonchalance, it should be clear that behind the success of the Community as an international mediator stand countless hours of dedicated study and hard work establishing and maintaining the "networks of friendship" at all levels. The spiritual discipline of regular prayer, worship in common, and performance of social service requires a measure of self-sacrificial commitment on the part of laypeople who must also work in regular jobs to support themselves financially. In essence, the members of Sant'Egidio offer their livelihood, and occasionally their lives, for the cause.[62]

These three illustrations of transnational advocacy networks and their profound impact demonstrate a growing phenomenon in political globalization: the explosion in nongovernmental organizations and the determination of many people to participate in shaping the world both close to home and far away. Most readers would probably agree that the anti-apartheid movement, the ICBL, and Sant'Egidio have made the world a better place to live. Not all TANs, of course, could claim such goals or accomplishments; that is, some NGOs use the instruments of globalization to bring more death and destruction to people near and far. Nonetheless, attention by activists to southern Africa has usually followed noble principles, inspired in part by some of the leaders in the region, a topic to which we now turn.

THE IMPACT OF INDIVIDUALS

The region of southern Africa stands out as having exceptional human beings who render remarkable leadership often under very difficult circumstances. For example, of the approximately 110 Nobel Peace Prizes awarded to men, women, and organizations since 1901, four were bestowed on South Africans: Albert Luthuli in 1960; Desmond Tutu in 1984; and F. W. de Klerk and Nelson Mandela in 1993. The famed writer and anti-apartheid activist Nadine Gordimer won the Nobel Prize for Literature in 1991. The list of widely acclaimed leaders from groups as diverse as the Communist Party, mainstream liberal parties, and Africanists, as well as scientists, religious leaders, writers, musicians, and others from the arts, grows long quickly when one examines the region. These exceptional people offer a rich opportunity to examine when and how hardship and struggle deepen character.

Few if any the world over, however, draw more publicity, respect, awe, admiration, and even reverence than Nelson Mandela. By his example of leadership and the gripping story of his life, Mandela offers a remarkable illustration of political globalization. He is the one of the most celebrated and written-about figures anywhere. As one analyst put it, "In an age of ethnic, religious and racial conflicts, societies of a very different character and history wish they had someone of his unifying qualities and unassailable standing."[63]

One scholar who studies revolutions, rebellions, and other forms of political violence has distinguished effective leaders from ennobling leaders, both being very important to accomplishing difficult political goals. Effective leaders bring "a variety of individuals and groups together to focus on a common cause," whereas ennobling leaders bring "a variety of individuals and groups together to focus on a common cause that does not immediately satisfy current desires. Instead, such leadership asks individuals and groups to make immediate sacrifices, and to tolerate immediate discomfort, by refocusing their interest on long-term gains."[64]

Mandela has always been both an effective and ennobling leader, even in prison, as the story of his life demonstrates. Born in 1918 to one of four wives of a Thembu chief, Nelson Rolihlahla Mandela grew up in Qunu, a small village in the eastern Cape and became the first in his family to attend school. Chief Jongintaba Dalindyebo, the regent or supreme leader of the Thembu people, took Mandela in at the age of nine after the death of his father. Although he attended Fort Hare University and began activist work there, he left before finishing his degree, which he completed through correspondence work at the University of South Africa. By then he had a job as an assistant in a law office in Johannesburg, arranged in 1941 by Walter Sisulu, another leader who would come to prominence in the ANC (along with Mandela's classmate from Fort Hare, Oliver Tambo). Immersing himself in political work, Mandela became acquainted with a range of activists, including members of the Communist Party. He joined the ANC in 1943 and together with Sisulu and Tambo founded its Youth League. Standing six foot two, from 1950 Mandela maintained his physique by being a heavyweight boxer. Famous for physical exercise, he continued such routines even during his prison years, part of the discipline for which he is also renowned.

By 1952, the South African government had already banned him until 1955 from all public gatherings, and then in 1960 the government banned the ANC. In 1961, Mandela went underground to help create Umkonto we Sizwe, the ANC's military wing. Captured in 1962, he went to prison. The apartheid government brought charges of treason against him in 1964 and sentenced him to life without the possibility of parole.

Mandela served his sentence on Robben Island, South Africa's most notorious prison, just offshore from Cape Town. For some years, officials forced prisoners to break rocks in the prison yard for hours daily, and Mandela could write and receive only one letter every six months. In 1982, the government moved him to Pollsmoor Prison, a less brutal place, and in 1988, officials transferred him to a private facility at Victor Verster Prison.

Beginning in the early 1980s, under international pressure to release the country's most famous political prisoner, the government began to make contact with Mandela and offered in 1985, in the midst of considerable domestic turmoil, to release him if he rejected violence as a political strategy. He refused, since to do so would alienate him from the ANC and others struggling against white minority rule. He continued secret talks with the government, however, and in 1990 a new South African president, F. W. de Klerk, released Mandela from prison after having lifted the thirty-year ban on the ANC. He had served more than twenty-seven years.

Mandela's family life has included an interesting mix of women and demonstrates what most people who know him say about him—he is not a saint but simply the closest thing that the world of politics has to a saint. As he stated in his autobiography, "[I]t seems to be the destiny of freedom fighters to have unstable personal lives. When your life is the struggle, as mine was, there is little room left for family. That has always been my greatest regret, and the most painful aspect of the choice I made."[65]

Leaving behind significant rural and tribal customs while at Fort Hare, he refused an arranged marriage pressed upon him by the Thembu regent. Instead, he married Evelyn Mase, a cousin of Walter Sisulu, who worked as a nurse and homemaker. Together they had three children, and she cared for his mother and other relatives who made their way to Johannesburg. The couple developed significant differences over his deepening political attachments as well as her withdrawal into religious movements. They got divorced. Soon thereafter, in the midst of one of his trials in 1957, Mandela fell in love with Winnie Nomzamo Madikizela, a social worker who had excelled at school and whose father was a headmaster in Pondoland. A year later, they married. Nelson not only wed Winnie, he politicized her into carrying significant responsibilities for campaigns, which she undertook with enthusiasm, creativity, and ambition. She provided the centerpiece of his support once he was imprisoned. By the time of his release, however, their separation and the extraordinary pressures on all their lives placed enormous stress on his ties to both Winnie and his children. Winnie had become quite a political force on her own and, more problematically, came to be accused of a variety of serious crimes. The couple separated in 1992, after she was convicted in 1991 of kidnapping and beating a young man from Soweto. In 1996, they divorced. Soon thereafter, Mandela began a serious relationship with Graca Machel, the widow of Mozambican president Samora Machel, and they married in 1998 on his eightieth birthday.

Words that journalists, biographers, and others use to describe Mandela include the following: powerfully disciplined; an aristocrat; one who "thinks with his brains, not his blood";[66] a reconciler; single-minded; pragmatic; realistic; patient; wise; unforgiving of betrayals; loyal; generous; magnanimous; a man of compromise; a man of deep convictions; a lucid mind; a keen sense of self-respect and self-confidence; a joker; calm and relaxed; a lawyer with keen respect for the law and for human beings; an autocrat and a democrat.[67] A few stories demonstrate these characteristics and the ennobling quality of his leadership.[68]

One is about his official house. When he became president of the country, Mandela renamed the presidential residence. It had been called Westbrooke, but he called it Genadendal as a symbol of South Africa's diversity and unity. Genadendal was the oldest Christian mission in the country, established in 1738 as a sanctuary for former slaves after the abolition of slavery. The Dutch dialect that eventually became Afrikaans originated in Genadendal.

Another is about Afrikaners. Blacks historically scorned South Africa's famous Springboks rugby team because Afrikaners dominated the sport. After taking office in 1994, President Mandela urged blacks to support the national team, particularly before World Cup matches, but they remained lukewarm. When South Africa made it into the final against New Zealand in 1995, Mandela went to the match, wore the team's green jersey, and startled the team in their locker room, wishing them luck. After an upset victory for the Springboks, Mandela walked onto the field to present the trophy, still wearing the green jersey. The Afrikaner crowd broke into a chant, "Nelson, Nelson, Nelson." More than a sports event, Mandela's symbolic act of visibly uniting the whole country reframed for many the picture of what he represented for their nation, thereby decisively undermining the appeal of far-right white groups. After his enthusiastic support for the Springbok victory, Mandela was clearly the president for Afrikaners, too.

A third is about his relationship with adversaries. Some activists in prison with Mandela held strong differences with him about politics, many considering him to be too moderate. He always showed them kindness and consideration, however, advocating a patient search for multiracial understanding, an end to the bitterness and hatred, and in the 1980s a willingness to negotiate with the enemy, suppressing personal feelings for the good of the country. Once released, Mandela sought no revenge against his jailers and even traveled to meet and have tea with the widow of apartheid's architect, Hendrik Vervoerd. Mandela also visited the prosecutor who had helped to send him to jail.

Lastly, a story about resolve and determination. Civil unrest and sporadic violence permeated the country throughout the time that leaders were negotiating for a transition to black rule. In July 1992, members of the Zulu-led Inkatha group massacred forty-five people, including children, in the squatter camp called Boipatong south of Johannesburg. Witnesses claim that apartheid police were involved, escorting Inkatha militants into and out of the camp. Mandela, along with most blacks in the country, blamed de Klerk. Mandela broke off negotiations with the government, then helped to lead massive demonstrations to protest the government's complicity in the ongoing violence among blacks. Negotiations did not resume for three months, at which point the government agreed to a number of ANC demands.

Through a process of long, careful, and tough negotiations, Mandela and de Klerk, the man who released him from prison, put in place a process that took South Africa from the brink of disaster to the possibility of a bright new future. Together they were awarded the Nobel Peace Prize in 1993, even though de Klerk's government remained deeply implicated in perpetrating horrific violence. Nonetheless, de Klerk provided effective leadership at a crucial moment in the country's history. Unlike any of his predecessors, he understood that the country had to change, and he brought people together to make it happen. The title of ennobling leader, however—the one who sets his or her vision on long-term gains, persuading followers to sacrifice, to endure, and to forgo current needs in a determined struggle to reach a higher goal—this title belongs to Mandela alone.

CONCLUSION

This chapter has examined a wide range of topics: the United Nations and peacekeeping, SADC, the unfinished agenda of creating democracy, South Africa's TRC, three different TANs, and ennobling and effective individual leaders. All of these illustrate transnational forms of power, authority, and rule, or political globalization. Local models for addressing civil conflict like the TRC and Mandela's leadership will likely continue to have some impact across the world. Regional decisions such as that of SADC to intervene in central Africa's war will continue to impose significant costs on the governments and people of southern Africa, as well as potentially shape the political economy of the whole continent. The UN and TANs demonstrate that southern Africa will continue to cope with a multilayered system of global governance that embeds governments' range of choices and decisions in complex structures of relationships and organizations over which individual states often have relatively little influence.

Although southern Africa has demonstrated the power of political globalization for centuries, the contemporary era brings complex challenges that no other period in history matches. Some aspects of globalization contribute to the possibility that people in the region will govern their own future, that is, live in democratic political systems that are participatory, consultative, transparent, and publicly accountable. Other aspects of globalization, however, undermine this possibility. This chapter shows some of the dilemmas the region faces in the crosscutting pressures of multiple layers of powerful political actors pursuing various, often conflicting, goals and policies. The discussion displays the range of organizations and their types of influence as a starting point for better comprehending and analyzing the local to global political interconnections that so profoundly affect the region.

As the first head of the new South Africa—the region's largest nation and the last to be transformed—Nelson Mandela led his country to a radically new place politically and inspired many others worldwide to believe that their long struggles would also eventually yield positive results. The entrenched economic legacy of apartheid and white minority rule in southern Africa, however, endures. Together with negative aspects of new and complex processes in economic globalization, this heritage threatens these countries' still fragile democracies. The next chapter addresses these issues.

Notes

1. Nelson Mandela, *Long Walk to Freedom: The Autobiography of Nelson Mandela* (Boston: Little, Brown, 1994), pp. 540–541.

2. David Held et al., *Global Transformations: Politics, Economics, and Culture* (Stanford: Stanford University Press, 1999), p. 32.

3. Frank L. Wilson, *Concepts and Issues in Comparative Politics*, 2nd ed. (Upper Saddle River, NJ: Prentice Hall, 2002), p. 8.

4. On a subnational level in southern Africa, village or tribal elders may exercise considerable legitimate authority through traditions and customs respected by their followers rather than through democracy.

5. Held et al., *Global Transformations*, p. 50.

6. David Held, ed., *A Globalizing World? Culture, Economic, Politics* (New York: Routledge, 2000), p. 164.

7. Held et al., *Global Transformations*, pp. 77–80.

8. Karen A. Mingst and Margaret P. Karns, *The United Nations in the Post–Cold War Era*, 2nd ed. (Boulder, CO: Westview Press, 2000), pp. 17–18.

9. Union of International Associations, *Yearbook of International Organizations, 1999/2000* (Munich: K. G. Sauer, 2000).

10. Ibid.

11. David Held, *Models of Democracy*, 2nd ed. (Stanford: Stanford University Press, 1996), p. 1.

12. Jan Aart Scholte, *Globalization: A Critical Introduction* (New York: St. Martin's, 2000).

13. Samuel P. Huntington, *The Third Wave: Democratization in the Late Twentieth Century* (Norman: University of Oklahoma Press, 1991).

14. Mingst and Karns, *The United Nations in the Post–Cold War Era*, p. 79.

15. Ibid., pp. 87–88; and Donald L. Sparks and December Green, *Namibia: The Nation After Independence* (Boulder, CO: Westview Press, 1992), pp. 46–56.

16. Tony Hodges, *Angola from Afro-Stalinism to Petro-Diamond Capitalism* (Bloomington: Indiana University Press, 2001), pp. 12–19.

17. Ibid., p. 16.

18. Thomas G. Weiss and Cindy Collins, *Humanitarian Challenges and Intervention*, 2nd ed. (Boulder, CO: Westview Press, 2000), p. 38.

19. Michael Wesley, *Casualties of the New World Order: The Causes of Failure of UN Missions to Civil Wars* (New York: St. Martin's, 1997).

20. Held et al., *Global Transformations,* pp. 76, 168.

21. Gilbert M. Khadiagala, *Allies in Adversity: The Frontline States in Southern African Security, 1975–1993* (Athens: Ohio University Press, 1994), p. 225. See also Margaret C. Lee, *The Political Economy of Regionalism in Southern Africa* (Boulder, CO: Lynne Rienner, 2003); Carol B. Thompson, "African Initiatives for Development: The Practice of Regional Economic Cooperation in Southern Africa," *Journal of International Affairs* 46 (Summer 1992): 125–144; Richard E. Mshomba, *Africa in the Global Economy* (Boulder, CO: Lynne Rienner, 2000), pp. 187–188; Nana Poku, *Regionalization and Security in Southern Africa* (New York: Palgrave, 2001); and Martin Holland, "South Africa, SADC, and the European Union: Matching Bilateral with Regional Policies," *Journal of Modern African Studies* 33 (June 1995): 263–283.

22. Khadiagala, *Allies in Adversity,* pp. 230–239; and Thompson, "African Initiatives for Development," pp. 130–135.

23. Poku, *Regionalization and Security in Southern Africa,* p. 103.

24. Ibid.

25. Mshomba, *Africa in the Global Economy,* pp. 177–187.

26. Logan Rangasamy et al., "Models of Economic Integration," in Jim Whitman, ed., *The Sustainability Challenge for Southern Africa* (New York: St. Martin's, 2000), pp. 48–51.

27. Neil J. Kritz, ed., *Transitional Justice: How Emerging Democracies Reckon with Former Regimes,* vols. 1, 2, 3 (Washington, D.C.: U.S. Institute for Peace Press, 1995). See also A. James McAdams, ed., *Transitional Justice and the Rule of Law in New Democracies.* (Notre Dame, IL: University of Notre Dame Press, 1997); Martha Minow, *Between Vengeance and Forgiveness: Facing History After Genocide and Mass Violence* (Boston: Beacon, 1998); and Naomi Roht-Arriaza, ed., *Impunity and Human Rights in International Law and Practice* (New York: Oxford University Press, 1995).

28. Priscilla B. Hayner, "Fifteen Truth Commissions—1974–1994: A Comparative Study," *Human Rights Quarterly* 16, no. 4 (November 1994): 597–655.

29. Minow, *Between Vengeance and Forgiveness,* pp. 55–56; see also Lyn S. Graybill, *Truth and Reconciliation in South Africa* (Boulder, CO: Lynne Rienner, 2002).

30. For their own accounts of the work of the Truth and Reconciliation Commission, see Desmond Tutu, *No Future Without Forgiveness* (New York: Doubleday, 1999), and Alex Boraine, *A Country Unmasked* (Oxford: Oxford University Press, 2000).

31. Minow, *Between Vengeance and Forgiveness,* p. 91.

32. R. Scott Appleby, *The Ambivalence of the Sacred: Religion, Violence, and Reconciliation* (Lanham, MD: Rowman and Littlefield, 2000), pp. 198–199.

33. Martin Meredith with Tina Rosenberg, *Coming to Terms: South Africa's Search for Truth* (New York: Public Affairs, 1999), pp. 287–289. See also Truth and Reconciliation Commission, *The Report of the Truth and Reconciliation Commission,* vols. 1–5 (South Africa: Truth and Reconciliation Commission, 1998); and Lyn S. Graybill, *Truth and Reconciliation in South Africa: Miracle or Model?* (Boulder, CO: Lynne Rienner, 2002).

34. Meredith, *Coming to Terms*, p. 289.

35. Minow, *Between Vengeance and Forgiveness*, p. 61.

36. Ibid., p. 66–72.

37. Pamela E. Oliver and Gerald Marwell, "Mobilizing Technologies for Collective Action," in A. D. Morris and C. M. Mueller, eds., *Frontiers in Social Movement Theory* (New Haven, CT: Yale University Press, 1992), p. 252, quoted in Margaret E. Keck and Kathryn Sikkink, *Activists Beyond Borders: Advocacy Networks in International Politics* (Ithaca, NY: Cornell University Press, 1998), p. 14.

38. Keck and Sikkink, *Activists Beyond Borders*, p. 9.

39. Ibid., pp. 8–9.

40. Ibid., p. 40.

41. Doug McAdam et al., "Introduction," in Doug McAdam et al., eds., *Comparative Perspectives on Social Movements: Political Opportunities, Mobilizing Structures, and Cultural Framings* (New York: Cambridge University Press, 1996), p. 6.

42. Keck and Sikkink, *Activists Beyond Borders*, pp. 25–26.

43. Ibid., pp. 16–17.

44. Ibid., pp. 23–24.

45. See Donald R. Culverson, *Contesting Apartheid: U.S. Activism, 1960–1987* (Boulder, CO: Westview Press, 1999); Audie Klotz, *Norms in International Relations: The Struggle Against Apartheid* (Ithaca, NY: Cornell University Press, 1995); Janice Love, *The U.S. Anti-Apartheid Movement: Local Activism in Global Politics* (New York: Praeger, 1985); Robert Kinloch Massie, *Loosing the Bonds: The United States and South Africa in the Apartheid Years* (New York: Doubleday, 1997); and George W. Shepherd Jr., *Anti-Apartheid: Transnational Conflict and Western Policy in the Liberation of South Africa* (Westport, CT: Greenwood, 1977).

46. Abdul S. Minty, "The Anti-Apartheid Movement and Racism in Southern Africa," in Peter Willetts, ed., *Pressure Groups in the Global System: The Transnational Relations of Issue-Orientated Non-Governmental Organizations* (New York: St. Martin's, 1982), pp. 28–29.

47. Love, *The U.S. Anti-Apartheid Movement*, pp. 1–51.

48. Klotz, *Norms in International Relations*, p. 109.

49. The South African government's claim to be a democracy rested on its citizenship policy. Only whites could be citizens under apartheid, and all citizens could vote to elect their government. Therefore, white rulers declared that the country was democratic.

50. Mandela, *Long Walk to Freedom*, pp. 540–541.

51. Maxwell A. Cameron et al., eds., *To Walk Without Fear: The Global Movement to Ban Land Mines* (New York: Oxford University Press, 1998), pp. 1–2.

52. Richard Price, "Reversing the Gun Sights: Transnational Civil Society Targets Land Mines," *International Organization* 52, no. 3 (Summer 1998): 618. See also Jody Williams and Stephen Goose, "The International Campaign to Ban Land Mines," in Cameron et al., *To Walk*, pp. 20–22, and Philip C. Winslow, *Sowing the Dragon's Teeth: Land Mines and the Global Legacy of War* (Boston: Beacon, 1997).

53. Price, "Reversing the Gun Sights," p. 620.

54. Ibid., p. 640.

55. Ibid., p. 628.

56. Appleby, *The Ambivalence of the Sacred*, pp. 155–157.

57. Cameron Hume, *Ending Mozambique's War: The Role of Mediation and Good Offices* (Washington, D.C.: United States Institute of Peace, 1994), p. 16.

58. Appleby, *The Ambivalence of the Sacred*, pp. 156–158.

59. Witney W. Schneidman, "Conflict Resolution in Mozambique," in David R. Smock, ed., *Making War and Waging Peace: Foreign Intervention in Africa* (Washington, D.C.: United States Institute of Peace Press, 1993), pp. 228–229.

60. Appleby, *The Ambivalence of the Sacred*, pp. 160–162.

61. Ibid., pp. 162–163.

62. Ibid., p. 164.

63. Anthony Lewis, "Mandela the Pol," *New York Times Magazine*, March 23, 1997.

64. Jack Goldstone, *Revolution and Rebellion in the Early Modern World* (Berkeley: University of California Press, 1991), p. 495. My thanks to Peter Sederberg for drawing this study and its relevance to southern Africa to my attention.

65. Mandela, *Long Walk to Freedom*, p. 523.

66. Taken from several sources, including Lewis, "Mandela the Pol."

67. Lewis, "Mandela the Pol"; Anthony Sampson, *Mandela: The Authorized Biography* (New York: Vintage, 1999); and Patti Waldmeir, *Anatomy of a Miracle: The End of Apartheid and the Birth of the New South Africa* (New York: W. W. Norton, 1997).

68. Lewis, "Mandela the Pol."

5

◄○►

Economic Globalization

IN 2003, ABOUT 14 MILLION PEOPLE IN SOUTHERN AFRICA WERE AT RISK of malnutrition and possibly starvation. Rains failed for two consecutive seasons in countries where subsistence farmers have no access to irrigation. They grow maize as a staple food, and it does not resist drought. A nonindigenous commercial crop, it has edged out hardier cereals that played key roles in traditional diets. The famine of 2003 arrived on top of a number of other pressures that jeopardize much of the population, such as deepening poverty in many parts of the region, government policy mistakes and inability or unwillingness to provide social services, and the spread of the HIV/AIDS epidemic. The UN World Food Programme (WFP) launched massive appeals for governments to supply food aid, and international nongovernmental organizations mobilized to help distribute it and provide other essential services. Yet some of the governments refused delivery of some of the grain because it was genetically modified (GM) in the United States. Their countries export maize to Europe, where GM crops are banned. These states feared that their farmers would save some of the grains to plant in the next season, thereby making future exports to Europe impossible. All parties reached a resolution when the governments agreed to accept milled GM food, thereby eliminating the possibility of using any seeds for future crops.

This illustration of how the international community tried to help local communities in crisis demonstrates some of the complexities of global aid and trade. Other examples illustrate different dimensions.

Southern Africa provides much of the world's gold, and the economies of the region have benefited enormously from the production of precious minerals. In 1997, however, central banks in Europe were rumored to be on the verge of selling their massive gold reserves. Gold prices plummeted as short-term speculators rushed in to take advantage of the potential central bank action, and tens of thousands of South African miners found themselves jobless. Mine workers accused the mine owners, who benefited enormously from white minority rule, of using the 1997 crisis to shrink the labor force and introduce greater mechanization. Even though mine workers' unions had played a pivotal role in the struggle against apartheid and the assumption of power by the ANC, the South African government had little solace to offer the workers. It was eager to be seen as friendly to business and economic globalization.

This chapter examines a number of the ways the interplay of local, regional, and global economic structures and processes shape the lives of the people and nations of southern Africa. As in previous chapters, the dilemmas in the economic domain resemble those in the political and military domains. If multinational corporations, global finance, and trade have had and continue to have an enormous impact on the economies of the region, what possibilities are there for the people and national governments of southern Africa to shape their own economic futures? What obstacles and opportunities do these countries face, and what policies might they adopt to lessen the obstacles and increase the opportunities?

Global economic institutions and patterns affect the nations of southern Africa profoundly and often negatively. National governments face significant dilemmas about who will shape their economic future as well as who will be held accountable for policy successes and failures. At the same time, in a reverse flow of influence, a few economic institutions and processes in southern Africa have far-flung impact across the world. Historically and currently, the region demonstrates vividly how local, regional, and global economic dynamics interact.

This chapter addresses a wide range of topics, all of which help to elucidate and provide context for the complexities associated with the prospects for sustained economic development in the region. The topics include: debates over the relationship of economies to governments; basic economic profiles of the countries in the region and their connections to the regional and world economies through trade, finance, debt, and multinational corporations; policies governments have undertaken to guide their economies, particularly in the context of larger debates in political economy; and an assessment of the countries' performance in addressing basic issues of survival, such as poverty and HIV/AIDs. In some respects, the picture painted here is bleak, in some respects hopeful.

CONTEMPORARY ECONOMIC GLOBALIZATION

Chapter 1 summarized economic globalization as trade, finance, and production. Trade consists of a system of regularized exchange of goods and services across regions and continents leading to the emergence of worldwide markets. Trade between any two countries may have an impact on trade relations among all the others. Finance is defined as the emergence of worldwide "flows of credit (such as loans and bonds), investment (foreign direct investment, equities) and money (foreign exchange)." Production is defined as the emergence of worldwide organization for producing goods and services, primarily through multinational corporations, companies that make and market goods or services in more than one country. As central players in economic globalization today, MNCs account for about two-thirds of all trade. Furthermore, up to one-third of world trade is intrafirm, that is, exchanges of goods and services between branches of the same company. In all three aspects of economic globalization, the reality of their genuinely worldwide reach constitutes the most striking feature of the contemporary era.[1]

Virtually all nations now find themselves deeply enmeshed in structures and patterns of global trade, finance, and production, which themselves have exploded in growth since World War II. As noted in chapter 1, some analysts assert that economic globalization lies at the heart of all other domains. Whether or not this is true, one significant feature of the economic domain is the number, power, coherence, and coordination of key institutions, both public and private, that promote globalization.

In the contemporary era, immediately after World War II, nations of the world created a number of IGOs, three of which came to be called the Bretton Woods institutions. Box 5.1 describes these organizations, including the World Bank Group (WBG), the International Monetary Fund (IMF), and the General Agreement on Tariffs and Trade (GATT, replaced in 1995 by the World Trade Organization [WTO]), as well as others that play a pivotal role in economic globalization. Although the membership of these three now encompasses almost all nations, historically these public organizations promoted the concerns, perspectives, and economic orientation of one part of the world, the West, and they have always lodged disproportionate power with one country, the United States. Furthermore, although there is substantial debate within the West and worldwide on how best to organize economic processes in global, regional, and national arenas, these IGOs have promoted a fairly narrow and rigid perspective. The debate revolves primarily around the relationship of governments to economies, often presented as the tension between states and markets.[2] The perspective these IGOs advocate is best understood in the context of the intellectual history of discussions of political economy, a brief discussion of which follows.

What role the state should play in the economy is a very old question. European powers of the sixteenth and seventeenth centuries, the early

BOX 5.1   Key Institutions in Economic Globalization

Bank for International Settlements (BIS)

Dating back to 1930 when European central bankers began meeting regularly, the BIS conducts operations through the central banks of member states, the advanced industrialized countries of the world. The United States Federal Reserve began cooperating with BIS in the 1960s but did not join until 1994. Headquartered in Basle, Switzerland, the BIS monitors monetary policies and financial flows and works with member states to regulate global banking. BIS has 49 members.

General Agreement on Tariffs and Trade (GATT)

The predecessory body of the WTO, GATT's purpose was to promote free trade by holding negotiations to reduce tariffs on trade in merchandise and by extending the most-favored-nation principle of nondiscrimination in trade relations. Absorbed into the WTO in 1995, GATT had been established in 1947 and headquartered in Geneva.

Group of Seven (G7) and Group of Eight (G8)

Initially formed in 1975 as the G5 (United States, Britain, France, Japan and West Germany), the group subsequently expanded to include Canada and Italy, too. After the fall of the Soviet Union, the group embraced Russia, to become eight. Although policy officials from these countries may hold more frequent consultations, the G8 government leaders meet in annual economic summits to collaborate on addressing world economic problems.

International Monetary Fund (IMF)

Established along with the World Bank in 1945 as one of the two international institutions of the Bretton Woods system, the IMF seeks to maintain monetary stability in part by providing loans to member states experiencing temporary balance of payments difficulties. In recent decades, the IMF has spearheaded stabilization policies and Structural Adjustment Programs (SAPs) for those nations suffering from chronic payments problems and debt. The Fund coordinates such programs with the World Bank and other financial institutions. Like the World Bank, the IMF is governed primarily by a system of weighted voting, which gives the greatest power to those governments making the largest contributions or subscriptions. Also like the World Bank, IMF headquarters are located in Washington, D.C. The Fund has 184 members.

(continues)

BOX 5.1 (*continued*)

Paris Club

The Paris Club consists of governments with large claims on various other governments. Its 19 members are drawn from the Organization for Economic Cooperation and Development. They meet periodically with individual debtor governments to negotiate debt-rescheduling agreements. The Paris Club applies terms defined in its Agreed Minutes but generally has no legal status, written rules, voting procedures or formal organizational structure.

World Bank Group (WBG)

The group consists of five lending agencies, the first of which (the International Bank for Reconstruction and Development—IBRD) was established along with the IMF in 1945 as one of the two international institutions of the Bretton Woods system. Headquartered in Washington, D.C., the Bank initially focused on rebuilding the economies shattered by World War II, but now it provides project loans for long-term development in poorer countries. Like the IMF, the Bank is governed by a system of weighted voting, which gives the greatest power to those governments making the largest contributions or subscriptions, primarily the advanced industrial countries. Member government subscriptions constitute one source of Bank funds, with borrowing in private capital markets providing another larger source. In recent decades, like the IMF, the Bank has become heavily involved in Structural Adjustment Programs in countries of the South. The WBG has 184 members.

World Trade Organization (WTO)

Established in 1995, with headquarters in Geneva, the WTO replaced GATT, and in contrast to GATT is a permanent institution with a formal legal structure on par with the World Bank and the IMF. With greater enforcement powers and a broader agenda than GATT, the purpose of the WTO is to promote greater cooperation in world trade, monitor the implementation of trade agreements, and settle disputes among trading partners quickly and decisively. Countries accused by the WTO of unfair trade practices can appeal, but the decision of the organization is ultimately binding. WTO has 146 members.

---

modern era of globalization, employed mercantilism as a guide to their policies. Mercantilism actively promoted the use of government to manipulate the economy in order to enhance the wealth and power of the nation, the state, and consequently, the monarchy. Few conceived of the possibility of any separation between political and economic activity until a sharp critique developed in the eighteenth century by such intellectuals as Adam Smith. He advocated that the state withdraw to hold a minimal role in the economy, giving it a much freer hand than had been envisioned before. This philosophy came to be known as liberalism, now often referred to as classical liberalism, the philosophical foundation of capitalism.[3]

In the nineteenth century, many analysts reacted negatively to the exploitation generated by capitalism and the industrial revolution, when these systems rose to prominence in the modern era of globalization. Charles Dickens, for example, chronicled the misery of ordinary people in the still popular stories he told of those times. To address such problems, Karl Marx advocated using the state to direct the economy for the good of the whole society, through, among other things, owning most of the means of production (i.e., land and capital) and deciding on how to use labor in a system sometimes called a command economy. The version of socialism he promoted was but one of several that envisioned alternatives to the exploitative system prevalent in the 1800s. By the twentieth century, especially in the wake of the Great Depression, some advocates of liberalism such as John Maynard Keynes argued that problems of market failure inherent to capitalism warranted substantial government intervention in the economy. By emphasizing the "demand side" of capitalism, they wanted to address issues such as unemployment and underutilized capital. However, they resolutely rejected Marxist calls for state ownership and central planning as well as other, less radical forms of socialism. This modified version of liberalism is often called Keynesianism, and it played a prominent role early in the contemporary era of globalization.

In the late twentieth century, building on Keynes's legacy, many West European governments remained committed to a substantial role for the state in the economy. In sharp contrast, however, in the 1980s Great Britain under Margaret Thatcher and the United States under Ronald Reagan rejected Keynesian policies. Instead, they advocated returning to more classical forms of liberalism where the state withdraws from prominence in guiding, regulating, or taxing the economy, a perspective known as neoclassical liberalism, which emphasizes the "supply side" of the system. A few years later, the world witnessed the collapse of the Soviet Union and effectively the abandonment of state-dominated command economies by most other Communist governments such as China and Vietnam. The long-standing global ideological debate between capitalism and socialism, or liberalism and Marxism, appeared to be coming to an end, with liberalism, whether in its neoclassical or Keynesian manifestation, winning the contest.

While neoclassical liberalism[4] gained ground in the West and Marxism collapsed in the East, substantially new versions of the oldest perspective on political economy—mercantilism[5]—were fueling remarkable experiments in public policy. The "Asian tigers," the newly industrializing countries (NICs) of South Korea, Taiwan, Hong Kong, and Singapore achieved booming economies in the 1980s and early 1990s through strong state involvement that created economic dynamism unmatched by other nations in the South and few in the North. This form of partnership between the government and the economy was labeled the developmental state by analysts.

Unfortunately, alongside the three traditional perspectives of mercantilism, liberalism, and socialism, as well as their modern variations, there is another model of the relationship between the state and the economy, one called the predatory state. As its name suggests, this perspective, which across time can be found in many parts of the world, is widely condemned by analysts from all three traditions as counterproductive to sustained development and national or international well-being. In a predatory state, governmental and other leaders use the country's political and economic organizations to extract societal resources for the leaders' personal use and accumulation. The state essentially "preys on its citizenry, terrorizing them, despoiling their common patrimony, and providing little in the way of services in return."[6] The government of Mobutu, the former dictator of Zaire (now Congo) discussed in earlier chapters, is often used to illustrate the archetype of the predatory state. Robert Mugabe's regime in Zimbabwe appears in recent years increasingly to offer another illustration of the same problem. As a group, however, the governments of southern Africa cannot be characterized as predatory, even if on occasion they experience corruption, a problem that plagues virtually every economy. The other three traditions of political economy offer more insight into these nations' past economic fortunes and possible futures.

In summation, from a practical point of view national governments in the contemporary era of globalization have chosen to pursue policies grounded in all three long-standing philosophical traditions (with a few predatory exceptions). On the whole, those in the West typically favored less state involvement in the economy, even though there is substantial variation, ranging from neoclassical liberalism to Keynesianism, among these countries. Those in the East, claiming to follow a Marxist path, adopted heavy state control. Those in the South, including those in southern Africa, typically chose more state involvement in the economy, basing those choices on one of the three: socialist or Marxist policy perspectives, mercantilist (developmental state) orientations, or the Keynesian version of liberalism, which allows only limited interventions.

From the point of view of economic and cultural (or more narrowly, ideological) globalization, however, this range of policy choices has all but disappeared, and one perspective has come to dominate all others. The IMF and WBG, two international financial institutions (IFIs) that profoundly influence the world's economy, enthusiastically and dogmatically promote the ideology of neoclassical liberalism in a one-size-fits-all approach to economic development. As noted earlier, for many the term "economic globalization" itself has come to mean the imperialistic imposition of neoclassical policy prescriptions on governments and people of the world who do not believe that such an orientation serves their interest.

The IMF and WBG attachment to liberal perspectives stems in part from their history of having been designed primarily by the United States and Britain at the close of World War II. Decisionmaking in both organizations concentrates power in the hands of a few. Through a system of weighted voting based on levels of contributions, the Group of Seven (United States, Great Britain, Canada, France, Germany, Italy, and Japan) hold more than 40 percent of the votes on the IMF and WBG boards of directors. The United States alone accounts for almost 20 percent and essentially holds veto power over the appointment of their leaders. As one analyst asserts, "the rich creditor governments . . . 'own and operate' the principal international financial institutions."[7] Across time the WBG has demonstrated more nuance of analysis and policy advocacy than the IMF, but the latter has always imposed conditions on borrowers basically in line with neoclassical liberalism. Moreover, the debt crises of the 1980s dramatically increased the power of both organizations to impose structural adjustment programs and thereby to accelerate the globalization of neoclassical ideology, often referred to as the "Washington consensus."[8] This perspective now powerfully frames policy discussions everywhere (see chapter 4 for a discussion of framing). Both the IMF and the WBG also work closely with the Paris Club, which also negotiates debt-rescheduling agreements (see box 5.1).

Structural adjustment programs (SAPs) pursue the goal of making both the state and the market more efficient so as to speed up growth and eliminate waste. The market takes center stage, with the state playing a secondary role. Considerable faith is placed in unfettered individual initiative, creativity, and ingenuity exercised through the market, which, according to neoliberalism, is made more effective through SAPs. Such policy prescriptions demand government reductions in spending, privatization of state-owned enterprises, trade liberalization, currency devaluation, and the general deregulation of the economy, including the sectors of finance and labor. Prior to the systematic global application of SAPs, a small number of governments in the South undertook their own initiatives to institute policies consistent with neoclassical policies. Most, however, including those in southern Africa, had them imposed from the outside by the IMF or WBG, or both.

How successful has this global one-size-fits-all approach been? Summarizing the literature in recent decades, John Rapley stated:

> Overall . . . the results of structural adjustment have varied widely. . . . SAPs have done the most good in Latin America, and the least good in Africa. . . . In addition to the moral concerns raised by structural adjustment, namely that SAPs have worsened the plight of the poor and deepened injustices in third-world societies, there appear to be serious economic and political drawbacks to neoclassical reform. It appears that neoclassical theorists, in focusing on the virtues of rolling back the state, overlooked some of the problems this process would beget. . . .
>
> Africanists have been among the harshest critics of structural adjustment, and they can draw upon a wealth of evidence to argue that it has done more harm than good in Africa. The aggregate evidence shows that during the 1980s, the decade when structural adjustment began across much of the continent, growth slowed and agricultural output failed to keep pace with population growth, leading in turn to increased food imports; manufacturing did not increase its share of total output, investment dropped, consumption plummeted, per capita incomes declined, and unemployment rose. . . . [B]y the end of the century, a strong economic recovery had yet to materialize in Africa. The most sanguine assessment now appears to be that if structural adjustment did not cause African's current economic woes, nor did it cure them.[9]

By 2000, a number of mainstream economic analysts as well as some WBG staff concluded that mechanistically imposing neoclassical economic policies, including SAPs, on all societies everywhere was an idea with dubious merit that had run its course. Emphasizing the role of culture and social values, Robert Gilpin has stated, "Contrary to economists' belief that economic activities are universal in character and essentially the same everywhere, the specific goals of economic activities are in actuality socially determined and differ widely over the face of the earth."[10] Joseph Stiglitz was the chief economist of the WBG in the late 1990s and co-winner of the 2001 Nobel Memorial Prize in Economic Science. Now a professor at Columbia University, he recently argued that the IMF discouraged frank discussion and expected developing countries "to accept fund prescriptions without question," more "on the basis of ideology rather than sound economic reasoning."[11] Others declared the Washington consensus to be unraveling,[12] but the IMF and, to a somewhat lesser degree, the WBG remain convinced that their basic approach is sound.

Many policymakers in southern Africa share this conviction. Economic approaches based on neoliberalism now play a prominent role in the region, in large part externally imposed by IFIs but in some cases adopted through more internally driven processes. In the context of predominant global economic trends, ideology, and reward structures, however, separating local and global tendencies from one another is difficult at best. When IFIs do not force a government to adopt SAPs, it still does so anyway. Does it do so because powerful international actors promote the ideology of SAPs and frame the range of options, legitimating some but stigmatizing others? Or do national decisionmakers genuinely believe that such policies will be good for their countries? Or is it perhaps a combination of these two?

Much of southern African suffers considerable economic woes, the causes of which are multiple and complex. Economic policies play an important role, but all of the countries of southern Africa face a number of structures and processes that work to limit the region's potential. Such structures and processes, both local and global, can only be changed across years, maybe decades. At the same time, however, there are some powerful economic possibilities for genuine, sustained development if coaxed and nurtured by creative initiatives.

Before examining national governments' policies and their changes across time, the next section provides a basic economic profile for each country, followed by a discussion of global links through production, finance, and trade. The analysis examines some of the constraints and opportunities these nations face, that is, the overall local, regional, and global economic structures in which they operate.

TABLE 5.1   Human Development Trends

	HDI rank out of 175 nations 2003	Human Development Index (HDI) value 2001	GDP per capita (PPP US$)[1] 2001
Angola	164	0.377	2,040
Botswana	125	0.614	7,820
Lesotho	137	0.510	2,420
Malawi	162	0.387	570
Mozambique	170	0.356	1,140
Namibia	124	0.627	7,120
South Africa	111	0.684	11,290
Swaziland	133	0.547	4,330
Zambia	163	0.386	780
Zimbabwe	145	0.496	2,280

SOURCE: United Nations Development Programme, *Human Development Report 2003* (New York: Oxford University Press, 2003).

[1]PPP US $ is a symbol for purchasing power parity, which is a rate of exchange that accounts for price differences across countries, allowing international comparisons of real output and incomes. PPPUS$1 has the same purchasing power as $1 has in the US.

THE POLITICAL ECONOMY OF SOUTHERN AFRICA

Table 5.1 demonstrates that five of the ten nations (Angola, Malawi, Mozambique, Zambia, and Zimbabwe) rank among the least developed countries in the world, according to the annual *UN Human Development Report*. Out of a total of 175 nations, these five fall below number 142, the point that separates the least developed from the rest. The other six fall low on the list of the countries in the category of medium human development. The UN Development Programme (UNDP) created the Human Development Index (HDI) in 1990. When compared to the traditional indicator of per capita gross domestic product (GDP), HDI performs as a multidimensional measure of countries' achievements. It takes into account, for example, life expectancy, adult literacy, and average local purchasing power. Countries such as China, Sri Lanka, Poland, and Cuba rank higher on the HDI than they do on per capita GDP, whereas countries such as Saudi Arabia and Kuwait rank lower on HDI than on GDP. A perfect HDI score would be 1.0, and countries such as Canada, Norway, and the United States have some of the highest HDI values, above 0.85. Data in Table 5.1 demonstrate an HDI score as low as 0.356 for Mozambique (with a rank of 170) compared to 0.684 for South Africa (with a rank of

111). A more crude measure, GDP per capita, assigns ratings according to purchasing power parity (PPP), in U.S. dollars. GDP is at a low of PPP US$570 in Malawi,[13] a bit higher at PPP US$780 in Zambia, and at PPP US$1,140 in Mozambique. In contrast, GDP per capita hits a high PPP US$11,290 in South Africa, with Botswana lower at PPP US$7820. The remainder of southern Africa lies in between, and their country economic profiles will begin to explain these differences.

Comparing National Economic Profiles

Proceeding in alphabetical order (except that South Africa will be last), a brief profile of the structure of each economy is followed by a summary comparison of the dynamics of political economy across the region. Table 5.2 summarizes some economic performance indicators for each country.

Although Angola is the seventh-largest country in Africa, less than 3 percent of the country is arable. Nevertheless, 80 to 90 percent of the population practices subsistence agriculture, which accounts for less than 15 percent of total GDP. Land mines, however, make many farmers reluctant to return to their fields. Crops produced include coffee, cassava, bananas, sugar cane, sisal, corn, cotton, manioc, and tobacco. Commercial crops (coffee, sisal, and cotton) make up some of the exports. In contrast to agriculture, offshore oil production and related activities contribute about 50 percent of total GDP and 90 percent of exports, the revenue from which in recent decades went to fund the government's war against the rebels. Industry consists of mining oil, diamonds, and other minerals, as well as fish, food, and other crop processing. Oil, diamonds, refined petroleum products, gas, coffee, and sisal make up the primary exports to the United States, the European Union (especially Portugal), and Brazil, the primary trading partners. Imports consist of capital equipment, food, vehicles and spare parts, textiles and clothing, medicines, and weapons as well as other military supplies.

Angola has enormous potential for wealth, with enormous reserves of oil, gas, and diamonds, as well as considerable hydroelectric potential. Overall, however, the economy remains in considerable disarray due to decades of war, with military expenditures making up about 22 percent of the GDP in 1999, down to 3.1 percent in 2001. Angola also suffers poor fiscal and monetary management. Much of the country's food must still be imported. Unemployment or underemployment affects more than half

TABLE 5.2   Economic Performance and Priorities

	GDP PPP US $ billions[1]	GDP per capita annual growth rate (%)		Household final consumption expenditure Average annual % growth		Public expenditure on education (as % of GDP)		Public expenditure on health (as % of GDP)		Military expenditure (as % of GDP)[2]		Government deficit/surplus (including grants) (% of GDP)
	2001	1975– 2001	1990– 2001	1980– 1990	1990– 2000	1990	1998– 2000	1990	2001	1990	2001	1999
Angola	27.5	-2.3	-1.1	-0.1	-3.8	3.9	2.7	1.4	2.0	5.8	3.1	-18.1
Botswana	13.3	5.3	2.5	5.9	6.2	6.7	8.6	1.7	3.7	4.1	3.5	-2.6
Lesotho	5	3.0	2.1	3.6	0.7	6.1	10.1	2.6	1.1	3.9	3.1	-3.5
Malawi	6	0.2	1.5	1.5	5.4	3.3	4.1	★★	3.6	1.3	0.8	-4.0
Mozambique	20.6	1.8	4.3	-1.4	4.3	3.9	2.4	3.6	2.8	10.1	2.3	-1.5
Namibia	12.8	-0.1	2.2	1.3	4.4	7.6	8.1	4.0	4.2	5.6	2.8	-3.8
South Africa	488.2	-0.7	0.2	2.4	2.6	6.2	5.5	3.1	3.7	3.8	1.6	-4.7
Swaziland	4.6	1.9	0.1	4.6	3.9	5.7	1.5	1.9	2.7	1.5	1.5	-2.1
Zambia	8	-2.2	-1.7	1.8	-2.8	2.4	2.3	2.6	3.5	3.7	0.6	-2.0
Zimbabwe	29.3	0.2	-0.2	3.7	0.0	7.7	10.4	3.1	3.7	4.5	3.2	-9.4

SOURCES: United Nations Development Programme, *Human Development Report 2003* (New York: Oxford University Press, 2003); *The World Bank, African Development Indicators 2001* (Washington, DC: The World Bank, 2001).

[1] PPP US$ is a symbol for purchasing power parity, which is a rate of exchange that accounts for price differences across countries. See table 5.1.

[2] As a result of a number of limitations in the data, comparisons of military expenditure data over time and across countries should be made with caution.

the population. Inflation has been brought down from over 300 percent in 2000 to about 110 percent in 2001. Yet because of oil, the GDP growth rate in 2001 was estimated to be about 5.4 percent. As shown in table 5.1, GDP per capita is PPP US$2,040, a figure that oil revenues badly distort, masking the extent of poverty in the country, as discussed later in this chapter. Table 5.2 displays long-term negative rates of per capita growth and consumption.

As with Angola, 80 percent of Botswana's population engages in agricultural production, which means raising both cattle and crops. Subsistence farming and cattle, however, provide only about 50 percent of the food required in the country and constitute only about 5 percent of total GDP. Crops grown include sorghum, maize, millet, pulses, and peanuts. In sharp contrast to Angola, diamond mining has fueled one of the world's highest sustained growth rates since independence in 1966, and as shown in table 5.2, overall growth has kept pace with population increases. The average growth in household final consumption has been the highest in the region for the last twenty years. The diamond industry now makes up about 40 percent of GDP and about 80 percent of export earnings. Other important minerals include copper, nickel, and coal. Besides diamonds, primary exports consist of copper, nickel, and meat, going to Switzerland, South Africa, and other countries in the region, as well as to the United Kingdom and the United States. Imports consist of food, vehicles and spare parts, textiles, and petroleum products. Estimates of unemployment range from 20 to 40 percent. Unlike the war-torn countries in the region, Botswana benefits from a thriving tourist industry. The growth rate in 2001 was almost 5 percent, down from previous years, and inflation reached only about 7 percent. Botswana's GDP per capita is second only to South Africa's, but almost 50 percent of the population live below the poverty line, despite the government's prudent management of resources as well as its investment in human and physical capital.

In Lesotho, about 85 percent of the resident population engages in subsistence agriculture, growing corn, wheat, pulses, and livestock, but agriculture accounts for only about 18 percent of GDP. However, about 35 percent of the active male wage earners migrate to work in South African mines, a number that has declined in recent years from 60 percent, and their earnings still contribute about 30 percent of the country's GDP. Water is the nation's main natural resource, and the completion of a major hydropower facility in 1998 generates royalties through sales of water to South Africa. Industry consists of food processing as well as a rapidly growing apparel-assembly sector, all of which account for about 38 percent of GDP and about 75 percent of export earnings. The primary trading partners are South Africa and North America. In 2001, the economy grew at less than 3 percent per year, although 1995–1997 saw rates of about 10 percent. Inflation was only about 7 percent in 2001. About 50 percent of the people live below the poverty line, and unemployment stands at about 45 percent. As shown in table 5.1, GDP per capita is only PPP US$2,420 and has grown very little in almost two decades, as with the average annual growth in household consumption (table 5.2).

About 90 percent of the people of Malawi live in rural areas. With some of the most fertile land in the region, crops include tobacco, sugar cane, cotton, tea, and corn. Agriculture constitutes almost 90 percent of export revenues, although it constitutes only about 40 percent of GDP. Trade partners include South Africa, Germany, the United Kingdom, the United States, and Japan. The country's imports include food, petroleum, and consumer goods. GDP per capita is only PPP US$570, and its growth is almost flat (table 5.2), making Malawi one of the poorest countries in the region and the world. More than half of the population live below the poverty line. The economy grew at less than 2 percent in 2001 and inflation approached 30 percent.

Mozambique is also one of the poorest countries in the world, with about 70 percent of its population living below the poverty line, despite the nation's vast untapped natural resources. Mozambique ranks below Malawi on the HDI but has a higher GDP per capita of PPP US$1,140. About 80 percent of the labor force works in agriculture, most of which is subsistence level. Together with commercial farming, this sector represents about 33 percent of the GDP. Crops include cotton, cashew nuts, sugarcane, tea, cassava, corn, and rice. Industry accounts for about 25 percent of GDP and consists of food processing as well as chemicals (fertilizer, coal, paints) and petroleum products. The outlook for greater development opportunities is positive and includes aluminum smelting, the discovery of natural gas, and new or restored electrical transmission lines to South Africa and Zimbabwe. Shrimp is an important export, along with cashews, cotton, and other agricultural products, which go to South Africa, Zimbabwe, Spain, and Portugal. Imports come from South Africa,

Portugal, the United States, and Australia and include machinery and equipment, mineral products, chemicals, and food.

Since the end of the war and the 1994 elections, inflation has declined dramatically (to about 10 percent in 2001, although up from even lower levels earlier) and growth rates have risen, averaging over 10 percent in the late 1990s (and about 9 percent in 2001). Per capita growth increases from 1990 to 2001 more than doubled the long-term averages (table 5.2), and figures for average growth in household consumption are even better. This growth is fueled in part by foreign and domestic investments and donor assistance, but the government remains dependent on foreign aid for most of its annual budget. Unemployment persists at about 21 percent, and the number of men who migrate to work in South African mines has declined in recent years. In 2000–2001, the country suffered from devastating floods that caused extensive damage to health care systems, schools, roads, railways, and utilities. Almost 500,000 people were displaced from their homes.

Namibia depends on the extraction and processing of minerals like diamonds, copper, gold, lead, zinc, uranium, tin, silver, and tungsten for 20 percent of GDP, but much of the wealth generated by mining leaves the country. Export partners include the United Kingdom, South Africa, Spain, and France, and minerals constitute the vast bulk of exports. Over half of the population depends on subsistence agriculture or cattle raising, which accounts for about 11 percent of GDP, but the country has one of the richest potential fisheries in the world. Now, however, the country must import food, in part a consequence of the desert climate, where less than 1 percent of the land is arable. Other imports include petroleum products, machinery and equipment, and chemicals, all of which come overwhelmingly from South Africa. Unemployment and underemployment stand at 30–40 percent. Industry consists of meatpacking and other food processing as well as mining and constitutes almost 30 percent of GDP. The economic growth rate is about 4 percent (2001), with inflation reaching about 9 percent (2001). Tables 5.1 and 5.2 show the GDP per capita as the third highest in the region and the HDI value as the second highest, with per capita growth improving slightly after 1990.

Like half the countries in the region, Swaziland is landlocked, and also like others, subsistence agriculture engages about 80 percent of the population but produces only about 10 percent of the GDP. Because of prevalent mountain terrain, only about 10 percent of the land is arable.

Unemployment is over 30 percent. Although in decline, mining continues to be the most significant industry, particularly coal and asbestos. Easily accessible diamond reserves are now depleted. All industry constitutes about 43 percent of the economy, with food processing, particularly sugar cane, and wood pulp also being consequential. The primary trade partner is South Africa, from which about 90 percent of imports come and to which more than 70 percent of exports go. Exports include soft-drink concentrates, sugar, and wood pulp, whereas imports include motor vehicles, machinery and transport equipment, food, and petroleum products. GDP grows at about 2.5 percent per year (2001), with inflation at about 7.5 percent. The GDP per capita is about PPP US$4,330, in the middle of regional values, as is the HDI score of 0.547. Per capita GDP growth worsened in the 1990s, as did growth in household consumption (table 5.2).

Bordered by half the nations in the region, Zambia, too, is landlocked. Copper mining and processing dominate exports (55 percent) and industry, with all industry accounting for about 25 percent of GDP. Exports include minerals other than copper, and they all go primarily to the United Kingdom, South Africa, and Switzerland. Imports include machinery, transportation equipment, and petroleum products, which come mostly from South Africa (almost 70 percent) but also from the United Kingdom, Zimbabwe, and the United States. Subsistence agriculture employs 85 percent of the population, but underemployment and unemployment plague about half the workforce. Only about one-fourth of GDP comes from agriculture, and only about 7 percent of the land is arable. An estimated 85 percent of the population lives below the poverty line, a reality reflected in an HDI value of 0.386 and a GDP per capita of only PPP US$780. Per capita income fell almost 5 percent annually between 1974 and 1990, due to a number of factors including a collapse in copper prices, oil price shocks, a contraction of food production, and economic mismanagement. The decade of the 1990s fares only slightly better but is importantly worse in declining rates of household consumption. Beginning to show some signs of recovery, the economic growth rate was about 4 percent in 2001, but inflation exceeded 20 percent.

Although traditionally in a good economic position compared to other nations in the region, Zimbabwe currently faces dramatic political and economic crises that threaten its future. Based on previous years' HDI scores, it used to be ranked by the UN in the category of medium human development. Inflation increased from about 30 percent in 1998 to about 100 percent in 2001, when the economy actually shrank, with a GDP growth of –6.5 percent due to several factors. These include declining prices for key exports, a decrease in tobacco exports following the invasion of large farms by those seeking access to land, a loss of investor confidence due to uncertainty about domestic policies, and economic mismanagement. Recent droughts and flooding in the region also have taken their toll, especially on the rural populations.

Almost 70 percent of the labor force works in agriculture, which accounts for about 11 percent of GDP. Important commercial crops are tobacco, cotton, and sugar cane, with tobacco representing about 30 percent of all exports. Minerals and textiles are also significant. These products go to South Africa, the United Kingdom, Japan, Germany, and China. Imports include machinery and transport equipment, other manufactures, chemicals, and fuels, and they come from essentially the same trading partners, with South Africa dominating (46 percent). Underemployment and unemployment stand at about 60 percent of the population, the same percentage that live below the poverty line. Especially because of its intervention in the war in the DRC, the government spends about 3 percent of GDP on the military. Zimbabwe has an HDI value of 0.496 and a per capita GDP of PPP US$2,280, in the middle of the region's range. In comparison to other nations in southern Africa (except South Africa), Zimbabwe has historically had fairly well developed financial, legal, communications, and transportation sectors. This vital infrastructure, however, has been put in jeopardy by the Mugabe regime. Table 5.2 displays some of the worsening picture.

The South African economy dominates all the others. In 2001, the region had a combined gross domestic product of PPP US$615.3 billion. Of this, South Africa accounted for PPP US$488.2 billion, or 79 percent. Table 5.1 shows an HDI ranking 111 for South Africa, 13 points better than the next-best score (for Namibia at 124). The GDP per capita in South Africa of PPP US$11,290 is about 45 percent greater than the next highest in Botswana (at PPP US$7,820). Yet when compared to the rest of the world, South Africa ranks as a middle-income, developing country. To its advantage, the nation has abundant natural resources and a modern infrastructure, which includes highly developed financial, legal, communications, energy, and transportation sectors. The Johannesburg Stock

Exchange (JSE) is among the ten largest in the world. To its disadvantage and like the rest of the region, South Africa suffers a high unemployment rate of about 37 percent, and about one-half the population lives below the poverty line, two of the many legacies of the system of apartheid.

About 30 percent of the labor force works in agriculture, which contributes only 3 percent to the GDP. Yet South Africa exports food products (for example, meat, fruit, wine, fish) in addition to feeding its own population. Industry accounts for about 31 percent of GDP and employs about 2 percent of the labor force, with mining being the largest industry. South Africa is the world's largest producer of platinum, gold, and chromium and is a leader in producing copper, iron ore, crude steel, lead, manganese, nickel, silver, uranium, diamonds, and others. Minerals constitute over one-half of all exports, and they go to the European Union (over 30 percent), the United States (about 20 percent), Japan, Mozambique, and others. South Africa ranks with Egypt as having the most advanced manufacturing sector on the continent, producing automobiles, machinery, textiles, chemicals, fertilizer, and foodstuffs. Imports consist of machinery, chemicals, petroleum, and scientific instruments, with primary partners being the EU (41 percent), the United States (11 percent), Saudi Arabia, and Japan.

Although South Africa has the largest economy in the region, GDP grew at only about 2.6 percent in 2001, a rate insufficient to address the widespread poverty and unemployment. Inflation in 2001 was basically under control at 5.8 percent.[14] Table 5.2 shows that the long-term trends of per capita growth and consumption as well as spending on education and health are not likely to raise the majority out of poverty.

When looking at the region's economies as a whole, some patterns and structures become evident. Except for South Africa, most households depend heavily on subsistence agriculture. Underemployment, unemployment, and poverty pervade every country, whether in the more industrialized economy of South Africa or in those with little industry. Except for Botswana and very recently in Mozambique, economic growth has been low or negative in recent decades. The same is true overall in growth rates for consumption. Mineral extraction plays a dominant role almost everywhere, as do a few large MNCs, which are discussed in more detail below. Because of its sheer size, what happens economically and otherwise in South Africa affects all the other countries profoundly. In addition, as is evident from Chapters 2 and 3, all of the discussion about economic challenges and opportunities must be put in the context of two long-standing realities: white minority rule premised on the deprivation of the black majority, and three or four decades of regionalized wars originating in the intransigence of this minority.

A closer examination of the region's global linkages will complement the national profiles and give a more complete picture of the structures and processes that shape the region's political economy.

Trade, Finance, and Debt

Trade provides a key link in the region's global connections. Following a pattern that dates back to colonialism, the economies of southern Africa rely heavily on trade, which supplies a high percentage of the governments' fiscal revenues. Just as important, most of these economies export primary commodities in return for importing manufactured goods, and overall the prices for many of their commodities have generally fallen in the last forty years or so (with oil from Angola being an important exception). This means that the region's terms of trade have generally deteriorated. "Terms of trade" refers to the relationship between the prices of a country's exports and the prices of its imports. The previous discussion showed that the major trading partner for many of the countries of the region is South Africa. Outside the continent, however, and for South Africa itself, trade flows primarily to and from Europe and the United States, where the region faces tough competition for export markets.

The United States and the European Union place a high priority on enforcing rules of the World Trade Organization when their own exports are at stake. Yet when poor countries attempt to export goods to the industrialized world, high tariffs, antidumping regulations, and technical barriers[15] get in the way, ironically violating the same ideology and policies of free trade that these governments advocate for everyone else. In June 2000, Peter Hain, the British minister of state for Africa, stated that such trade obstructions "cost sub-Saharan African countries $20 billion annually in lost exports—$6 billion more than they receive in aid."[16]

Table 5.3 summarizes the structure of trade in the region. The table includes the value of exports and imports, as well as exports and imports as a percent of GDP and changes in each country's terms of trade. In seven of the ten economies, the value of exports has risen from 1990 to 2000, in some cases dramatically. In all but two cases, however, the terms of trade have declined. In other words, except in South Africa and Zimbabwe, the prices received for goods and services these countries sell to the world have generally fallen (dramatically, for some) compared to the prices of the goods and services the countries buy from the world. Consequently, these countries cannot pay for the goods and services that they buy with the money they earn from selling their products. Furthermore, as is evident from the previous section, much of what these nations buy remains essential for their economic well-being, for example capital equipment such as machinery, transportation vehicles, petroleum (except Angola), food, and medicine. When nations need to buy more than they sell, trade deficits and debt become almost inevitable.

Table 5.4 displays capital flows into the region. To grow economically, countries need to accumulate money for investment, and several sources exist. Some are domestic, such as people's personal savings stored in local banks or the profits of local companies that provide opportunities for expanded or new businesses. International sources include individuals or corporations from abroad that purchase shares in local companies (portfolio investments), foreign direct investment (FDI, which involves the ownership and control of assets, usually by MNCs), loans from international commercial banks, multilateral loans or grants from IFIs, and bilateral loans or grants from governments.

Table 5.4 shows the region's key global sources: official development assistance (ODA,[17] loans primarily from Western nations often channeled multilaterally through IFIs but sometimes made bilaterally), FDI, and other private flows (e.g., from NGOs). The table also includes total debt service. Overall, the trends for FDI are positive, in part reflecting the cessation of warfare, the end of apartheid and the increased freedom of South African MNCs to invest outside their own country, as well as governments' adoption of policies that welcome FDI. Although increasing, investment in the new, democratic South Africa has been disappointing overall. FDI and MNCs will be discussed in greater depth in the next section.

ODA translates into one of the most powerful tools of economic globalization because it requires that local governments respond to the policy recommendations of IFIs. As is evident from the table, the region receives considerable sums in multilateral and bilateral loans and in some cases has

TABLE 5.3   Structure of Trade

	Merchandise Exports $ millions		Imports of goods and services (as % of GDP)		Exports of goods and services (as % of GDP)		Public expenditure on health (1980 = 100)
	1990	2000	1990	2001	1990	2001	2000
Angola	3910	7,858	21	62	39	74	182
Botswana	1,784	2,670	50	35	55	51	**
Lesotho	59	200	121	86	17	34	59
Malawi	417	350	33	38	24	26	61
Mozambique	126	235	36	44	8	22	57
Namibia	1,085	1,455	57	66	44	54	**
South Africa	23,549	29,983	19	25	24	28	103
Swaziland	556	900	74	81	75	69	106
Zambia	1,309	800	37	37	36	27	49
Zimbabwe	1,726	1,670	23	21	23	22	108

SOURCES: United Nations Development Programme, *Human Development Report 2003* (New York: Oxford University Press, 2003); *The World Bank, World Development Indicators 2002* (Washington, DC: The World Bank, 2002).

** denotes missing data.

TABLE 5.4 Flows of Aid, Private Capital, and Debt

| | Official development assistance (ODA) received (net disbursements) | | | | Net foreign direct investment flows (as % of GDP) | | Other private flows (as % of GDP) | | Total debt service | | | |
| | Total (US$ millions) | Per capita (US$) | As % of GDP | | | | | | As % of GDP | | As % of GDP exports of goods and services | |
	2001	2001	1990	2001	1990	2001	1990	2001	1990	2001	1990	2001
Angola	268.4	21.0	2.6	2.8	-3.3	11.8	5.6	-2.3	3.2	19.7	7.1	26.0
Botswana	29.1	16.6	3.9	0.6	2.5	1.1	-0.5	(.)	2.8	1.0	4.4	1.7
Lesotho	54.0	30.1	22.8	6.8	2.7	14.7	(.)	-0.5	3.7	8.6	4.2	12.4
Malawi	401.5	34.5	26.8	23.0	1.2	3.3	0.1	0.0	7.1	2.2	28.0	15.5
Mozambique	934.9	51.3	40.7	25.9	0.4	13.3	1.0	-0.8	3.2	2.4	26.2	2.7
Namibia	109.1	56.5	4.4	3.5	**	**	**	**	**	**	**	**
Swaziland	29.3	27.6	6.1	2.3	3.4	1.7	-0.2	1.1	5.3	2.2	5.3	2.5
South Africa	428.5	9.6	**	0.4	-0.1	6.3	**	-0.5	**	3.8	**	6.8
Zambia	373.5	35.3	14.6	10.3	6.2	2.0	-0.3	1.5	6.2	3.6	6.2	13.4
Zimbabwe	159.0	12.5	3.9	1.8	-0.1	0.1	1.1	-0.4	5.4	1.5	5.4	3.4

SOURCE: United Nations Development Programme, *Human Development Report 2003* (New York: Oxford University Press, 2003).

** denotes missing data

TABLE 5.5   Debt of Southern Africa's Least Developed Countries

	Debt *$ millions*			*Debt Service* *$ millions*			*Ratio (percentage)* *Total Debt/GDP*		
	1985	*1990*	*1999*	*1985*	*1990*	*1998*	*1985*	*1990*	*1998*
Angola	3045	8348	8314	372	328	588	45	81	97
Lesotho	169	469	999	22	29	122	58	75	114
Malawi	1034	1557	2594	120	116	108	91	86	143
Mozambique	2276	4168	7001	184	125	123	51	166	176
Zambia	4532	5462	6153	219	246	162	201	166	195

SOURCE: United Nations Conference on Trade and Development, *The Least Developed Countries Report 2002* (New York: United Nations, 2002).

staggering amounts of debt. In its last four columns, Table 5.4 displays the total debt service as a percentage of GDP and as a percent of the value of goods and services exports. For example, the total ODA as a percent of GDP in Angola remained fairly steady from 1990 to 2001 (from 2.6 to 2.8). The total debt service payment as a percent of exports of goods and services rose by a factor of more than three (from 7.1 to 26). Debt service payments as a percent of GDP more than quadrupled in the same time period. Table 5.5 demonstrates the debt load on the poorest five countries, including the total amount of debt, the money paid as interest (debt service), and the ratio of total debt to GDP. In this table, from 1985 to 1999, Angola more than doubled its total debt as well as the ratio of debt to GDP and increased its debt service by about 60 percent. As alarming as these figures are, however, other countries included in the table fare worse in many respects. Chronic debt crises threaten the long-term viability of their economies and societies.

In the 1980s the global debt crisis deepened in Africa, Asia, and Latin America due to repeated increases in the costs of oil, rising interest rates, and declining global prices for many primary commodities, problems that were compounded by war and instability in southern Africa. (Many in the region consider the portion of the debt incurred by the apartheid government of South Africa to be illegitimate, a problem all newly established democracies face when inheriting the legacies of bad policies from dictatorships.) IFIs and creditor governments began trying to address the global crisis through the widespread use of SAPs that they hoped would stabilize and restructure debtor economies to ensure repayment. In 1989, the Paris Club became more active as an arena where creditor governments coordinated their bilateral rescheduling of payments with debtor countries. With indebtedness and the threat of default growing, the IMF and the World Bank launched the Heavily Indebted Poor Countries (HIPC) initiative in 1996 as the first comprehensive framework to bring together private and government creditors and the IFIs. In 1999 the Group of Eight (G8) wealthy nations put their weight behind the HIPC initiative, giving it more momentum and tacitly acknowledging that previous work to restructure and reschedule loans had not resolved the now chronic situation many nations face.

HIPC targets debt relief and aid to the poorest countries in an attempt to reduce their debt burden to sustainable levels, defined as a debt-to-export ratio of between 200 and 250 percent and a debt-service-to-export ratio of between 20 and 25 percent. HIPC governments must demonstrate sound economic and social policy reforms through SAPs and other means as well as negotiate a Poverty Reduction Strategy Paper. Four nations in southern Africa qualify for the HIPC (out of a total thirty-four initially named in Africa): Angola (paying 26 percent of its export earnings to debt service in 2001), Malawi (paying 28 percent of its export earnings to debt service in 1990), Mozambique (paying 26 percent of its export earnings to debt service in 1990), and Zambia (paying 47 percent of its export earnings to debt service in 1999). By 2001, Mozambique had received about $4.3 billion to dramatically lower its debt service payments. The World Bank is in the process of implementing a program in Malawi (where the debt service to export earnings ratio fell to about 10 percent in 2002) and more recently began working with Angola and Zambia. To get this relief, however, the countries are drawn further into the economic globalization of neoclassical liberalism as they adopt the IFI policy recommendations.[18]

Many analysts and activists alike argue that the HIPC, with its limited approach and slow-moving negotiations, has offered too little, too late to address poor African countries' chronic indebtedness, which poses a monumental, if not fatal, obstacle to their development. Transnational advocacy networks, led by churches and organizations such as Oxfam campaigned vigorously under the banner of Jubilee 2000[19] to cancel poor countries' debt by the turn of the millennium. In 1998, for example, 70,000 people formed a human chain around the Group of Eight summit in Birmingham, Britain. The activists did not succeed on the timeline they projected, but the G8's 1999 endorsement of HIPC was evidence that the political globalization of TANs can have impact on the worldwide economic processes. Jubilee 2000 TANs continue to put pressure on wealthy nations to provide effective leadership on debt issues.

In 2000, UN general secretary Kofi Annan called for "an independent panel of experts not unduly influenced by creditor interest to reassess the debt burden of developing countries and the international measures taken to deal with them."[20] He also called for the immediate suspension of debt service payments by all HIPCs. Similarly, increasing numbers of scholars argue that even if debt service payments decline substantially, the decades-old creditor-dominated approach to chronic debt will consign the poorest countries to long-term impoverishment. HIPC, they charge, essentially amounts to writing off loans that would never have been paid anyway, while at the same time extracting the maximum possible repayments through rescheduling.

Harvard economist Jeffrey Sachs sharply criticized the IFIs as leading a "creditor grab race" that undermines economic stability in debtor nations. For example, the IMF loans funds to debtor nations to help them maintain debt servicing to private banks. This practice has been "widely seen as creating moral hazard, encouraging future indiscriminate lending by creditors to weak borrowers on the basis of expected future bailouts." Moreover, the approach provides "the minimum possible to prevent outright disaster, but never enough to solve the debt crisis."[21] Countries like most of those in southern Africa, Sachs has argued, are vulnerable to a "poverty trap, which can be caused or exacerbated by an excessive foreign debt burden," making sustained economic growth impossible and a variety of key goals (poverty alleviation, reduction of hunger, reduction of disease burden) unattainable. Governments end up servicing their debt but spending very little on investments in human capital (primary health care and education) and basic infrastructure (roads, sanitation, water). This diminishes significantly the likelihood of FDI or even investment from insiders with wealth.

To make his point, Sachs traced the number of IFI restructurings and debt reschedulings (R&Rs) for a number of countries. For example, since 1982, Malawi has had at least three R&Rs but its average growth of GNP per capita was –0.2 percent from 1975 to 1999. Although its recent growth rates are higher, Mozambique has experienced an average growth of GNP per capita of 1.3 percent from 1975 to 1999 under at least seven R&Rs since 1984. Zambia has had at least six R&Rs since 1983, with an average growth of GNP per capita from 1975 to 1999 of −2.4 percent.[22] Furthermore, as will be even more evident later in this chapter, indicators of this kind signal that the whole region suffers from a serious deterioration of social conditions.

Something is very wrong with this picture, according to Sachs.[23] He proposes an internationally monitored plan whereby the poorest nations could declare themselves insolvent, similar to declaring bankruptcy within a country. The goals of such an international insolvency would be: to provide a "fresh start" for the "insolvent sovereign," which would have access to considerable resource transfers (through debt cancellation or new grants); to set and achieve broad development objectives such as investments in health, education, and basic infrastructure (monitored by an review panel appointed by creditors and debtors); and to repay creditors.[24] Rather than simply blaming debtor nations, this proposal, like others, accepts the global dimensions of chronic debt as a significant part of the problem and provides global solutions that would more appropriately respond to the needs and aspirations of poor and indebted countries such as those in southern Africa. Sachs concluded: "The idea of linking debt reduction to a detailed assessment of the financial requirements for meeting the debtors' essential needs may seem obvious, even trivial, but it is radically different from what the creditor-donor nations have done during the past quarter century."[25]

Production and MNCs

In addition to trade and finance, production is the third key element of economic globalization. Southern Africa provides a very interesting context for studying the local and regional connections to the global production of goods and services through multinational corporations. During the modern and contemporary era of globalization, southern Africa drew in large amounts of FDI from Britain, the United States, and the European continent. A succession of oil companies, for example, operated in Angola under Portuguese colonial authorities and then under the MPLA government, as discussed in chapter 3. Most FDI went to South Africa, however, linking many well-known business names in Britain, the United States, and other industrialized countries (e.g., Shell, British Petroleum, Mobil, Caltex, Ford,

GM, Datsun, Toyota, Chrysler, Union Carbide, U.S. Steel, Chase Manhattan, Citibank, Bank of America, Barclay's) to one of the most profitable parts of the world for MNCs and one of the most odious regimes. Many companies pulled out in the 1980s under pressure of divestment campaigns and the imposition of international sanctions. Most of the homegrown MNCs, however, had few other places to go, although a few cleverly managed to navigate international business waters through a variety of partnerships, despite boycotts and sanctions. Two of the largest, De Beers and Anglo American, provide fascinating tales of how companies based in the region came to be global economic powerhouses.

In 1947, a young copywriter working in a New York advertising firm on an account for the South African De Beers corporation penned the famous line seen in magazines and newspapers and on television, "A diamond is forever." In 1999, the U.S. magazine *Advertising Age* named this catch phrase the top advertising slogan of the century. This award acknowledged the extraordinary global power, creativity, and reach of the diamond mining, holding, and financial corporation begun in 1888 by English immigrant Cecil John Rhodes, who managed to achieve a virtual monopoly over diamond production and marketing in southern Africa. At the end of World War II, most people believed that only the rich could enjoy the luxury of diamonds. The ad campaign created demand for De Beers products by convincing middle-class couples that they, too, could afford diamonds as a sign of their love. The use of a New York firm to promote a South African mining interest followed a long-standing pattern of joint undertakings among businesses from the United States, Britain, and South Africa. This campaign, however, marked the consolidation of a global strategy by De Beers not only to mine, but more important, to control the selling of diamonds worldwide. For this purpose, De Beers established the Central Selling Organization (CSO) in 1930, a producers' cooperative that limited the quantity of diamonds on the market and, from the company's point of view, stabilized the trade.

By the 1950 and 1960s, as the contemporary era of globalization unfolded, De Beers reached agreement with the Soviet Union, a major source of diamond mining, whereby it would use the CSO. De Beers also purchased major shares in Canadian mines, a second significant source of production that would funnel sales through CSO. The company also invested in western and central Africa, Namibia, Australia, and Botswana and began making synthetic diamonds in Ireland. Advertising campaigns extended into Japan in 1967 (where retail sales reached $18 billion by 1995) and later, East Asia. The discovery in Botswana proved to be one of the largest in the world, and in 1969 De Beers and the government of Botswana formed a joint venture (Debswana) to develop the mine. This fueled a period of sustained economic development in Botswana, evident in the economic indicators and discussion elsewhere in this chapter. Namibia forged a similar joint venture in 1994 (Namdeb). Other countries where De Beers has investments include Angola, Tanzania, Belgium, and Britain.

De Beers registered its non–South African assets in Switzerland in 1990 because of unrest in South Africa, the divestment and boycott pressures of the global anti-apartheid movement, international sanctions, and the apartheid government's intransigence in the late 1980s, among other uncertainties. Furthermore, the collapse of the Soviet Union and civil war in Angola and other parts of the world that produce diamonds disrupted the CSO and caused a glut on the world market. In the face of such competition, the company adopted a new business strategy to brand its gems, shifting the focus of the CSO from being a "buyer of last resort" to being a "supplier of first choice." The company continues to be responsible for about two-thirds of the world's trade in rough diamonds. In 2001, De Beers separated from Anglo American Corporation, with which it had been intimately allied since 1926. The Oppenheimer family reached a $17.6 billion agreement with Anglo American Corporation to take the company private, delisting it from the Johannesburg Stock Exchange.[26]

Sir Ernest Oppenheimer founded Anglo American in 1917, having immigrated from London in 1902, to expand the gold mining interests of his family's company, Dunkelsbuhlers. He raised the necessary capital from British and U.S. sources, which also gave the venture its name. A future U.S. president, Herbert Hoover, helped Oppenheimer set up share subscriptions through J.P. Morgan & Company, as well as its British affiliate. After establishing itself in gold mining, in 1926 Anglo American became the largest single shareholder in De Beers, and Oppenheimer took over its helm in 1929. In turn, De Beers came to be the largest shareholder in Anglo American, and ever since, the two companies have presided over a complex interlinking of financial, mining, and industrial businesses in southern Africa. Expanding to the north, in 1928 Anglo American drew again on U.S. and British investors to begin copper mining in Northern

Rhodesia (to become Zambia). Industrial ventures had already begun in the 1920s and 1930s, as had coal mining. With considerable expansion of gold mines in South Africa, by the 1940s and 1950s Anglo American had become one of the world's most important mining operations.

Harry Oppenheimer, who had been involved in politics as an opposition member of the South African parliament, took over leadership of both companies when his father died in 1957. After the Sharpeville massacre in 1960, the South African government instituted domestic exchange controls restricting Anglo American and other conglomerates from investing abroad. Although both Anglo American and De Beers circumvented these to some degree, the controls pushed the large South African companies to diversify further inside the country, expanding from mining into manufacturing, finance, and other services. Anglo American established new, closely tied companies to consolidate its operations in steel, timber and paper, coal, and other endeavors. In the 1970s and 1980s, when the global anti-apartheid movement pressured businesses to withdraw their FDI from South Africa, Anglo American bought a number of these assets, such as Barclay's National Bank, Ford, and Chrysler. By the late 1980s, Anglo American controlled about 85 percent of the companies quoted on the JSE. In the meantime, Anglo American acquired mines in Canada in 1961 and in Latin America in the 1970s, using a new company, Minorco, for FDI in Latin America. During the contemporary era of globalization, Anglo American became the world's largest natural-resource company with operations in six continents. In 1993, the company consolidated all its non-African international businesses under the heading of Minorco, retaining the name Anglo American to continue investing on the African continent.[27]

De Beers and Anglo American are only two of a number of giant conglomerates that originate in southern Africa. Others include Gencor, an old Afrikaner-based rival of Anglo American and the world's fourth largest producer of gold, and Billiton, a partner of Gencor. Lonrho is another platinum mining company that profits from a variety of other ventures. Yet in the history of the region, the power of large mining companies such as De Beers and Anglo American made an impact on shaping overall patterns of political economy. Late in the 1800s and early in the 1900s, for example, these businesses' particular demands for labor made possible controls such as passes, migrant workers, and housing compounds for migrant workers separated from their families. This instituted a pattern that white minorities adopted in one form or another in most of the region and sowed the seeds of the apartheid system that Afrikaners so rigidly instituted in the mid-1900s in South Africa.[28]

The Oppenheimer family and their businesses, however, provided support for political parties based primarily in the South African English-speaking white community, and after 1948 these parties were in permanent formal opposition to the government. As regional pressures mounted in the 1970s and 1980s to end white minority rule, Harry Oppenheimer asserted repeatedly that government controls in the form of apartheid structures needed to give way to unimpeded opportunities for capitalist development, including skilled African labor. He established the Urban Foundation in 1976 to contribute to welfare projects in the African townships, and he recommended that educated Africans be incorporated into the political system. The 1980s brought recession, a decline in the price of gold, and the pressure of divestment and economic sanctions, depriving the South African economy of much-needed capital. Many business leaders, including those from Anglo American and De Beers, began to seek alternatives to apartheid in part to end the geographical restrictions on their ability to make profits. By 1990, for example, U.S. corporations were earning about 30 percent of their profits abroad, whereas South African firms gained only 7 percent from overseas investments.[29] In 1985, Gavin Relly, Harry Oppenheimer's successor as head of Anglo American, met with ANC leader Oliver Tambo and others in Zambia. Similar meetings of white South African business, intellectual, and church leaders (including Afrikaners) with exiled ANC officials followed soon thereafter, some with the approval of the government.[30]

With the end of sanctions and the liberalization of the South African economy, the conglomerates and others immediately seized opportunities for investing outside of South Africa. "From 1991 to 1995 South African firms increased their total investment in Sub-Saharan Africa fivefold to account for 25 percent of the total. From 1994–1998, African countries received 42 percent of the outward investments by South African companies, while the European Union received 18 percent."[31] This equates to an average of $1 billion each year in South African FDI in other African countries since 1994, among other things, to run the national railroads in Cameroon and Madagascar; manage power plants in Mali and Zambia; brew local beer in Mozambique and Ghana, provide cell phone service in Nigeria,

Uganda, and Cameroon; and provide banks and supermarkets in Tanzania, Mozambique, and Kenya.[32] From 1994 to 1999, South Africans invested $9.8 billion abroad. Only $8.2 billion flowed into the country.[33] As one analyst put it, the South African companies used "the region as a springboard to globalise."[34]

In addition, many conglomerates moved their primary stock market listings and headquarters to London in the 1990s in order to get access to cheaper capital, to facilitate greater foreign expansion, and to improve global competitiveness, including denominating their assets in a more secure hard currency. Among those who moved were Anglo American, Old Mutual, SA Breweries, Billiton, and Dimension Data. The shift increased these corporations' asset values and share prices[35] and returned them to relationships reminiscent of the region's imperial history, when Britain played a primary role in the region's economies.

With the South African government's blessings, some conglomerates have also sold some of their "non-core" South African assets to foreign MNCs, some of whom had left during the 1980s, as well as to about 200 emerging black business leaders through a process of "black empowerment." From 1995 to 1998, the proportion of shares on the JSE owned by black-empowerment companies rose from an estimated 0.5 percent to about 20 percent, whereas the five largest conglomerates dropped to controlling only 55 percent of the shares on the JSE. In addition, prominent former anti-apartheid leaders such as Mamphela Ramphele and Cyril Ramaphosa were added to the boards of directors of such conglomerates as Anglo American.[36]

Whether originating in the region or coming from outside, MNCs have a profound economic, political, and social impact on southern Africa. Maintaining investment and attracting more is increasingly important for government policies. Having examined the basic economic profile of each country and the region's connections to economic globalization through trade, finance, and production, the discussion now shifts to concrete policy choices, particularly the growing role of neoclassical liberalism.

GOVERNMENTS' ECONOMIC POLICIES

The previous sections discussed how international financial institutions used SAPs to impose neoclassical economic policies in Malawi, Mozambique, and Zambia. Various aspects of the Mozambican and Zambian cases warrant further examination together with Zimbabwe. Botswana and South Africa adopted neoclassical policies through more internally driven processes, however, making their experience also analytically useful.

Historically, during and after their hard-fought struggles to achieve black majority rule, some of the region's governments embraced a vision of socialist economic policies. They hoped to ensure greater national economic control and higher levels of basic services to ordinary people. As time progressed and as the Asian "tigers" succeeded so remarkably under developmental state policies, some in southern Africa advocated similar models. Analysts sympathetic to such alternatives agree that the governments that pursued them sometimes made mistakes that hindered the social vision they had hoped to implement. None, however, could be classified as predatory (until perhaps very recently in the case of Zimbabwe).

Any economic policy failures of the newly independent countries in the last twenty to thirty years must be judged in the context of regionalized warfare fueled by the confluence of desperate white regimes and Cold War politics. What economic policy initiatives would have succeeded under such circumstances? Moreover, the region's fairly recent widespread embrace of neoclassical liberalism and thereby its repudiation of socialist, developmental, or even Keynesian alternatives must also be seen in the context of the persistent promotion of neoliberalism by the most powerful governmental and business institutions in the world. As Paul Williams and Ian Taylor have suggested, this assertive global promotion frames the policy choices, delegitimizing alternatives and stifling much-needed debate within these societies and their governments, as well as across the whole region.[37]

Outside of ideological disputes among politicians and policy analysts, however, the more pressing questions are these: What works, and for whom? What helps to alleviate the immensurable poverty that guarantees that most people in the region will not live to be fifty? The remainder of the chapter addresses some of these issues in part by briefly describing both the successful and the failed experiments a few countries made with neoliberal policies.

Mozambique represents something of a showcase for the IFIs and their SAPs, which seem to have achieved their immediate goals. For example, in the 1990s Mozambique dramatically decreased government regulation of the economy in foreign exchange, trade, crop marketing, and the privatization or restructuring of more than 1,200 state enterprises, including banking. Growth rates averaged over 10 percent, except when floods ravaged the country. FDI has increased significantly (table 5.4), and new initiatives in infrastructure are underway. Yet except for the very welcome relief of the end of warfare, the economic plight of average citizens in the country has improved only marginally. Mozambique continues to be not only one of the poorest nations in the world but one of the most dependent on international aid. Therefore, it suffers the long-term consequences of indebtedness.

Despite its showcase status, Mozambique won a dispute with the IMF over cashews. This victory demonstrates the power and wisdom of persistent local officials faced with determined IFI trade liberalization. In 2000, after a five-year campaign by the government, the IMF and WBG finally allowed Mozambique to ban the export of unprocessed cashew nuts and to protect its expanding sugar industry. The government wanted to create and safeguard tens of thousands of industrial jobs processing cashews and sugar. The IFIs had argued that free trade, that is, allowing unrestricted export of unprocessed cashew nuts to India, would bring more long-term benefits, including higher prices to farmers, even though thousands of industrial workers would lose their jobs to Indian processors. Contrary to IFI predictions, however, under free trade the income for farmers fell when, as a monopoly buyer, India pushed cashew prices down. Therefore, both the farmers and the workers in Mozambique lost out. Eventually the IFIs capitulated to the government's pressure to reverse course.[38]

Policy recommendations backfired in a similar way in Zimbabwe in the 1990s in SAPs applied there. Padraig Carmody documented the systematic collapse of Zimbabwe's textile and footwear industries, which the IFIs predicted would grow rapidly after the introduction of liberal reforms. By the late 1980s, some degree of policy change became necessary and inevitable. The country suffered high unemployment, low private investment, shortages of foreign exchange, and low levels of economic growth. Commercial farming stood to gain the most from SAPs, and the government adopted the reform package in part because a number of government ministers owned such farms. However, the IFIs deemed export-oriented, labor-intensive manufacturing industries to be already fairly efficient and potentially very efficient if labor costs were lowered and new investment undertaken. The SAP provided for, among other things, financial, exchange rate, and trade liberalization intended to make textiles and footwear more competitive internationally. Contrary to predictions, a boomerang effect occurred that basically deindustrialized the country in these sectors. By 1995, the World Bank acknowledged that trade liberalization was linked to significant losses of industry in countries such as Zimbabwe.[39]

Moreover, since the mid-1990s things have only gotten worse due to policies unrelated to SAPs, that is, the country's involvement in the Central African war, gross mismanagement accompanied by severe political repression by the Mugabe government, and disastrous manipulation of land reform policy.

Zambia's case provides an interesting mix of externally imposed and internally generated SAPs. After independence in 1964, the government of Kenneth Kuanda nationalized the copper mines and other foreign-held assets in an attempt to pursue policies more socialist in their orientation. By the early 1980s, however, President Kuanda had accepted structural adjustment imposed by IFIs, but he reversed course in 1987. As a consequence, all other sources of international finance dried up. In the country's first multiparty elections in 1991, the opposition group Movement for Multiparty Democracy (MMD) campaigned vigorously against Kuanda in part on the basis of failed economic policies, including high inflation and reluctance to privatize government-owned industries. The MMD offered voters a radical reorientation toward neoclassical liberalism, likening a new Zambia to a vision of Western-style democracy and capitalism. When MMD's candidate Chiluba won, the government normalized relations with the IFIs and reinstituted SAPs. Therefore, in Zambia's case, the adoption of neoclassical liberalism resulted in part from electoral politics in which the opposition party successfully convinced citizens that they should try something entirely different.[40] Since 1991, the government has leaned considerably on the economic expertise offered by the IFIs and has privatized or commercialized more than 300 state-owned enterprises. By 2000, the nation had lost some of its appetite for liberal reforms. Furthermore, the country is now deeper in debt. The economy grew a bit since 2000, but Zambia's economic fortunes continue to be highly dependent on erratic international copper prices. The country remains one of the poorest in the world.

Botswana also embraced neoclassical liberalism without external imposition of SAPs, but in contrast it is in many respects a success story, "an

African miracle."[41] In the last two decades the growth rate has been about 7 percent per year, the highest sustained in the developing world. As indicated earlier in the country profile, such growth rates are fueled in large part by the discovery soon after independence of remarkably rich diamond deposits, mined in a joint venture with Anglo American. The government consistently gets high marks for sound management, prudent budgetary policies, avoiding rampant corruption, the accumulation of substantial foreign exchange reserves, and keeping the small amount of debt under control. Investments in human capital and infrastructure have taken the country from one of the poorest in the world at independence to a middle-income country today. Despite these noteworthy accomplishments, however, most of the population continues to live in poverty, suffering high unemployment and, as will be seen in the next section, one of the highest rates of HIV/AIDS in the world.

In the early 1990s in anticipation of the 1994 elections, the ANC in South Africa campaigned vigorously for an economy based essentially on a Keynesian or demand-side model of capitalism wherein the government would spend considerable sums for social services such as housing and education. Such a vision built on the principles contained in its 1955 Freedom Charter, which outlines a benevolent state that works to provide justice, equality, and economic prosperity. Unlike the charter, however, which reflected a more socialist and nationalist orientation, the 1994 platform essentially embraced capitalism.[42]

The ANC's primary election opponent, the National Party (NP), campaigned for neoclassical liberal economic policies such as the supply-side orientation advocated by IFIs. Ironically, this stood in sharp contrast to the more mercantilist policies (dramatically skewed in favor of the white minority) on which the NP government had run the country for many decades. When apartheid officials realized the inevitability of black rule, they quickly began to embrace what they saw as the virtues of privatizing publicly held enterprises.

Once elected, the ANC adopted a Reconstruction and Development Program (RDP) that reflected a Keynesian approach. RDP emphasized housing, training, jobs, and services that responded to the concerns and interests of the party's constituents, including the powerful labor unions that were so key in ending apartheid. From the start, however, President Mandela and the ANC signaled that they were more open to neoclassical liberalism than their campaign might have indicated. In 1996, only two years after the election, in the face of strong opposition from the labor unions that helped to put them in power, the ANC government replaced the RDP with Growth, Employment, and Redistribution (GEAR), a new blueprint that shifted policies decidedly in favor of neoliberalism. Some in government and business argued that from the perspective of economic globalization, neoliberalism was "the only game in town."[43]

GEAR favors, among other things, privatization, improving the climate for business and foreign direct investment, trade liberalization, restrained government spending on social programs, and low indebtedness. Analysts explain this apparent sudden change as an indication of the government's "acute awareness of the importance of foreign investment and the importance of the IFIs' 'good housekeeping seal of approval' in luring foreign investment." The ANC has strengthened its relationship with the large conglomerates at the same time that it has risked its close alliance with labor. Furthermore, the government has embraced and promoted the arms and weapons industries built in the apartheid years as a reliable and easy means of making money in the world economy.[44]

The results of GEAR so far are mixed. Among the positive outcomes are low inflation, a reversal of the negative growth rates of the 1980s to low levels of growth in the 1990s, modest levels of FDI, the transfer of economic opportunities and wealth to a small black elite, and increased prosperity for wealthy Afrikaners (with their businesses surging from 24 to 36 percent of the JSE). Some of the negative outcomes are the loss of about 500,000 jobs in the first five years, with unemployment already running very high; the provision of more than 1 million houses for the over 4 million poor people the government intended to help; a slow start on the promised land redistribution program; high levels of crime; and the privatization of water utilities with the consequence of the outbreak of cholera and other waterborne diseases in some areas, as well as water being cut off for those who cannot afford to pay.[45]

In 2001, Thabo Mbeki led the presidents of Nigeria, Algeria, Senegal, and Egypt to launch an initiative known as the New Partnership for Africa's Development (NEPAD). Billed as a Marshall Plan for Africa, NEPAD invokes the U.S. government's model of massive infusion of aid to rebuild Europe after World War II. The partnership's goals are to restore peace and security, to eradicate poverty, and to place African countries, individually and collectively, on a path of sustainable growth and development. NEPAD aims to halt the marginalization of Africa in economic globalization by attracting resources, financing, and technology partnerships and by stimulating human and institutional capacity building. The presidents promised to hold each other accountable to political standards of supporting democracy within their own countries and across the continents. Many find such collaboration and accountability between African governments to be a promising and creative aspect of NEPAD. Its development strategy basically embraces neoclassical liberalism, which critics argue will undermine its other goals. Although its recent launch makes a full evaluation impossible, one analysis suggested:

> NEPAD is in many respects a marketing strategy for Africa that attempts to overcome the negative image and sentiment that Africa generates in the consciousness of many political, business, and civil society circles outside the continent. It has, for whatever reasons, received much acclaim and has won international political respectability that could be harnessed for the benefit of the continent.[46]

Whatever the region's internally generated or externally imposed economic policies, the fundamental issue for most people is how well these economies address basic needs. The next section ends the chapter by investigating some indicators of quality of life for the people of southern Africa and by examining the role of women in development. The discussion therefore now turns to concrete outcomes that affect the lives (and deaths) of people every day, in some respects the culmination of both the policies that governments choose as well as the global, regional, and local structures and processes that frame their range of options.

POVERTY AND SURVIVAL

For the majority in the region, life is short, often lived in brutal conditions. A minority, however, have a standard of living as high as that found in any Western country. A few people have extraordinary wealth. Some economic conditions have worsened in recent years, while others have improved. Tables 5.6 and 5.7 show data on life expectancy, health, and poverty. For example, access to improved sources of water and health services is much better in South Africa and Botswana than in the other countries. South Africa, Swaziland, and Zimbabwe suffer the most unequal income distribution. Although the mortality rates for children under five are improving overall, life expectancy is declining, as are population growth rates. For example, as of 2000, people from Malawi, Mozambique, Swaziland, Zambia, and Zimbabwe could expect to live on average into their thirties. Thirty years earlier, many would have lived into their fifties, a figure that is no longer typical for any country in the region and an appalling trend. The percentage of the population living in urban areas has grown in recent decades, and one consequence is overcrowding and sanitation problems. Two diseases that ravage poor people everywhere are tuberculosis and HIV/AIDS, both of which are alarmingly high in the region.

For decades, the nations of southern Africa have faced with mixed success substantial challenges in addressing poverty and creating sustained economic development. Regional wars and entrenched racial discrimination have compounded the difficulties associated with these challenges. Now, however, the globalized pandemic of HIV/AIDS has struck with a vengeance. It threatens to reverse many of the hopeful signs that life would improve for the majority of the people in the region.

HIV/AIDS

HIV/AIDS affects Africa worse than any other part of the world. In 2001, 28.5 million people across the continent were living with HIV/AIDS—about 70 percent of the world's total—even though Africa has only about 10 percent of the world's population. The epidemic is most severe in southern Africa, and it has not yet reached a plateau, a "natural limit" beyond which it will not grow further. The number of AIDS-related deaths among young adults aged 15–34 is projected to peak in 2010–2015, when there will be more than seventeen times as many deaths as there would have been without AIDS. In Botswana, as shown in table 5.6, more than one-third of the adults are infected, with the rates rising to about 45 percent for pregnant women in urban areas. In South Africa, the percentage of adults is lower (about 20 percent), but because of the large differences in total population, the absolute numbers are higher and growing, about 4.7 million (compared to 300,000 in Botswana). This gives South Africa the distinction of having the highest number of HIV-positive people in

TABLE 5.6 Survival: Progress and Setbacks

	Life expectancy at birth (years)		Under-five mortality rate (per 1,000)		Tuberculosis cases (per 100,000)	Prevalence of HIV			Annual population growth		Urban population (as % of total)		
						Adults	Young people						
							Male	female					
						% age 15-49	% age 15-24	% age 15-24					
	1970	2000	1970	2000	2001	2001	2001	2001	1975-2001	2001-2015	1975	2001	2015
Angola	38	40	300	260	197	6	2.23	5.74	2.8	2.9	17.8	34.8	44.1
Botswana	56	40	142	110	224	39	16.08	37.49	2.9	0.2	12.8	49.4	56
Lesotho	50	35	190	132	277	31	17.40	38.08	1.8	0.3	14	26.7	32.7
Malawi	41	38	330	183	242	15	6.35	14.89	3.1	1.9	7.7	15.1	21.3
Mozambique	41	38	278	197	125	13	6.13	14.67	2.1	1.5	8.7	33.2	48.2
Namibia	50	44	155	67	221	23	11.10	24.29	2.8	0.9	20.6	31.4	39.4
South Africa	54	48	115	71	237	20	10.66	25.63	2.1	0.3	48.0	57.6	67.2
Swaziland	47	34	196	149	627	33	15.23	39.49	2.8	0.1	14	26.7	32.7
Zambia	50	32	181	202	445	22	8.07	20.98	2.8	1.3	34.8	39.8	45.2
Zimbabwe	56	33	138	123	493	34	12.38	33.00	2.8	0.2	19.6	36	45.9

SOURCES: United Nations Development Programme, *Human Development Report 2003* (New York: Oxford University Press, 2003); UNAIDS, *Report on the Global HIV-AIDS Epidemic 2002*, www.unaids.org/barcelona/presskit/barcelona%20report.

TABLE 5.7 Poverty

	Population w/o access			Share of income or consumption		Daily per capita supply of calories	Food production index (1989–91=100)	Children 10–14 in the labor force % of age group
	To improved water (%)	To health services (%)	To sanitation (%)	Poorest 20% (%)	Richest 20% (%)			
	2000	1981–1993	1990–1998	1993–1997	1993–1997	1997	1998	2000
Angola	62	76	60	**	**	1,903	143	26
Botswana	5	14	45	2.2	70.3	2,183	91	14
Lesotho	22	20	62	1.4	70.7	2,243	100	21
Malawi	43	20	97	4.9	56.1	2,043	116	31
Mozambique	43	70	66	6.5	46.5	1,832	140	32
Namibia	23	**	38	1.4	78.7	2,183	124	17
South Africa	14	**	13	2.0	61.5	2,990	97	0
Swaziland	**	45	41	2.7	64.4	2,483	96	12
Zambia	36	25	29	3.3	56.6	1,970	94	16
Zimbabwe	17	29	48	4.6	55.7	2,145	93	27

SOURCES: United Nations Development Programme, *Human Development Reports 2000 and 2003* (New York: Oxford University Press, 2000 and 2003); World Bank, *World Development Indicators 2002*. (Washington, D.C.: World Bank, 2002).

[1] Data refer to the most recent year available during the period specified in the column heading.

the world. Twenty-five percent of young women in South Africa suffer infection, as do 300,000 children. Estimates suggest that 1.5 million children in South Africa will be orphaned by the year 2010 as a result of AIDS.

One in every three adults in Zimbabwe has the virus, one in every five in Zambia, and one in about seven in Mozambique. Life expectancy is dropping in every country in the region. A person who turned fifteen in 2000 in Lesotho has a 74 percent chance of becoming infected with HIV by the age of fifty, and as already stated, most people in southern Africa cannot expect to see their fiftieth birthday. Many will not reach forty. Some analysts assert that the world has not witnessed a plague this severe since the Black Death killed at least one-fourth of Europe's population in the fourteenth century.[47]

No single factor accounts for the rapid spread of HIV/AIDS in southern Africa. The primary means of transmission still appears to be heterosexual intercourse, but recent studies suggest that unsafe blood transfusions, unsafe injections, and other tainted health-care treatments account for more transmissions than had previously been known.[48] Sexual transmission increases under certain conditions such as warfare; population displacement due to war; large numbers of single, migrant men (as in the mining communities in the region); long-term travel along transit routes for commerce; and insecure livelihoods, driving women especially to become commercial sex workers. Although as of 2002 the wars in or near the region have all abated, one estimate suggests that as many as 60 percent of the military personnel in Angola have the virus. Outside of the military, however, all of the conditions that enhance transmission pertain to southern Africa.[49]

The economic impact is staggering. HIV/AIDS strikes hard at the 15–45 age group, those who constitute the most productive members of society and who play a critical role in stabilizing families. In Zambia, for example, 65 percent of households where the mother died had dissolved. Monthly disposable income fell by more than 80 percent in two-thirds of families where the father died. In the Free State Province of South Africa, medical expenses and funerals related to HIV/AIDS absorbed an average of twenty-one months of savings. In rural areas, fewer people are able to work the fields.[50]

The region's already fragile social service delivery systems have become overloaded. In Zimbabwe, for example, 50 percent of all patients in hospital wards suffered from AIDS, and the number of beds needed for such patients exceeded the total number available in Swaziland by 2004 and will in Namibia by 2005. Meanwhile, the inadequate number of health-care staff have become overwhelmed by stress and the danger of work. In Malawi and Zambia, rates of illness and death among health-care professionals have increased more than fivefold. In all of southern Africa, training for doctors and nurses would have to increase by 25–40 percent in 2001–2010 to compensate for the losses. Children who do not attend school either stay home to tend to sick family or can no longer afford school fees. In Swaziland, school enrollment has fallen 20–36 percent because children have been lost to or orphaned by AIDS, with girls affected most. One study in Zimbabwe found rates of HIV to be 19 percent for male teachers and 29 percent for female teachers. The South African Democratic Teachers Union claims that in 2000–2001, AIDS-related deaths among teachers rose by over 40 percent.[51]

Businesses report that HIV/AIDS hinders their operations because of increases in absenteeism and loss in productivity. One study in the region estimated that "the combined impact of AIDS-related absenteeism, productivity declines, health-care expenditures, and recruitment and training expenses could cut profits by at least 6–8 percent." Other research reports that 23 percent of skilled workers in South Africa will be HIV positive by 2005.[52]

At the same time that the pandemic requires more resources and services from all sectors of society, including the government, it also undermines the capacity to provide such resources and services. A number of studies on the macroeconomic impact of the pandemic conclude that the net effect on GDP is large and negative. The UN estimates, for example, that "[b]y the beginning of the next decade, South Africa, which represents about 40 percent of sub-Saharan Africa's economic output, faces a real gross domestic product 17 percent lower than it would have been without AIDS."[53] But AIDS will not likely lower unemployment, despite the fact that the unskilled laborers suffer disproportionately from the disease. Furthermore, the economic risk for potential foreign investors in the region has increased substantially. With such monumental impact across entire societies, massive social dislocation and civil unrest could easily follow.

How are governments and other institutions inside and outside the region responding? As might be expected, their responses demonstrate the interaction of local, regional, and global factors. Compared to other governments in Africa (such as in Uganda and Senegal) or elsewhere in the world (such as in Brazil), policymakers in southern Africa have been slow to address the crisis. A number now pioneer prevention and treatment programs, however, having been hounded by activists in INGOs such as Oxfam, Médecins Sans Frontières (Doctors Without Borders), and the International HIV/AIDS Alliance and aided by outside funding organizations such as the Kaiser Family Foundation and the Bill and Melinda Gates Foundation. UNICEF, UNAIDS, the World Health Organization (WHO), and other UN-related agencies also play a major role. Recognizing the toll the pandemic takes on the productivity of their workers, large multinational corporations have also begun to institute programs.

President Mbeki of South Africa proved to be the region's most controversial leader in his resistance to address the pandemic. Soon after he took office, he questioned the crucial link between HIV and AIDS and subsequently went further to assert that AIDS caused only a tiny proportion of deaths in the country. Many in his own government, in addition to church leaders and activists, severely criticized his statements as well as the policies that blocked needed medical efforts to address the crisis. The Pretoria High Court, for example, ruled against some of Mbeki's apparent obstructions to treatment.

In contrast, the government of Botswana has exercised considerable political will to marshal local and global resources to offer both treatment and prevention. For example, in 1999, Botswana became the first country in Africa to implement a mother-to-child transmission (MTCT) program combined with voluntary counseling and testing. By 2001, the health clinics across the whole country had embraced the approach. When a mother knows she is HIV-positive, she might choose to use preventative antiretroviral (ARV) drugs, elective cesarian section, or replacement feeding instead of breast feeding, all of which have proven to decrease dramatically the chances that newborns will become infected. When ARV drugs became more widely available, Botswana quickly took advantage of this access and worked to get over 100,000 people into treatment within the first year. With the largest number of HIV cases in the world, the government of South Africa has come under considerable pressure from inside and outside the country to stem the pandemic, in part because what happens there has an impact on the region, the continent, and the world.

Multinational corporations in South Africa have moved more quickly and decisively than the government to address the issue in their own work arenas. The automaker Ford South Africa, for example, put condom distribution machines in workplace toilets, dramatically increasing usage. Under some pressure from its unions, the mining conglomerate Anglo American announced in 2002 that it would provide ARV drug therapy to its HIV-positive employees. The company employs about 90,000 workers in the region, about one-fourth of whom have HIV. Although the company will spend considerable sums each year for treatment, officials expect to see the returns on their investment. Anglo estimated that HIV/AIDS cost their operations between $4 and $6 (and rising) per ounce of gold produced. Most miners come from poor and remote regions and live in hostels, separated from their families. Under such conditions, the sex industry thrives. Therefore, for some years companies such as Anglo American have implemented mass distribution of condoms, awareness campaigns, and some medical treatment for the sex workers. Providing ARV takes their ongoing efforts to a new level.[54]

Contention over ARV offers an interesting illustration of the connection between global and local actors in the provision of health care, as well as the interplay of the economic and political domains of globalization. ARV drug therapies reduce the need to treat opportunistic infections (e.g., tuberculosis) that plague those who have HIV/AIDS, reduce the amount of care necessary to treat patients' primary disease, and effectively inhibit transmission. People in rich countries have had access to ARV drugs for many years. Access for people in poor countries came only recently as the result of a concerted transnational advocacy campaign to lower the price of these drugs. The campaign was spearheaded by activists inside and outside of southern Africa, along with INGOs and UN agencies.

By 2000, the campaign began to show results, which accelerated in late 2001 when the 142 members of the WTO issued the Doha Declaration on the Trade-Related Aspects of Intellectual Property Rights (TRIPS) Agreement and Public Health. TRIPS are international legal patent protections mandated by the WTO to safeguard governments and businesses from the theft of their intellectual property, a problem acutely compounded by globalization. Prior to the creation of the WTO, many countries in Africa, Asia, and Latin America had no intellectual property laws. This meant that nations such as Egypt, Brazil, and India could develop generic drug industries with little or no regard for other nations' legal protections for intellectual property. Under WTO rules, however, all members must honor drug patents.

A court case brought by the Pharmaceutical Manufacturers Association (PMA) against a South Africa law limiting this strict intellectual property regime directed the glare of global attention to the emotionally charged debate over profits and returns on investment for pharmaceutical MNCs versus the need to provide public health in poor countries. Activists pointed out that in a historical precedent dating back to 1928, penicillin was considered so crucial to public health across the world that it was never patented. Eventually the PMA dropped its suit against South Africa, and the WTO addressed the issue comprehensively in a global agreement forged at its meeting in Doha, Qatar.[55]

Although not yet fully implemented because of the opposition of some governments and companies, the Doha Declaration states that governments have a right to protect public health and to promote access to medicines for all, even when patents are at stake. In the face of public health crises such as those of HIV/AIDS, tuberculosis, malaria, and other epidemics, governments can issue a compulsory license authorizing the use of patented products. This means that a non-patent-holding local manufacturer may produce the necessary drugs for domestic use with reasonable compensation being paid to the patent holder.[56] Thus, the international legal system relaxed patent regulations a bit to give more license to national governments to provide health security for their people.

The debate over affordable drugs, however, often gets pitted against the debate over how to deliver effective health care. The region has never had sufficient resources to forestall diseases for which prevention or cure is routine elsewhere, such as malaria and tuberculosis. Pandemics like HIV/AIDS provide a much greater challenge. Clearly, poor countries need additional funds to cope.

The UN began operating the Global Fund to Fight AIDS, Tuberculosis, and Malaria in 2002 and by 2003 had $2.1 billion to spend out of an estimated $10 billion needed annually. In his State of the Union address in 2003, President George W. Bush called for the U.S. government to spend $15 billion across five years to address HIV/AIDS. Actual funding is not likely to reach this level, and most of it will be spent bilaterally, not through the UN Global Fund. Meanwhile, in 2002 overall levels of aid through official development assistance from rich countries to poor ones as well as from private sources continued to decline to their lowest levels in twenty years.[57] The UN estimates that up to 80 percent of the resources necessary to address the AIDS epidemic in Africa will have to come from international sources, but those with the most resources have yet to commit them to such a cause.

Furthermore, the globalization of neoclassical economic policies counteracts the ability of governments in poor countries to provide social services to address the crisis. In the last decade or so, southern African governments have been slow to embrace both prevention and treatment, but when they have, they run into difficulties of limited budgets for health care. Moreover, in countries like Mozambique where the IMF and WBG have imposed SAPs, the cutbacks in government spending on health care have been exacerbated by rules that prohibit supplementing government expenditures with outside funds for addressing HIV/AIDS (unless the domestic budget is slashed further). Therefore, even if the Global Fund does raise sufficient money to tackle these problems appropriately, IFIs may obstruct recipient governments' ability to make maximum use of the aid.

When focusing on prevention with or without help from outside the region, one of the most effective measures to prevent HIV/AIDS is to address the status of women. Gender lies at the heart of the pandemic, according to Stephen Lewis, the UN special envoy for HIV/AIDS in Africa, who stated that "there has rarely been a disease which is so rooted in the inequality between the sexes."[58] Table 5.6 demonstrates that across the region of southern Africa, young women are more than twice as likely as young men to be infected. Due to economic dependency and social norms, women have difficulty denying men sex. Furthermore, teenage girls suffer higher infection rates than boys because older men prey on girls. Yet women and girls often bear primary responsibility for caring for sick family members and get neglected when they become sick. The status of women relates closely to many other socioeconomic problems in the region as well, and for this reason, the discussion now turns to gender-related development issues.

Women and Development

Table 5.8 displays data on women and development. Like the Human Development Index (HDI), the Gender-Related Development Index (GDI) includes such measures as life expectancy at birth, education, and standard of living, but the GDI adjusts these for disparities between women and men. Both indicators use 1.0 as the highest score (an indication of equality between the sexes) and 0 as the lowest. Scores for southern African countries vary between a low of 0.341 for Mozambique and a high of 0.678 for South Africa.

Life-expectancy patterns show slight advantages for women, a rate that could change with young women's higher levels of HIV/AIDS infection. Literacy shows greater disparities, however, with at least four out of the ten countries reporting significantly lower rates for females than males. (Interestingly, females have higher rates in two cases, Botswana and Lesotho.) In Mozambique, men are more than twice as likely to be literate than women are. Malawi also shows a very serious distortion. Birth rates are declining across the region as a whole, however, generally a sign of progress for women.

There is considerable debate over the impact of colonialism on women. Some analysts contend that African women lived in more equal relations with men prior to colonialism. For example, chapter 2 mentioned the famed resistance of Queen Nzinga of Angola to Portuguese colonialism. However, there was substantial variation in women's precolonial status. The Tswana and Shona (now in Botswana and Zimbabwe) considered women to be "legal minors" in very subordinate positions, whereas women could be "headmen" in the Tonga (now in Zambia). Most analysts conclude, however, that imperial conquest on the whole either undermined women's power and roles or caused them to decline further within an already subordinate position. For example, April Gordon has stated:

> The commercialization of agriculture through the introduction of cash crops altered the customary gender division of labor in ways mostly disadvantageous to women. Men were taught to grow new cash crops . . . for export, while women continued to grow food crops for the family and local consumption. Men were forced into the wage economy to work in the mines, on the plantations, or in town; most women remained in the rural areas, often assuming the responsibilities their absent menfolk could no longer perform. Schooling and the teaching of new skills were made available primarily to males. All in all, although both men and women were exploited within the colonial economy, men gained some access to important resources such as money, skills, land, and education less available to women.[59]

TABLE 5.8 Gender-Related Development

	Gender-related development index (GDI)	Life expectancy at birth (years)		Adult literacy rate (% age 15 and above)		Total fertility rate (births per woman)	
	2003 Value	2001 Female	Male	2001 Female	Male	1975	2000
Angola	**	41.6	38.8	**	**	6.6	7.2
Botswana	0.611	46	43.3	80	75.3	6.7	3.7
Lesotho	0.497	41.7	35.4	93.9	73.3	5.7	3.8
Malawi	0.386	40.2	40.4	45.3	73.8	7.4	6.1
Mozambique	0.341	40.9	37.4	30	61.2	6.6	5.6
Namibia	0.622	49	45.5	81.9	83.4	6.6	4.6
South Africa	0.678	54.4	47.7	85	86.3	5.4	2.6
Swaziland	0.536	39.9	36.5	79.4	81.3	6.9	4.5
Zambia	0.376	33.4	33.3	72.7	85.8	7.8	5.6
Zimbabwe	0.489	35.4	35.5	85.5	93.3	7.6	3.9

SOURCES: United Nations Development Programme, *Human Development Report 2003* (New York: Oxford University Press, 2003); World Bank, *World Development Indicators 2002*, (Washington, D.C.: World Bank, 2002).

Regardless of these debates about what happened in the past, considerable research now quite clearly demonstrates the link between the status of women and the overall well-being of a society. The World Bank asserts that women's education is the single most influential investment that can be made in the developing world. Women's education and literacy are clearly important. Education gives women more power over family decisions. Women who are better educated have greater freedom to pursue work other than continuous child rearing, have increased opportunities to widen their horizons in the future, and more practically, have better access to information on family planning, thereby reducing fertility rates as well as the mortality rates of children. This makes the literacy gaps in countries such as Malawi, Mozambique, Zambia, and Zimbabwe all the more alarming.

Central to the debate about women and development and to the women themselves is the question of how to increase women's access to and control over resources. In rural areas, women's ownership of land and access to credit often yields more crops for family use. The commercialization and mechanization of agriculture often works against land ownership by women and the family's food supply. In Zimbabwe, for example, on the whole, women remain excluded from control over land and cattle, and men still control women's access to economic resources. Women's ownership of businesses and access to credit also add considerably to the welfare of their families. In both Zimbabwe and Lesotho, for example, women already run more than 65 percent of the informal sector businesses, but in Lesotho as well as Botswana, Namibia, and Swaziland, men hold permanent guardianship over their wives, who have no right to manage property on their own.[60]

Yet important changes have been made. In Mozambique, women have begun to acquire land titles, have expanded their economic activities into nontraditional jobs, for example becoming electricians and masons, and began to open their own bank accounts in the early 1990s. A predominantly female organization, the General Union of Cooperatives, built more than 200 farm cooperatives that supply Maputo with most of its fruits and vegetables. In Zimbabwe, the government enacted a law on estates in 1997, making a man's wife and children his automatic beneficiaries when he dies and allowing the matrimonial home to remain with the surviving spouse.[61]

The nation in the region with the highest GDI is South Africa (0.695). One analyst characterizes South Africa as one of two "trailblazers in efforts to achieve gender equity in formal politics." (Uganda is the other.)[62] The South African constitution's Bill of Rights guarantees equal rights for women (although, as in other parts of the region, these can be challenged in local communities by customary African law enforced by traditional authorities). Since 1994 and its first democratic elections, South Africa has consistently ranked in the top ten nations in the world for women's numerical representation in national parliaments. In 1999, women held about 30 percent of the seats in both houses of the South African legislature, and they held about 38 percent of executive cabinet positions. In contrast, in the United States in 1999, women held about 14 percent of the seats in Congress and made up about 32 percent of the cabinet.[63] Women's political strength in South Africa results in part from their key roles in the anti-apartheid movement.

South Africa also leads the whole continent on two issues that women's human rights organizations often promote: reproductive rights and criminalizing violence against women. The country's Bill of Rights guarantees women access to reproductive health services as well as the right to make decisions regarding the number and spacing of children. Legislation was passed in 1996 ensuring the legal right to abortion on request during the first trimester of pregnancy. In 1993, the government outlawed marital and statutory rape.[64]

Whether coping with poverty, HIV/AIDS, education, or sustained economic development, the government leaders could increase their prospects of success by responding to the concerns and perspectives of women, improving their access to and control over resources, and thereby uplifting the entire society.

CONCLUSION

The interaction of local, regional, and global economic structures and processes has significant impact on the lives of the people and nations of southern Africa, as has been true for more than 300 years. The end of the Cold War and the fall of apartheid hastened an even greater integration of the region into the global economy. For example, some institutions that had very local origins in the colonial economies have now become global, such as minerals-based MNCs. Some local concentrations of global phenomena, for example the HIV/AIDS pandemic, threaten the health of both the region and the whole world.

Although there are significant differences across these ten political economies, regionally they all face many common problems and possibilities. Most of the governments have shifted their economic orientation across recent decades to comply with the prevailing global ideology of neoclassical liberalism promoted by IFIs and other powerful world actors. Some of the governments, however, occasionally exhibit the willingness to resist such pressures, opting for more locally driven policies or more appropriate models of development.

This chapter began by stating a dilemma: If global forces have such a powerful impact on the economies of southern Africa, what possibilities are there for the people and nations to shape their future in response to their own concerns and perspectives? In contrast to the political, military, and cultural domains where, on balance, people and governments seem to be gaining greater control, in the economic domain they are increasingly relinquishing it. Whatever the similarities and differences are among these ten local economies, their ties to the world economy have all become tighter. Regional trends and organizations do not offset this reality. To the contrary, they reinforce it.

Disaster potentially looms, if it has not already hit. The majority of people in southern Africa experience their cruel state of poverty deepening and widening with the HIV/AIDS pandemic. Between the world economy and the plight of ordinary people stand the region's governments. In the context of accelerating economic globalization, can they and will they demonstrate the ingenuity to harness the extraordinary wealth and capacity of their environment and people to build prosperity for all? Will they be able to transform the extraordinary challenges they face into opportunities for creating a new future? In such complex circumstances, answers to these questions do not come easily. No doubt they will be mixed.

Early in the new century, discussions among the most prominent actors in economic globalization have been framed and dominated by only one out of a number of perspectives of political economy—neoclassical liberalism. As previous chapters have shown, however, other domains of globalization such as the political and cultural dimensions often offer alternatives. Globalization is not a monolith, even in the economic domain. The international community has the capacity to provide powerful, productive partnerships that strengthen the possibility of people in the region deciding and profiting from their own future. With such potential, perhaps disaster can be averted for many living in southern Africa. To state this more hopefully, perhaps many will see their children have a much better future.

Notes

1. David Held et al., *Global Transformations: Politics, Economics, and Culture* (Stanford, CA: Stanford University Press, 1999), pp. 150, 190, 236–237.

2. A market can be defined as the place where the forces of supply and demand in an economy determine prices, output, and methods of production. Gilpin argues that markets are populated with powerful actors such as large businesses, including agribusiness, and powerful labor unions that exercise enormous influence over the market. See Robert Gilpin, *Global Political Economy: Understanding the International Economic Order* (Princeton, NJ: Princeton University Press, 2001), especially chap. 2.

3. The term "liberalism" can be confusing. From the perspective of political economy, liberalism denotes the philosophical foundation advocated by Smith and others such as David Ricardo, all of whom wanted a much smaller role for the state. In contemporary po-

litical parlance, "liberal" is often contrasted with "conservative" as terms distinguishing, for example, the Democratic Party from the Republican Party in the United States. This is *not* the way in which the term "liberal" is being used here. In terms of economic policies, both the Democratic and Republican parties are liberal in the classical sense being used here.

4. The term "neoclassical" or "neoliberal" will be used as shorthand for neoclassical liberalism.

5. In its original form, mercantilism represented less a coherent philosophy than a set of policies aimed at strengthening the nation and the monarch through political manipulation of economic processes. The term, sometimes renamed neomercantilism, however, continues to refer to the philosophical perspective that the government can and should intervene in the economy for the sake of the overall well-being of the nation. Alexander Hamilton and Friedrich List in the late eighteenth and early nineteenth centuries advocated forms of economic nationalism, a historical tradition and philosophical perspective in keeping with what is generally called mercantilism or more recently, neomercantilism.

6. Peter Evans, *Embedded Autonomy: States and Industrial Transformation* (Princeton, NJ: Princeton University Press, 1995), p. 45.

7. Jeffrey D. Sachs, "Resolving the Debt Crisis of Low-Income Countries," *Brookings Papers on Economic Activity* 1 (2002).

8. John Williamson, "Democracy and the 'Washington Consensus,'" *World Development* 21, no. 8 (1993): 1329–1336.

9. John Rapley, *Understanding Development: Theory and Practice in the Third World,* 2nd ed. (Boulder, CO: Lynne Rienner, 2002), pp. 73–76.

10. Gilpin, *Global Political Economy,* p. 41.

11. Michael Massing, "Challenging the Growth Gurus," *New York Times,* October 19, 2002. See also Joseph E. Stiglitz, *Globalization and Its Discontents* (New York: W. W. Norton, 2002).

12. See Paul Krugman, "Austerity Good Economic Policy for Every Country but Ours," *State Newspaper,* July 19, 2001; and Robert J. Samuelson, "Brazil's Election Illustrates Tide of Free Markets Turning," *State Newspaper,* October 16, 2002.

13. PPP US$ is a symbol for purchasing power parity, which is a rate of exchange that accounts for price differences across countries, allowing international comparisons of real output and incomes. PPP US$1 has the same purchasing power as $1 has in the United States.

14. Data for the discussion on each country came from several sources: Tables 5.1 and 5.2; Kwame A. Appiah and Henry Louis Gates Jr., eds., *Africana: The Encyclopedia of the African and African American Experience* (New York: Basic Civitas, 1999); F. Jeffress Ramsay, ed., *Global Studies: Africa,* 9th ed. (Guilford, CT: McGraw-Hill/Dushkin, 2001); U.S. Government, CIA, *The World Factbook 2002* (www.odci.gov/cia/publications/ factbook); and World Bank, Country Briefs (www.worldbank.org).

15. Dumping is selling a product as an export at a lower price than that charged in the home market or below the cost of production; tariffs are taxes levied on imports, particularly to protect local businesses, such as textiles in the United States; technical barriers often relate to quality controls, environmental protection, or similar regulations.

16. Quoted in David Simon, "Trading Spaces: Imagining and Positioning the 'New' South Africa Within the Regional and Global Economies," *International Affairs* 77, no. 2 (2001): 396.

17. To qualify as ODA, the loans must be concessional, that is, they must have lower interest rates, longer grace periods, and longer repayment periods than commercial or hard loans. The grant element of these loans should be at least 25 percent to count as ODA. Wealthy nations pledged in the early 1990s to raise their aid donations to 0.7 percent of their GDP. Denmark spends almost 1 percent of its GDP, followed by Norway (0.9), the Netherlands (0.8), Sweden (0.7) France (0.4), Australia (0.28), Japan (0.28), Britain (0.27), Germany (0.26), and the United States (0.1).

18. International Development Association and the International Monetary Fund, *Heavily Indebted Poor Countries (HIPC) Initiative—Statistical Update, April 11, 2003,* www.worldbank.org/hipc. The most recent data on Mozambique's HIPC participation comes from www.worldbank.org/afr/mz/ctry_brief.htm.

19. The name is inspired by Hebrew scripture, which calls for jubilee, the reorganization of land rights to benefit the poor, every fifty years.

20. Quoted in Africa Action, "Towards a New State on Debt Cancellation," September 25, 2002, www.africaaction.org/desk/debt0209.htm.

21. Sachs, "Resolving the Debt Crisis," pp. 4, 19.

22. Table 5.2 shows a slight improvement in all these cases when growth rates are averaged 1975–2001 rather than 1975–1999, as in Sach's data.

23. Sachs, "Resolving the Debt Crisis," pp. 12–16.

24. Ibid., pp. 24–28.

25. Ibid., p. 23.

26. See www.debeersgroup.com/; www.mbendi.co.za/codb.htm; and Alan Cowell with Rachel L. Swarns, "$17.6 Billion Deal to Make De Beers Private Company," *New York Times,* February 16, 2001.

27. William Minter, *King Solomon's Mines Revisited* (New York: Basic Books, 1986), pp. 47–51; www.angloamerican.co.uk/; Padraig Carmody, "Between Globalisation and (Post) Apartheid: The Political Economy of Restructuring in South Africa," *Journal of Southern African Studies* 28, no. 2 (June 2002): 262–263.

28. Minter, *King Solomon's Mines*; and Nigel Worden, *The Making of Modern South Africa: Conquest, Segregation, and Apartheid* (Cambridge: Blackwell, 1994).

29. Carmody, "Between Globalisation and (Post) Apartheid," p. 262.

30. Leonard Thompson, *A History of South Africa,* rev. ed. (New Haven, CT: Yale University Press, 1995), pp. 206–207, 243–244.

31. Carmody, "Between Globalisation and (Post) Apartheid," pp. 262–263.

32. Rachel L. Swarns, "Awe and Unease as South Africa Stretches Out," *New York Times,* February 17, 2002; www.uneca.org/era2002.

33. "Jobless and Joyless," *Economist,* February 24, 2001.

34. Carmody, "Between Globalisation and (Post) Apartheid," p. 263.

35. Ibid., p. 263.

36. Ibid., pp. 264–265.

37. Paul Williams and Ian Taylor, "Neoliberalism and the Political Economy of the 'New' South Africa," *New Political Economy* 5, no. 1 (2000): 21.

38. Joseph Hanlon, "Mozambique Wins Long Battle over Cashew Nuts and Sugar," *Review of African Political Economy* 28, no. 2 (March 2001): 111–112. See also Joseph Hanlon, "Power Without Responsibility: the World Bank and Mozambican Cashew Nuts," *Review of African Political Economy* 27, no. 83 (March 2000): 29–45.

39. Padraig Carmody, "Neoclassical Practice and the Collapse of Industry in Zimbabwe: The Cases of Textiles, Clothing, and Footwear," *Economic Geography* 74, no. 4 (1998): 319–342.

40. Margaret Hanson and James J. Hentz, "Neocolonialism and Neoliberalism in South Africa and Zambia," *Political Science Quarterly* 114, no. 3 (1999): 479–502.

41. Abdi Ismail Samatar, *An African Miracle: State and Class Leadership and Colonial Legacy in Botswana Development* (Portsmouth, NH: Heinemann, 1999).

42. The Freedom Charter called for nationalization of the country's large conglomerates, but when legalized, the ANC moved away from advocating such policies in favor of retaining a capitalist form of economy.

43. Williams and Taylor, "Neoliberalism," p. 37.

44. Hanson and Hentz, "Neocolonialism and Neoliberalism," pp. 501–502.

45. Carmody, "Between Globalisation and (Post) Apartheid;" Solomon R. Benatar, "South Africa's Transition in a Globalizing World: HIV/AIDS as a Window and a Mirror," *International Affairs* 77, no. 2 (2001): 347–375; Rachel L. Swarns, "Farmland Battle Tests South African Leaders," *New York Times*, July 14, 2001; Rachel L. Swarns, "For South African Whites, Money Has No Color," *New York Times*, April 20, 2000; www.icij.org/dtaweb/water.

46. The South African Council of Churches, "Un-blurring the Vision: An Assessment of the New Partnership for Africa's Development," www.africaaction.org/docs02/nepa0206.htm; see also www.nepad.org.

47. Tina Rosenberg makes this comparison to the Black Death in "Look at Brazil," *New York Times Magazine*, January 28, 2001. The data on Africa and specific countries comes from United Nations Development Programme, *Human Development Report 2001* (New York: Oxford University Press, 2001), and UNAIDS (Joint United Nations Programme on HIV/AIDS), *Report on the Global HIV/AIDS Epidemic*, www.unaids.org/barcelona/presskit/barcelona%20report.

48. David Gisselquist et al., "HIV Infections in Sub-Sahara Africa Not Explained by Sexual or Vertical Transmission," *International Journal of STD and AIDS,* Royal Society of Medicine, October 2002, www.rsm.ac.uk./pub/std.htm.

49. UNAIDS, *Report on the Global HIV/AIDS Epidemic*, p. 25.

50. Ibid., pp. 47–50.

51. Ibid., pp. 50–53.

52. Ibid., pp. 54–58.

53. Ibid., p. 57.

54. Ibid., pp. 87, 111.

55. Hugh McCullum, "Patient Rights Priority over Pharmaceutical Profits," Southern African Research and Documentation, www.sardc.net/editorial/sanf/2001.

56. UNAIDS, *Report on the Global HIV/AIDS Epidemic*, p. 149.

57. Ibid., p. 170.

58. United Nations Integrated Regional Information Network (IRIN), "Interview with Stephen Lewis, UN Special Envoy," www.irinnews.org/ December 3, 2001.

59. April A. Gordon, "Women and Development," in April A. Gordon and Donald L. Gordon, *Understanding Contemporary Africa* (Boulder, CO: Lynne Rienner), p. 276.

60. Ibid., pp. 283–289.

61. Ibid., pp. 287–289.

62. Anne Marie Goetz, "Women in Politics and Gender Equity in Policy: South Africa and Uganda," *Review of African Political Economy* 76 (1998): 241–262.

63. United Nations Development Programme, *Human Development Report 2001* (New York: Oxford University Press, 2001), pp. 226–227.

64. Gordon, "Women and Development," pp. 284–287.

6

∘

Conclusion

THIS BOOK BEGAN BY INDICATING SOME OF THE CONTROVERSIES IN THE debates over globalization. Subsequent chapters analyzed some of the dilemmas faced by the nations of southern Africa in the contemporary era, with earlier history providing a context. This chapter summarizes how the region elucidates the interaction of global, regional, and local dynamics in world affairs.

All of the domains enumerated by Held et al. (i.e., political, military, economic, migrational, cultural, and environmental) apply to globalization, regionalism, and localism in southern Africa. The reach of political power, authority, and forms of rule in political globalization becomes evident through examination of regional history. European powers ventured contacts with the region's coastal areas in the fifteenth century and had fully imposed colonial occupation by the late nineteenth and early twentieth century. In the contemporary era, Africans embraced wholesale the nation-state system of governance initially imposed on them by the Europeans, including awkward and contentious territorial boundaries. Many in southern Africa died in violent confrontations, which had significant regional and global dynamics, over who would govern these nation-states under what forms of rule, a set of issues that is not yet fully resolved in places like Zimbabwe. Furthermore, these states' membership in regional and global IGOs such as the United Nations or the Southern Africa Development Community effectively gave outside actors permission to meddle in the internal affairs of these seemingly sovereign nations. Such multilayered "meddling" may or may not be welcome, but it is now legitimate in the era of contemporary political globalization.

Moreover, some southern African states do their own meddling abroad. For example, South Africa has sent troops to participate in various

UN peacekeeping missions and has sought diplomatically to mediate civil conflicts in a number of places, including Zimbabwe. In its constitution, South Africa has enthusiastically embraced the global norms of civil and political human rights and has extended them to include gays and lesbians. This unusual legal provision stakes out a clear position in a debate that remains deeply contentious for other governments, particularly in Africa, Asia, Latin America, and the Middle East.

The cultural globalization of the ideology of democracy and human rights is now so widespread that authoritarian and ruthless forms of local rule often evoke considerable attention from governmental and non-governmental actors abroad, as was the case with white minority regimes in the past and with Zimbabwe now. The global anti-apartheid movement and other transnational advocacy networks demonstrated convincingly that the political domain is a powerful arena in which ordinary people can organize to effect change across the world. Furthermore, individuals such as Nelson Mandela and Jonas Savimbi clearly illustrate the point through example that charismatic leaders wield considerable power and authority, for good or ill, in world politics.

The history of southern Africa also displays vividly the network of worldwide ties and relations in the military domain. The colonial conquest, the white minority's well-armed intransigence, and the imposition of the Cold War onto regional conflicts all played roles in military globalization. The seemingly intractable violent confrontation in Angola demonstrated that when Cold War sources of support for warring parties ended, the confrontation could transform into a new form of warlord-like struggle fueled by international marketing of diamonds and oil. Furthermore, the arms industry fostered by the South African government as a mechanism for economic development continues to proliferate weapons across the world.

The discussion in this book touched only briefly on the cultural flows and institutions across regions, civilizations, and continents related to southern Africa, that is, cultural globalization. Mention was made of the significance of Christianity, both in colonialism and in motivating many who worked for majority rule. Southern Africa also demonstrates the power of the local-to-global interplay of ideas, sometimes expressed through more formal ideologies. Multiracial and Africanist perspectives continue to contend in the region, although unlike other parts of the continent, ethnonationalism, a particularly virulent form of localism, has been remarkably rare. Socialist ideology seems to have lost out to capitalist ideology, but some other new system of ideas focused on the basic needs of people may come along to address the deep, seemingly entrenched material deprivations of most in the region. In other aspects of culture, more attention could be devoted to local and global interactions in music, literature, art, cinematography, archeology, and other areas about which this text has been able to provide only a few hints.

The same is true to a lesser degree in the environmental domain, the transformation of ecosystems that adversely affects the economic or demographic conditions of the life and health of human beings. Much more could be said about the earth and its plant and animal inhabitants in the region, as well as the impact of atmospheric conditions. The discussion here, however, has focused primarily on the spread of a disease, HIV/AIDS, which threatens to depopulate entire nations and perhaps the region. Such dramatic demographic changes in southern Africa could affect the rest of the world in a number of ways.

Like the other domains, the economic realm of trade, finance, and production demonstrates intimate local to global ties. When Europeans discovered the wealth available across southern Africa, many displayed a keen determination to capture and exploit these resources. The movement of large numbers of settlers to the region from the seventeenth to the twentieth centuries illustrates the migration domain of globalization, whereas the systematic recruitment of African labor to fit the needs of the white-owned mining industries elucidates the regionalization of migration. Land, capital, and production facilities in South Africa still remain largely in white hands. Since the end of apartheid, large South African companies have been acquiring significant assets in other parts of the region, further spreading their influence abroad. So far, South Africa has made only small attempts at internal land redistribution, whereas hasty, violent, and deeply politicized seizures of white farms in Zimbabwe, more than twenty years after independence, appear only to have achieved economic chaos and collapse.

Even if endowed with extraordinary natural resources, nations in the region predominantly export primary commodities, and the prices for many of these have declined overall in recent decades (except for oil). The value of these countries' imports regularly exceeds the value of exports, leading a number of them into chronic debt. Deep and lasting debt invites the global oversight of international financial institutions, which take considerable control over national economic policy decisions. Structural adjustment policies, sometimes externally imposed and sometimes internally embraced, mold virtually all the region's economies according to the perspective of neoclassical liberalism, the prevailing ideology of economic globalization. Under such guidance, governments postpone, perhaps indefinitely, their commitment to provide their populations with basic social services. Furthermore, all of these problems get compounded when governments, such as those of Mugabe in Zimbabwe or dos Santos in Angola, exhibit corrupt tendencies to enrich themselves and their loyalists at the expense of the nation.

Under the combined stress of the HIV/AIDS pandemic, the decline in social services, and recent warfare in some areas, insufficient investment has been made in human capital, that is, people's education, training, and skills. Poverty remains deeply embedded and pervasive in southern Africa, and life expectancy has dropped dramatically. IGOs and INGOs have mobilized substantial resources to address the HIV/AIDS crisis, and the World Bank's HIPC program has provided some short-term debt relief. Yet the material conditions in which most people live today do not provide a firm foundation upon which to enhance national or regional development.

Regionally, South Africa dominates in industry, trade relations, investment, and some other areas of finance. However, coordination through SADC, facilitated by aid from external sources, has improved infrastructure in some countries and may hold promise for strengthening their relations with both their large neighbor to the south and the global economy.

In summary, if judged by the plight of the majority of people, economic interactions across local, regional, and global arenas on the whole have not served southern Africa very well. Some significant signs of improvement can be found in a few places such as Botswana and Mozambique. The war in Angola ended only very recently, however, and South Africa's democracy is still quite new. Now that, for the first time in forty years the whole region is benefiting from a cessation of armed conflict, perhaps southern Africa will begin to show greater signs of translating majority rule into broadly shared and sustained prosperity in economics.

Southern Africa can demonstrate the significance of all domains of globalization, but the question still remains: Is one domain dominant? Much of the literature on globalization suggests that the economic domain eventually trumps all others. Clearly, economic dynamics are powerful and crucial, but the analysis in this book shows that globalization is both multidimensional and complex.

Across time, the political, military, migrational, and cultural (or ideological) domains have all had substantial impact. In the modern era, when colonialism and white minority rule took firm hold in the region, the political, military, cultural, and migrational arenas dominated. The contemporary era demonstrates shifting domains. At first, after World War II and until the end of the Cold War (1989–1990), the military, political, and cultural domains dominated. Furthermore, whereas political regionalization and globalization in the modern era meant the subjugation of blacks in the region, in the contemporary era regional and global political forces helped to bring freedom from white minority rule. After World War II, shifts in the cultural domain, with its powerful impact of ideas and ideology, buttressed these political movements.

The aftershocks of militarization that intimately linked local, regional, and global forces early in the contemporary era continue to be felt in the region. As wars subsided, however, economic globalization began to forge its way into the region with a renewed and more powerful presence. Indeed in some wars (e.g., the case of Mozambique), such economic penetration was a concession extracted as a condition for the cessation of hostilities. Therefore, the economic domain has become prominent only late in the contemporary era. This suggests that it may not remain dominant indefinitely.

However powerful they may be, economic factors alone rarely shape how local, regional, and global interactions unfold. For example, the impending possibility of large-scale depopulation due to HIV/AIDS demonstrates a massive impact in the environmental arena. This spills over dramatically into the economic, political, and cultural domains.

Is the global more important and powerful than the local? Are local actors capable of producing, affecting, or refusing to participate in world trends? Again, the analysis of southern Africa would suggest that there are no easy answers to these questions. The local-to-global interactions are multidimensional and complex across various domains. Sometimes the local, regional, and global contend against each other, with one or the other winning. Sometimes they synergistically reinforce one another. Sometimes they produce positive outcomes, sometimes negative, and an assessment of the overall positive or negative impact usually depends on the values of those doing the assessing.

Moreover, the penetration of global forces into local places is uneven, particularly in the poorest parts of southern Africa. Many in Mozambique and Malawi, for example, do not have reliable access to electricity, much less to the Internet. As the quote from Rosenau suggested in the first chapter, "[T]he local entity . . . is likely to mark the human landscape as far as one can see into the future even as it will also be continuously assaulted by the requirements of a global economy and the intrusion of communications technologies."[1]

The hallmark of the contemporary era is that the world has never before experienced such an "assault" of globalization that reaches so extensively across so much territory, functions with such strong intensity, and operates with such speed and impact in virtually every domain. Southern Africa demonstrates the substantial innovations in the technological, institutional, and legal infrastructure since World War II, changes that promote and reinforce the movement of goods, services, people, ideas, religion, culture, and so on across the region and the world. Global networks and relations have become embedded in the practices and operations of the governments, businesses, NGOs, and other organizations in southern Africa as well as across many of the households and individuals. These states, like others, face the challenge of navigating the multilayered governing structures of the contemporary world in a way that previous generations could not have imagined.

Yet the region's governments have not been rendered impotent by the new, faster paced, and more complex world. Some are better equipped and more powerful than others, but to varying degrees they all make choices. They choose how they will engage with regional and global arenas as well as the terms under which these interactions will take place. At the turn of the millennium, on the whole, most states in southern Africa have chosen to facilitate the penetration of globalization. The economic arena illustrates this vividly and perhaps paradoxically, since some of the regimes now in power promised their citizens a different vision of the future. On balance, openness to global and regional interaction in all domains now outweighs the instances when such interchange has been discouraged or blocked.

Across centuries, globalization and regionalism have played crucial roles in the nations of southern Africa, just as southern Africa, in turn, has been significant in global relations. This remains true today. Only the future will reveal whether local leaders will choose to forge terms of engagement with the region and the world that benefit the few or the many.

Notes

1. James Rosenau, *Along the Domestic Foreign Frontier: Exploring Governance in a Turbulent World* (Cambridge: Cambridge University Press, 1997), p. 96.

Acknowledgments

Many people contributed to this book, and I want to thank them. Some years ago, George Lopez and Jennifer Knerr first imagined a book on the region of southern Africa and believed that I should write it. I have exhausted their patience in the time it has taken to complete the book, but I am grateful for the task they entrusted to me.

I have benefited enormously from the advice and counsel of Steve Catalano at Westview Press, as well as his predecessor, David Pervin. I am grateful for the comments of two anonymous reviewers, whose feedback helped to sharpen the analysis. Other colleagues gave generously of their time to read the manuscript at various stages and to offer feedback. They are Trond Bakkerig, Chester Brinser, Betty Glad, Prexy Nesbitt, Donald Puchala, and Peter Sederberg. Dan Sabia also provided insights that facilitated the analysis. On occasion, I chose not to heed some of the advice given by these many readers, and any mistakes in the book, of course, are entirely mine.

Many years ago, Chad Alger got me started on the path of what was then called transnational relations. Although he had no input on this book, my professional life will always reflect some of the intellectual heritage he bequeaths. This book continues the intellectual perspective Chad encouraged: that one might see the world as more interesting and messy than most would like to believe.

Mardi McCabe used her remarkable technical skills to add the maps and other figures in the book. She also provided considerable assistance in a range of other technical matters, and most important, she always complemented her competence with cheer and optimism. Ann Lucht provided good spirits and practical help, too. Gray Stevenson tracked down figures, made charts, and otherwise provided invaluable research assistance.

The Department of Government and International Studies at the University of South Carolina granted a much-needed sabbatical for research and writing. The former chair of the department, Mark DeLancey, also provided encouragement for the project and practical support.

I have dedicated this book to three institutions that enormously deepened and broadened my understanding of the world. They demonstrate in very practical ways the kinds of local to global connections that I write about here. The Women's Division of the United Methodist Women introduced me to the region of southern Africa when I was seventeen and still living in the unfolding civil rights movement in Alabama. The World Council of Churches introduced me to people who gave their lives for freedom and justice, causes integral to and embodied in their faith conviction, and from whom I continue to take great inspiration and strength. Wesley United Methodist Church in Columbia kept me grounded in the intersection of faith and justice at home.

In the creation of this book, however, my deepest thanks and most profound gratitude belongs to the Department of Religious Studies at the University of South Carolina, and particularly its chair, Carl Evans, for rescuing me from a brutal academic war. After having taught international relations in political science departments for twenty-one years, I moved to the Department of Religious Studies. My new colleagues took a giant leap of faith that I might make a contribution to their mission and their lives. They surrounded me with a rich, nurturing, and stimulating intellectual environment, which enormously lifted my spirits as well as my productivity, and redeemed the academy for me.

Peter Sederberg, my husband, always deserves thanks for being who he is—one of the most gifted intellectuals to be found anywhere, from whom I will continue learning for the rest of my life, and an indispensable partner in all my pursuits. His big heart and quick wit regularly inspire me. He also bought me a computer, without which the book would never have been written! Thanks, too, to Per Sederberg for being a cheerleader and a model eager investigator and to Rachel Love for demonstrating in her still young life degrees of courage, strength, love, generosity, creativity, patience, and hope that the rest of us will probably never fully comprehend or attain.

For all these contributions to this book, I will always be grateful.

Index